FRINGE BENEFITS

OTHER BOOKS BY ANITA GATES

90 MOST PROMISING CAREERS FOR THE 80S
90 HIGHEST-PAYING CAREERS FOR THE 80S

FRINGE BENEFITS

THE FIFTY BEST CAREER OPPORTUNITIES FOR MEETING MEN

by Anita Gates and Shelley Klein

DONALD I. FINE, INC.

NEW YORK

Library of Congress Catalogue Card Number: 85-80627
ISBN: 0-917657-48-9
    Manufactured in the United States of America
    10 9 8 7 6 5 4 3 2 1

This book is printed on acid free paper. The paper in this book meets the guidelines for permanence and durability of the Committee on Production Guidelines for Book Longevity of the Council on Library Resources.

To RDF
"Present mirth hath present laughter."
—*Twelfth Night*
AG

To my husband Brad
who continues to make all my dreams come true
SK

"In that day seven women shall take hold of one man."

Isaiah 4:1

Acknowledgments

Most of the working people who contributed their insights, experiences and candid opinions must be thanked anonymously. From the fireman to the psychiatrist, from the chemist's wife to the lawyer's ex, their names have been changed or omitted to allow them the freedom of complete honesty.

Thanks also are due to the many professional associations across the country who supplied us with salary and membership surveys, among other materials, perhaps not realizing that this book might poke some fun at the career in question. We hope they see it, as we do, as good-natured fun.

Special thanks to Ethel and J.C. Gates and to Betty and Bob Klein, our parents, for their love and support. And to Lorrie Klein for her creative contributions.

Finally, thanks to Richard Flagg, our research associate who set aside his objections that this was not the most scholarly project he had ever worked on, and did a superior job—from locating people in many career fields to finding reference books we never knew existed.

And to all the guys we ever loved, thanks. We warned you you'd end up in a book someday.

Contents

11

Introduction

I remember Jenny Curtis coming into my room at the Delta Zeta house one night almost 17 years ago. She was in tears. She and her longtime boyfriend, Eric, had broken up. But she was not crying at the thought of never laying eyes on Eric again as long as she lived. A much more devastating prospect had crossed her mind.

"I am twenty-one years old," she announced between sniffles (somehow making age 21 sound, even in my memory, just one step away from menopause). "In less than six months, I'm going to graduate from college. *Then* where am I going to meet anybody?"

Jen was always a practical girl.

Some of us have begun to ask that question more recently, as we approach 30 or 40 or mandatory retirement. And now even Phil Donahue can't give us an answer.

Luckily I later met another practical woman, Shelley Klein. I met her through work, when she and I had both attended a photographer's combination cocktail party and slide presentation. I'd just done one of my first TV talk show appearances to publicize my first book on careers, and Shelley was a media consultant with lots of advice.

Soon, Shelley was managing the publicity and lecture side of my writing career. And one day an idea was born. "Well, I could talk about the careers where women really have great opportunities, because there are so few women in the field," I suggested, when she'd asked me for new ideas for a talk show segment. "You know, careers like engineering and architecture where ninety percent of the work force is still male. They need women, so you actually can get better starting salaries than the men."

She nodded and thought for a minute. "You know, Anita, wouldn't those be good places for women to *meet* men, too?"

Oh. Yeah.

All we knew at first was that it went against the golden rules of being serious working women in the 1980s:

1. Don't mix business with pleasure.
2. If the romance becomes public knowledge, it's always the woman who gets fired.
3. Look at Mary Cunningham.

Look at her? The woman's name is a household word since her alleged affair with her then-boss at Bendix. Do you know how much that's worth on the open job market or the lecture circuit? But more about that in chapter 14.

The absurd thing, in retrospect, was that we'd bought these rules—hook, line and sinker—while ignoring the factual evidence around us.

At the last corporation I worked for, there were enough office romances going to keep a daytime soap in scripts for years. There was the bubbly college recruiter/interviewer who married the brooding product manager. The cute guy in budget control who married a young sales rep. The two terribly competent marketing managers who married each other, and even managed to find time to reproduce. My own former secretary who married the new guy in personnel. And there was Molly, the publicist who took up with Jim, the R&D executive, when both were married to other people. They got their respective divorces, took an apartment together in New York, and have been living in sin for more than 12 years. They're also both vice presidents now.

Who, we asked, was kidding whom? These people seemed to be doing just fine. Hadn't anyone told *them* about the golden rules?

Shelley looked back at her own career path. A sociology major, she'd started her adult work life as a social worker for an adoption agency. It was rewarding, yes, but the only people she met during her work days were happily married couples hoping to be approved as adoptive parents. Watching these people hold hands and look wistfully into each other's eyes all day got a little routine.

Shelley didn't think of herself as changing careers for social reasons at the time, but that's how it turned out. She found a production job at a local TV station and her date book started filling up again. A year later, now working as a television producer, she was calling out instructions and suggestions to a TV news crew outside a Manhattan apartment building when one of the building residents walked by—and into her life. They moved in together shortly thereafter, and were married in May, 1984.

Looking at my own social life (normally not one of my favorite hobbies), I found that the same pattern held true. When I'd worked in a public relations department of 14 women and one man, I hardly ever met an available man through my work. When I started doing travel writing, there was a distinct improvement. First the tall, dark and handsome editor I discussed Eastern philosophies with in Stockholm. Next the cute, curly-haired guy on a trip to Italy, the one who looked like actor John Shea. And then there's my best friend in the world, a man I met when I interviewed him for my second book.

Come to think of it, my old friend Meredith met Frank at an orientation luncheon when they both worked for the same ad agency. Our mutual friend Helen met Gary when she was a United Nations guide and he brought his special ed class for a tour of the facilities. Why, even Phil met Marlo (definitely their real names) when she did his show!

So we set out to learn more, to look for interesting careers where you have a great chance to meet men as co-workers, clients or passing customers. We talked to people who met their spouses or lovers through work, and to people who knew the kind of men you might meet in each career. And, just to be safe, we changed virtually everybody's name before quoting them.

At times, we disagreed on what this all meant—about the relative importance of business and personal life, about feminism, about changing social and sexual roles and all the rest.

> Shelley: How would you feel if we put you on a talk show with a real women's libber?
>
> Anita: Shelley, I *am* a real women's libber.

* * *

But we were sure of one thing. This was the way courtship was going to have to work in the late 1980s and maybe beyond. With yuppie-ism approaching plague proportions, every young(ish) American woman honestly can say, "My career is my life."

This, too, shall pass.

Not that she's going to leave her job in favor of white picket fences. But let's hope that, in the 1990s, we'll at least try to strike a *balance* between our work and personal lives!

Meanwhile, however, where else is she going to spend enough time to meet a man?

> — Anita Gates
> Shelley Klein
> New York City
> May 1985

P.S.—Don't worry about my old sorority sister, Jen. She found herself a new boyfriend, accepted his fraternity pin, made Eric very jealous as a result and they (she and Eric) were secretly married before the end of her senior year.

Why Meet Men At Work?

Fact 1: You spend at least 50 percent of your waking hours at work, and so does the man of your dreams—wherever he is.

That's why the American workplace has become the most fertile love-and-marriage hunting ground of the 1980s. "Where are all the men?" ask single and divorced women from Maine to California, as they survey the disappointing supply of males found at singles bars, married friends' cocktail parties, night courses in computer literacy and church socials.

They're working late at the office, of course, probably meeting the objects of their next Primary Relationship there. After all, now that attractive, intelligent, educated and interesting women make up such a large percentage of the work force, why should men have to look any further for love than the next office or desk? The best catches don't have to bother with bars, co-ed health clubs or personals ads.

Exactly where are all the men? The greatest number of them are in engineering offices, in brokers' offices on Wall Street and in financial districts around the country, behind the drawing boards at architectural firms, behind the control panels of 747s, behind schedule at major metropolitan hospitals and in several dozen other careers that we're going to tell you about.

Ambitious women have realized for years that certain occupations offer them special hiring and advancement opportunities because of a shortage of female workers there. Those same careers now offer even more exciting social and romantic opportunities. Get ready to make your move.

Fact 2: Proximity breeds familiarity.

In a simpler era, nice girls married the boy next door. Statistics showed that, in a majority of weddings, the bride and groom walking down the aisle already lived within a few miles of each other.

The same natural law applies to the ambition-conscious 1980s, but with a twist. Since we're marrying later and devoting more time to the workplace, we're marrying the man in the office next door instead.

And if you don't believe us, just turn on your TV. Back in the days of *Ozzie and Harriet* and *Leave It To Beaver*, viewers never even knew what Dad did for a living. American life appeared to take place in the living room, the eat-in kitchen, on the lawn and occasionally at school.

In recent years, however, our favorite shows have become office- or workplace-based. *Mary Tyler Moore*, aka Mary Richards, never became seriously involved with Lou Grant or any of her other co-workers, but her life revolved around the WJM-TV newsroom. She once dated Murray's father and when she had a party, Rhoda was normally the only person on the guest list who didn't work with her. On *Cheers*, a master's degree never stopped Shelley Long from falling in love with her bartender boss, Ted Danson. On *Hill Street Blues*, the liaisons are too numerous—and confusing—to mention. The nighttime soaps, from *Dynasty* to *Dallas*, are all about personal relationships—revolving in and around the family business. And even *M*A*S*H* had its social message: War may be hell, but it's a great place to meet new people.

For real-life proof, read company newsletters: "Wedding bells rang last month for Kevin Monello of Materials Distribution and Tiffany Blodgett of Information Services." We have seen editorial assistants lose their heads over the new men in employee benefits and men in operations analysis commit all to secretaries with word processing skills. We have admired the rings, listened to the details of the leases and the mortgages—and paid for the wedding presents.

Yes, people still do meet occasionally on blind dates and end up pledging eternal love. We actually know one woman who met a man in a New York East Side singles bar and married him three weeks later. We can tell you the story of a lonely magazine editor (female) who joined a religious social organization in May, met a nice accountant in June and was married, pregnant and living in a big house in New Jersey by the following September.

But we also know that these incidents are mere subterfuge on the part of cruel gods, taunting us from Mount Olympus (where they've all been happily paired up since 4000 B.C.) with false hopes of candlelight and romance.

Face it. You're probably first going to see the man of your dreams under flourescent panels, surrounded by metal files, not at Top of the Mark with the sunset over the Golden Gate Bridge behind him. He'll probably be talking about promotional budgets or electronics trade shows, not reciting Byron or reminiscing about his childhood in southern France. And the first thing he will hand you is more likely to be a Xeroxed flow chart than a dozen yellow roses.

Fact 3: Offices are better than singles bars.

When men arrive at their offices each day, they are looking for financial reward, status, professional identity and promotion opportunities. Sometimes they are even looking for the men's room. But they are almost never looking for a fast fling.

You're at your best at the office. True, you may have raised your voice on occasion, or dropped every piece of paper in the folder you were carrying, and watched the report be run over by the coffee wagon. But these occurrences are rare, unless you're reading this at the unemployment office. (And if you are, cheer up. We're going to tell you where to find work next time.)

At work—unlike some bars, parties and other social situations— you do speak in complete sentences. You do not enter conference rooms for meetings, then promptly avoid eye contact with every man in the room and announce that you've never come to this sort of place before. And no American business conference has ever been opened with the question, "What's your sign?"

In all fairness to the outside world, however, strange encounters do occur in office buildings on company time. One woman we know recalls strolling down the hall to a product manager's office for a two o'clock meeting. The man asked her if she'd ever considered transferring to the marketing department (a suggestion that had nothing to do with the supposed topic of their meeting), pointed out that he could put in a word for her, closed the office door and began kissing her on the mouth.

It had been so long since she'd had a date that she started to respond, but decided to pull away, brush off the incident with a joke and get back to business. Six months later, the product manager married a woman from the personnel department. One can only assume that it all began with a similar two o'clock meeting.

Fact 4: There are great advantages to meeting men at work.

Office romances have gotten a bad name without good cause. They generally do not ruin careers, hardly even turn you into the subject of a *People* magazine scandal and are as rampant as the common cold. So let's consider all the positive aspects of meeting a man at work.

1. *You'll get to see him in daylight.* In a dark and crowded room, with Culture Club's latest hit turned up to scream level in the background, it's easy to become confused. Men who look like Richard Gere by bar-lamp at midnight have been known to bear startling resemblances to Chubaka the Wookie when they turn on the bathroom light in your apartment.

2. *You know what you're getting.* Meet a man at the workplace, and you'll already have friends and acquaintances in common. There's nothing like meeting someone handsome, sensitive and articulate, spending three weeks holding hands and cooking intimate dinners together, only to discover that he has some nasty secret. Just as you're planning a small wedding, choosing the right street-length white dress and consulting your gynecologist to see if women really can have children at your age, his parole officer turns up at the door. Or he confesses that there are three sixes engraved on his scalp, and your Pekingese reminds him of his mother. At the office, these little surprises are almost impossible. He's been checked out by Personnel and the company doctor.

3. *When the subject is business, you can do the asking*. We don't care what those elegant women in Harvey's Bristol Cream ads say. When you put on a sexy outfit, turn the lights down low, set out two glasses on your living room coffee table and pick up the phone to ask him over (in your best breathy voice), men do not always consider it "downright upright."

Even worse, men sometimes will turn you down. And by the time you've recovered from the emotional blow, you'll be too old to date.

When it comes to work-related get-togethers, however, men have grown accustomed to role reversal. You can suggest a meeting, schedule it, set up an interview or request a brainstorming session. If he says no, you can stress just how important your getting together will be to the third quarter ad campaign/ annual sales meeting/ new fall sportswear line/ Syracuse test market, or excuse of your choice.

Even if he suspects your interest in him goes beyond his data base, he'd be unprofessional to confront you about it. So the meeting is arranged. Salespeople call this getting your foot in the door.

At the office you're not in a seduce-or-forget-it position, as you would be at a singles gathering. With a co-worker or client, there's always next week. You can psyche him out by analyzing the kinds of personal items he keeps in his office, too. And experts (shrinks, advice columnists, et al.) agree that the best kinds of matches are made at work. The two of you are starting off with a strong common interest—just as real as sharing the same hometown, socioeconomic background, political leanings or religion.

Of course, some of the men in the office will be married, but that's not the end of the world. Just keep in mind that men always know other men to introduce you to, and that America's high divorce rate is holding steady. If there are 20 married men in your department, and one out of three marriages in the U.S. breaks up, at least six of those men will become available at some point in the future.

Fringe Benefits wasn't written to suggest a new and untried approach to meeting great men. This is the way adult dating works in the 1980s. This is how many of those happily-attached women you know got that way. And it's our suspicion that all this talk against office romances is just a scheme devised by other women to keep you away from a good thing.

This is a book for feminists and nonfeminists alike. It is not for you, however, if you've known since kindergarten that you wanted to be a nuclear physicist. Or a prima ballerina. Or a third-grade teacher.

Most of us aren't that focused. Many American women, like most American men, start out unsure of exactly where and how we want to make our marks professionally. And most of us could be good at any number of careers. So why not take advantage of the careers in which you can end up surrounded by prospective lovers?

If you find that we take the whole subject lightly in the pages ahead, all the better for you to have fun as you read. Just rest assured that the statistics and the other hard facts are real and can be put to any use you choose.

Chapter 2

Careers With The Highest Percentage Of Men

The simplest way to meet men at work is to be surrounded by them, as co-workers, at every turn. Here are the hard numbers. Here are the 50 best career opportunities for meeting men.

9 OUT OF 10 WORKERS ARE MEN

Airline Pilots	98%
Dentists	94%
Engineers	94%
FBI Agents	95%
Firefighters	99.9%
Optometrists	93%

8 OUT OF 10 WORKERS ARE MEN

Architects	89%
Doctors	84%
Engineering Technicians	82%
Financial Planners	85%

Foreign Service Officers	82%
Geologists/Geophysicists	86%
Lawyers	84%
Photographers	80%
Police Officers	89%
Surveyors	88%

7 OUT OF 10 WORKERS ARE MEN

Advertising	77%
Chemists	77%
College Teachers	73%
Insurance Sales	74%
Musicians	72%
Pharmacists	71%
Product Managers	77%
Purchasing Managers	77%
Stockbrokers	76%
Systems Analysts	70%

6 OUT OF 10 WORKERS ARE MEN

Association Managers	64%
Bankers	62%
Biological Scientists	69%
Economists	60%
Market Researchers	61%
Computer Programmers	65%
Science Technicians	65%

AT LEAST 5 OUT OF 10 WORKERS ARE MEN

Accountants	59%
Buyers	58%
Editors/Reporters	54%
Educational Administrators	56%
Health Care Administrators	50%

Hotel Managers	59%
Meeting Planners	53%
Personnel Managers	54%
Physician Assistants	59%
Public Relations	51%
Real Estate Sales	52%
General Sales	52%
Technical Writers	59%
Underwriters	52%

CAREERS WITH A LOT OF MEN—BUT YOU'D BETTER MEET THEM IN SCHOOL

Clergy	94%
Athletes	82%
Foresters	88%

9 Out of 10 Workers Are Men

> *"...neither children nor Gods, but men in a world of men!"*
> RUDYARD KIPLING
> *England's Answer to the Cities*

AIRLINE PILOT

98% are men   2% are women

+ An 18-hour work week, seeing the world for free.

− Layovers can be lonely. And when they aren't, you could get into trouble.

"The airline pilot is a man who likes to be in control, he likes to be in the driver's seat. He thinks of himself as macho," says a former employee of a major airline.

"It would be very hard to find a homosexual pilot," adds a gay man.

"Pilots are very detail-oriented, very compulsive," suggests a former flight attendant who flew internationally for more than a decade. "They're also very military."

A restaurateur, who has served many flight crews in his time, agrees. "You have to have Army training, and they turn you into a soldier. Then, when you're on the ground, you're like a soldier on leave."

A pilot has to be alert, clear-headed and sober on the job. Afterward, he may make up for it. "Oh, they would have three or four drinks each, knocking it back seriously," recalls a former waiter. "And they tend not to be very good tippers."

"Very tight with their money," the flight attendant agrees.

Rumor even has it that their infidelity record is as high as their divorce rate. "They all are terrible philanderers," observes another airline employee. "But the pressures are different than if you go home to your wife every night. And flying a plane is really doing something against God and nature. Every time you go to work, you could die—and take a lot of people with you."

There are three positions in the pilot's profession. The *Captain*, who runs the show, requires an Air Transport Pilot (A.T.P.) rating from the Federal Aviation Administration (F.A.A.). Average age: 49. Average years of service: 22. The *First Officer* (co-pilot) must have a commercial pilot's license with an instrument rating from the F.A.A. Average age: 40. The *Second Officer* (flight engineer) doesn't actually fly the aircraft, but is required to have a valid pilot's license. He monitors and operates many of the plane's instruments and systems. Average age: 38.

Aviation is big business. An American commercial flight takes off every three and a half seconds, and more than 400 million passengers fly every year. Women are a very small part of it all.

It's not that women don't learn to fly. Amelia Earhart was the first president of The Ninety-Nines, a group of that many female pilots who organized in 1929. Today, the organization has more than 6,000 members, and their figures show that there are more than 46,000 female pilots in the U.S. currently qualified to fly. The greatest number of them, however, don't make a living at it. They hold only students' or private pilots' licenses. Only 679 hold A.T.P. credentials, the greatest number of them in California (128), Florida (62) and Texas (48).

Three out of four of these women aren't even working for the airlines. As of August, 1984, there were 145 female pilots employed by ALPA airlines. Of those, only 16 were captains. USAir employed the greatest number, with 16 first officers and six second officers. United had 15 female second officers on its payroll. Piedmont had six captains, six first officers and two second officers. Republic had three captains. Other captains were with Air Wisconsin, Comair, Frontier, Imperial, Metro and Ozark.

Some of those other women are working as corporate pilots, flying corporate executives in company-owned planes. Not long ago, 99 *News* profiled one member who flies a Learjet for an Idaho company that maintains a fleet of five Lears, a Falcon and a helicopter.

Another career possibility is a job with a commuter airline. You'd be most likely to pilot a plane that seats under 20 passengers on routes of 150 miles or less. With revenue increases of 30 percent a year, this is aviation's fastest-growing area.

JOB SECURITY: It all depends on the health of the airline industry. And despite much-publicized financial troubles, the industry appears to be in good shape. International airlines showed a $800 million profit in 1984 and appeared headed for a 1985 total of $1.5 billion. According to an item in *U.S. News & World Report* (March 11, 1985), a shortage of airline pilots actually could develop during this decade. In 1984, leading airlines had hired 5,346 new pilots and had called almost 1,900 furloughed pilots back to work.

The Bureau of Labor Statistics predicts 23 percent occupational growth for a total of 103,000 jobs by 1995.

MONEY: You might start as a flight engineer for as little as $16,000 a year. Airline pilots at all levels average $75,000 per year, however. According to ALPA figures, the average flight engineer earns $46,000 per year; the average co-pilot, about $60,000; the average captain, about $90,000. Captains with international routes for major carriers can earn $200,000 or more.

When United Airlines ran want ads during their 1985 strike, they offered starting salaries of $50,000 and $75,000 for first officers and captains (respectively) experienced in flying 727's, 737's, 747's, 767's, DC-8's or DC-10's.

Outside the airlines, earnings are considerably lower. Corporate pilots average $29,000-$48,000 per year, depending on rank.

LIFESTYLE: If you become an airline pilot, you're likely to fly no more than 16 days a month, but layovers will keep you away from home on many off-days. If your husband or lover is a pilot too, attempts to work the same flights may present considerable challenge. But as one observer points out, "If you want two-thirds of a marriage, fine."

Your paychecks will make up for a lot. You'll be able to live well— and of course you and the family will fly free or nearly-free at vacation time. You can take the kids to see the Disneyland in Tokyo more easily than most American parents can get to Orlando or Anaheim.

More than one-third of all pilots work at airports near seven major cities: New York, Los Angeles, San Francisco, Chicago, Dallas/Fort Worth, Miami and Atlanta. You'll need to live in or near one of those, but you do have a choice between city or suburban living.

WHAT IT TAKES: Youth, for one thing. You could have begun your aviation career at age 16, when you were first old enough to apply for a student pilot's license. You have to be at least 23 to apply for an A.T.P. rating, but this is not the sort of career men and women switch into at age 40 or 50. ALPA took a look at airline hiring practices and concluded . . . that "an applicant's chances drop to almost nothing after age 32."

You have to be in good health, mentally and physically. A medical certificate is required for a commercial or A.T.P. license. Heart, lungs, physical dexterity and eyesight are the main concerns. Although some airlines will now hire pilots who wear eyeglasses or contact lenses, most still require 20/20 vision or better, uncorrected. And if you can't pass the psychological tests, for obvious reasons no one will want to put you at the controls of a DC-10. Decision-making ability and good judgment under pressure are important parts of the job.

GETTING HIRED: About half of all pilots work for commercial airlines, but these are the hardest jobs to get. Female applicants, however, may find a little less competition just because there are fewer qualified women than men in line ahead of them.

Your first step: a college degree. When airlines can pick and choose, the first people they'll count out are those without the educational background they're looking for. College will also help get you into officers' training if you join the military for your flight training. The high cost of training in large, multi-engine aircraft makes this the most sensible path, even if khaki is not your idea of high fashion. Pass the exams, demonstrate your ability to fly and get 1500 hours of flying time, and you can get your A.T.P. license. After another 500-1000 hours in the air, it'll be time to apply for an airline job. (Getting in all that flying time on your own would be very expensive. Fortunately, you're most likely to accumulate it during training, and then on the job.)

If you're looking for an alternative to a stint in the armed forces, ALPA suggests the Air National Guard, the air reserves, a job with a commuter airline or a job as a corporate pilot. Of course you'll have to get your initial pilot training at a civilian school beforehand.

TRAINING: No matter where you choose to get it, pilot training is no piece of cake. Taking the controls of a plane and proving you can take off and land is just the beginning. You'll be tested for your ability to think clearly in times of stress (and you'll be put under considerable real stress to prove it). In addition to the hands-on experience, there'll be classroom instruction in topics such as aerodynamics, aeronautics, navigation and meteorology.

EDUCATION: College degree plus flight training, preferably from the military. License.

EARNINGS: $75,000 national average.

WORKSTYLE: 18 hours a week average plus layovers. Constant travel. Enormous responsibilities.

DIRECT INTERACTION OPPORTUNITIES: Long hours together in the cockpit, while the computers do most of the work.

FOR MORE CAREER INFORMATION: Air Line Pilots Association, 1625 Massachusetts Avenue NW, Washington, DC 20036.

For airline information, write to: Air Transport Association of America, 1709 New York Avenue NW, Washington, DC 20006.

DENTIST

95% are men   5% are women

+ Both of you will have movie-star smiles.

− You'll work alone, and children will hate you.

Jake Hunt, D.D.S., is 28 years old, looks a little like a young William Hurt and sings rock 'n' roll to his patients. You have not lived until you've had a molar filled to the tune of "I Want to Know What Love Is."

Hunt sees himself as a prime example of the "new dentist." His theory goes something like this: In the past, dentists had a PR problem. They were known to have bad marriages, an unusually high suicide rate (all that solitary work, all those people who hate visiting them), and a decidedly unsexy image.

"Kind of like CPAs and optometrists, they'd gotten a bum rap," Hunt explains. "Of course some of it might have been accurate, because of the nature of the profession. It's a precise specialty. And it deals with a part of the body that the public doesn't think of as attractive—the mouth. But there really are human beings in the profession."

The way Hunt sees it, dentists were so in demand until 15 or so years ago that dental schools could pick and choose applicants. Naturally, they picked and chose the most scholarly—academic grinds, if you will. Since competition to get into dental school has dropped considerably, the admissions committees have loosened up. As a result, they're getting "well-rounded individuals, people with other interests."

The increased marketing of dental services has had an impact, too. Today's private practitioner has to compete with low-cost dental clinics and the practitioner down the street who shows sci-fi movies on his ceiling, so he has to offer something extra. And now that so many dental visits are for cosmetic reasons (some cosmetic treatments like bonding didn't even exist 15 years ago), patients' attitudes toward both the services and the profession are changing.

The "new dentist," Hunt says, is very involved in physical fitness, very understanding and empathetic, yet knows how to have a good time. Dentistry can attract well-rounded people because it's "a great profession, but you don't have to marry it."

"It doesn't have to choke you like medicine," he explains. "I'm done at five o'clock and I don't have to take my work home." In fact, the average dentist works 42.2 hours per week.

Although at least nine out of ten American dentists are men, the numbers are changing—and that's most evident at dental schools. One out of five dental students today is a woman. Of his class of 400, Hunt estimates that there were about 40 women. In fact, he dated a fellow dental student for two years.

"Dental school is hell," he recalls. "It's a period of intense study, and you don't have time to develop outside relationships. You get horny and another dental student is right there." Perhaps not the most romantic of attitudes, but decidedly realistic.

Hunt finds it easy to imagine marrying a female dentist. He points out that it's an honored professional tradition to have one's wife involved in the practice—as a nurse, a receptionist, a bookkeeper— because of the solitary nature of the work. So why not a fellow practitioner?

If he meets her now, it may be at a seminar or conference. Or it just may be through general socializing. Most of his close friends are dentists—old school friends practicing in the same city.

The average independent dentist today is 47 years old, and your chances with him are good. In Texas, for instance, there are 6,494 male and only 215 female professionally active dentists. Things are even better in Idaho, where there are 495 men practicing and only one woman.

JOB SECURITY: There are already 132,000 dentists practicing in the U.S., but there's plenty of room for growth. The need for dentists is expected to grow by almost 30 percent in the decade ahead. Although it's true that your income could be affected by a bad economy (people tend to put off dental work, because overbites are rarely life-threatening), remember that the number of Americans covered by dental insurance has tripled in recent years. So the future looks secure. All the dentists' office waiting rooms should be full of patients of all ages in the 1990s.

MONEY: With an average income of $65,900, dentistry is among the ten most highly-paid occupations in the country. If you want to make even more, become a specialist (the average income rises to $86,420). Your choices include endodontics (root canal therapy), periodontics (treating gums), orthodontics (straightening teeth), prosthodontics (making artificial teeth or dentures) and oral and maxillofacial surgery. The nation's top dental earners are in Hawaii and Alaska.

LIFESTYLE: As a dentist, you and your true love can lead comfortable, relatively stress-free lives. You're both probably likely to be self-employed, so you can schedule vacations when and where you like. You can keep normal office hours, with the freedom to block out days and half-days for personal time whenever you need it. And with a household income of over $130,000, you'll probably never have to take in laundry to survive.

WHAT IT TAKES: You should start off with certain skills and abilities— good visual memory, good judgment of space and shape and a high degree of manual dexterity.

Chances are, you'll be a businesswoman too. Most beginning dentists either start their own practices or buy a practice from an established dentist. This means spending most of the day alone or with only one assistant, working one-to-one with patients, many of whom would rather be on a blind date with Godzilla than in a dentist's chair.

The average patient's dental anxiety has been known to take the form of hostility toward the dentist her- or himself. And a lifetime of having grown men quake with fear when you enter the room and being bitten by small children can take its toll emotionally. Maybe the profession's high suicide rate will decline, now that more and more patients are turning up for cosmetic dentistry, rather than for gum surgery and root canals.

If you prefer being part of a team, consider working in a group practice. Or take a job in a hospital, clinic or dental school. All the better to meet your fellow dentists, too.

EDUCATION: You'll become a Doctor of Dental Surgery (D.D.S.) or Doctor of Dental Medicine (D.M.D.), and you must be licensed in the state where you practice. Dental school normally takes four years, after two or four years of college. Training for specialties takes at least two years longer.

EARNINGS: $65,900 national median; higher for specialists.

WORKSTYLE: One-on-one with patients. Controllable schedules with few emergency appointments.

DIRECT INTERACTION OPPORTUNITIES: Seminars and conventions. Informal office contact in hospitals, clinics, schools and group practices.

FOR MORE CAREER INFORMATION: American Dental Association, Council on Dental Education, 211 East Chicago Avenue, Chicago, IL 60611; American Association of Dental Schools, 1619 Massachusetts Avenue NW, Washington, DC 20036.

ENGINEER

94% are men   6% are women

+ You can name your own salary and your own terms. You're in demand.

− Those big salaries level off, if you don't make it into management.

It was 1981, during the darkest days of America's most recent job market slump. She was a soon-to-be engineering graduate, fresh from classes at Georgia Tech, with no related business experience. The interviewer on the other side of the desk represented one of the nation's largest and most successful high-tech firms.

She: "I have to have three things. First: I have to be able to leave the office at any time when my daughter needs me, and not hear any arguments or criticism about it. Second: I'm willing to relocate, but I'll only do it during the summer so that it doesn't interfere with my daughter's school year. Third, I will not relocate in an area that doesn't have a suitable religious school for her."

They: "Yes."

This scene is not an exercise in how not to behave at a job interview. It's a slice of real life, related by a woman who had two job offers to choose from and thought that, by making demands, she could narrow the field. Both companies agreed to her requirements.

If there were as great a shortage of fascinating single women in America as there are of qualified female engineers, *Fringe Benefits* never would have occurred to us. Women in engineering can make demands these days, salary demands included. This is one of the few fields where female college graduates are offered better starting salaries than men. (Companies are often compelled to pay well in order to snare one of the few qualified women and thereby comply with equal opportunity laws.)

It seems only fair, however, to warn you about the public image of the profession you're about to enter, and of the men who people it. "Engineers are sort of quiet and introspective," says a Birmingham, Alabama, man whose sister married one. "There were times my brother-in-law would rather solve a logarithm—or whatever you do with logarithms—than sit down with a nice bottle of wine. You remember, in school, they were the ones who ran around with slide rules on their belts. But their prospects are good!"

Dress-for-success expert John Molloy (who, in all fairness, gently ridicules almost every occupation) suggests that engineers are turned off completely by even a hint of high fashion. They are looking for a realistic, down-to-earth sort of woman to whom one and one always add up to two. She is a woman whose wardrobe choices never veer from the incredibly appropriate and who wears solid colors because patterns never quite look neat enough.

Of course, there are almost as many kinds of engineers as there are kinds of men in general. A little more than 1.2 million working engineers make it the nation's second largest profession, beaten out only by teaching.

There are chemical, civil, computer, electrical, industrial and mechanical engineers (the specialties in which most women are enrolled, by the way). There are aeronautical, ceramic, mining, nuclear and petroleum engineers. Specialties with particularly strong growth or shortages in the mid-1980s include the following.

• *C.A.E.* *(Computer-Aided Engineering).* This sub-industry, which provides electrical engineers with computerized work stations so they can design and engineer silicon chips and integrated circuits, is "red-hot," according to one executive expert. As of 1984, C.A.E.'s three major companies employed only about 600 people. Forecasts are that, by the end of this decade, tens of thousands will be working in the industry. The three—Daisy Systems in Sunnyvale, California; Mentor Graphics in Beaverton, Oregon; and Valid Logic Systems in Mountain View, California—sell hardware too, but software is their specialty. They're looking for people with good general training in electrical engineering and computer science. Starting offers range from $25,000 to $35,000, with stock options that soon could be worth a mint.

• *Environmental Engineering.* With all the new problems brought on by toxic chemicals, acid rain and assorted other pollutants, why are there only about 15,000 environmental engineers in the U.S.? And as of 1984, there were only about 2700 graduate students in the field nationwide. Possible subspecialties include hazardous-waste management, solid-waste engineering (for nonhazardous waste disposal) and industrial hygiene. Most environmental engineers major in civil or chemical engineering, then go on to specialized graduate degrees. Thanks to a shortage in the field, points out an Engineering Manpower Commission spokesperson, new graduates are not having any trouble finding jobs. Salaries are competitive with other engineering specialties.

• *Metallurgy and Materials Science Engineering.* The field has a definite shortage and 100 percent job placement right now, according to a Carnegie Mellon professor. Students may think of materials science as part of the decidedly unglamorous steel and copper industries, but new materials have broadened it into a high-tech area. One example: polymers, which can make airplanes lighter, help get oil out of underground rocks or act as membranes in biotechnology. Starting salaries range from $22,000 for bachelor's degree graduates to as much as $45,000 for those with Ph.D.'s.

JOB SECURITY: Engineering is a boom-or-bust kind of career. One year, you can choose between several handsome job offers; the next year, you can't get arrested. To compound the problem, every time a shortage in a certain engineering specialty develops, so many people come in to take advantage that a glut soon exists. And all the time the employers are complaining about an engineering shortage, plenty of older engineers are standing in the unemployment line. The problem, presumably, is that they haven't kept up with changing technology. Why hire the old guys, when you can have a new kid—one who's up on the latest high-tech talk?—for the same money or less?

The solution: careful career planning, with an eye on the changing job market at all times. The reality right now: "Most engineering students don't retire as engineers," says one college student. They go into management instead.

For the record, the Bureau of Labor Statistics forecasts above-average occupational growth for several engineering specialities. They include civil (47 percent), mechanical (52 percent), metallurgical (47 percent) and nuclear (48 percent) engineers. One industry survey predicts that by 1987 there won't be enough engineers to go around in three specialities: aeronautical/astronautical (35,000 short), electrical/electronics (31,000 short) and computer engineering (a grand 137,000 short).

MONEY: When you have a brand-spanking-new engineerng degree, you can impress your old college friends with your new paycheck. Not only do engineers in general have extremely high starting salaries among all college graduates, but new female engineers get higher starting offers than their male fellow graduates.

Engineering graduates today receive average starting salaries of $25,200-$36,200, depending on whether they're entering the job market with a bachelor's, master's or doctoral degree. The highest-paying specialty to start, according to the Bureau of Labor Statistics, is petroleum engineering at an average of just under $30,500.

The national average for all experienced engineers is $36,726, but the average salary for those at senior supervisory levels is more impressive: $66,938. If it seems that the average salaries aren't much higher than the starting figures, that's the way it works in this constantly changing career field.

LIFESTYLE: Manage your money well and you'll be able to enjoy all the upper-middle-class luxuries you can think of. If you're like most dedicated engineers, however, you may spend more time at your work than you have to.

WHAT IT TAKES: The most important prerequisite is a thirst for problem-solving. You need to be creative, but with an analytical mind and a good head for details. Don't go into engineering if you prefer to sit in a room alone and work. In this career, teamwork is the name of the game.

EDUCATION: A bachelor's degree in engineering, which may be a four- or five-year program. Certain specialties, however, are taught primarily at the graduate level.

EARNINGS: $36,726 national average.

WORKSTYLE: Could be almost anything, depending on your specialty. There are desk jobs, outdoor jobs, hard-hat jobs and lab jobs, among others.

> **DIRECT INTERACTION OPPORTUNITIES:** Teamwork has its special compensations. Or consider a job on an oil rig (see our section on Secretaries, page 267).
>
> **FOR MORE CAREER INFORMATION:** Society of Women Engineers, 345 East 47th Street, New York, NY 10017.

FBI AGENT

95% are men   5% are women

+ He's sure to be college-educated, in good physical condition and can probably protect you from muggers. But then, as soon as you become an agent, so can you.

− Decide fast. You can't join up after age 35. And don't even think about cheating on him; he's a trained investigator.

Scene: A deluxe hotel's bridal suite, its focal point a king-sized bed with satin headboard. Beside the terrace doors, which overlook ocean and moonlight, are a tall vase of red roses and a just-opened bottle of champagne with two glasses. A handsome, clean-cut young man (Mr. FBI Agent) is standing beside the doors, smoking a cigarette. Then the dressing room door opens and an attractive woman (Mrs. FBI Agent) emerges, dressed in a white silk gown and peignoir. Demurely, she approaches him.

Mrs. FBI Agent: "Darling, there's something I must tell you. You were not the first man in my life."

Mr. FBI Agent: "Don't be silly, dearest. I know, and I forgive you. For Jim Barnes in your senior year of college. For Steve Parrish from April through November of 1982. For Ben Overton at the Bel Air Hotel last July 7th. For Alan—"

A pair of newlywed FBI agents will have few secrets left to reveal to each other on their wedding night. G. Gordon Liddy admits in his autobiography, *Will,* that he had a check run on his new fiancée, right after proposing. But other agents had a simpler system: "We wouldn't want to bring the wrong person into the FBI family," Liddy wrote. "For that reason, FBI agents tended to date and marry female Bureau personnel; they could be presumed cleared, and it saved a lot of trouble."

If your ideal man is one who, like Liddy, would ask about your parents' height and weight and your ancestors' nationality to be sure you'll produce exceptional children, don't say we didn't warn you.

But let's be fair. The FBI's approximately 8,000 special agents are the cream of a certain crop. Line them all up, pick one of them for your next date while blindfolded and you're virtually assured of getting a college graduate, probably a lawyer or an accountant.

Obviously, an agent needs to know about law. How can you collect the right kind of evidence if you have no idea what's going to be legally admissible? The need to know about accounting, however, comes as something of a surprise to prospective applicants. It seems that so much Federal law-breaking today is of the white-collar variety, particularly computer crime, that it takes someone with a financial or computer background to do the job right. If you've envisioned your FBI career as one Bonnie-and-Clyde car chase after another, come back to reality. The culprit you're after is more likely to be hunched over a computer terminal and wearing a three-piece suit.

JOB SECURITY: Become an FBI agent and marry one and the two of you probably will have jobs for life. More than 40 percent of all agents have been with the Bureau for ten years or longer. And the FBI always promotes from within. Just keep in mind that, in a job like this, burnout is a real possibility; there are plenty of 45-year-old retired agents around.

MONEY: You can count on regular salary increases. You and he will start in the mid-$20,000s during training. Supervisory agents start at $37,800, and the FBI even pays overtime.

LIFESTYLE: If the two of you should work on cases together, you can talk about work over dinner at home. Otherwise, learn your lesson now. Agents take the FBI's rules about secrecy very seriously.

During courtship, just try mentioning the job in your correspondence with him. You're almost sure to find your love letters turned over to headquarters.

When and if you have children, you'll have to put corks in their ears while you chat about the office. Then see to it that they never learn to lip-read. Or just save all the shop talk for the bedroom. Most FBI cases do have some element of risk involved so, if danger turns you on, this could be the career for you.

Let's hope you love redecorating regularly, because FBI families are apt to be moved around. You'll be assigned either to Bureau headquarters in Washington, D.C. or to one of the organization's 59 field offices throughout the U.S. Later on, this can be a little wearing on the kids. But now, while you're still looking for Mr. Agent Right, it can be a distinct advantage. You'll be constantly transferred to new hunting grounds and, even while you're staying in the same place, you'll have a steady flow of new fellow agents to look over as they're transferred in.

Bonus: The FBI is one big happy family. They're the kind of folks who'll help you find a house when you've just moved into town.

WHAT IT TAKES: Luckily, although the FBI is a competitive organization to get into, acceptance is somewhat easier for women than for men. Until 1972, there were no female agents, and the Bureau is still trying to make up for lost time by actively seeking out qualified women.

You'll have to go through the same selection process men do, however. You must be between the ages of 23 and 35, in good physical condition and have excellent vision, hearing and a valid driver's license. (Forget leaping into moving taxis and screaming "Follow that car!" You'll be driving yourself to and from most assignments.) You'll also need a college degree (see "Education" below).

GETTING HIRED: Apply at the nearest FBI office and take a batch of exams. If the computer likes your scores, you'll be granted an interview. If you're chosen, the Bureau will check out your background before hiring you.

TRAINING: Then it's off to Quantico, Virginia (the FBI Academy is on the Marine Corps base, which should tell you something); for 15 weeks of rigorous training. Your physical fitness program will be a modified version of the men's. You'll have classroom sessions in constitutional law, Federal criminal procedure, collection and preservation of evidence and the like.

You won't get out of Quantico without firearms instruction, of course. And if you should meet the man of your dreams here, think how romantic it will be to look back on the day your eyes first met—over his-and-hers .45 caliber submachine guns—at target practice.

Then you'll start at the GS-10 civil service level, investigating violations of certain Federal statutes, including bank embezzlements, highjackings, kidnappings and espionage. But if this all sounds a little too perilous for your career tastes, consider a headquarters job as a computer programmer, lab technician, fingerprint examiner or secretary instead. (You don't need to go through the agents' training program for these positions. Just get the kind of education you'd need to do these jobs for any company.)

And if you're not sure the clean-cut FBI type is your type, do some spying of your own. The J. Edgar Hoover building in Washington offers guided weekday tours. Just turn up at E street between 9th and 10th during office hours, and keep your eyes open as you roam the halls.

EDUCATION: A law degree or a bachelor's in accounting, foreign languages or science will get you off to a good start. Even English majors get in, however, and a bachelor's degree in anything—plus three or more years of full-time work experience (preferably executive, professional or investigational) is considered more than adequate.

EARNINGS: $20,000 and up to start; $37,800 and up as a supervisory agent.

WORKSTYLE: Technically an office job, but you'll spend a lot of time away from the desk on investigations, and some travel is likely. Subject to call 24 hours a day.

DIRECT INTERACTION OPPORTUNITY: 15 weeks of training, partnership assignments, office contact and general socializing.

> **FOR MORE CAREER INFORMATION:** Federal Bureau of Investigation, U.S. Department of Justice, Washington, DC 20535.

FIREFIGHTER

99.9% are men   0.1% are women

+ They're the last of the American heroes

− Their idea of a woman's place is anywhere but the firehouse.

"Firemen? They're a little bit crazy," Peter Bates, a veteran New York City fireman, announces with a smile. "They tend to be less than grown-up, you know. They're practical jokers."

In fact, if the between-alarms atmosphere of the average fire department looks and sounds a little like the Sigma Chi house on a Saturday afternoon, the fellows would like to keep it that way. "That was one of the biggest conflicts with women coming on the job," explains Bates. "The guys thought it was going to break up the gang, I think that was the biggest threat to them." Well, boys will be boys.

When firemen aren't lounging around the firehouse cancelling their girlfriends' *Ms.* subscriptions, they're out doing serious and often dangerous work. When they respond to an alarm, they operate firefighting equipment, rescue fire victims, administer emergency medical aid and try to save the contents of buildings.

Bates estimates that his company made more than 4,000 runs last year. Of those, 2,500 were "workers" (fires that the men actually fought). In the other cases, they left—either because other companies had arrived and were able to handle the fire, or because the run was a false alarm.

Most of the nation's 252,000 firefighters work for city fire departments. Fewer than one out of ten work at Federal or state installations, such as airports.

Fall in love with a fireman, and you may not get a Rhodes scholar. He probably hasn't been to college at all. He's likely, however, to be honest, brave, true and in good physical shape—with just a dash of mischievousness to keep things interesting.

JOB SECURITY: Firefigthers usually join the local fire department with no formal education beyond a high school diploma, and only a few weeks of official training. Turnover is remarkably low.

Job security is equally high. Because fire protection is an essential service by anyone's definition, firefighters rarely get laid off. When budgets are cut, that often means no new people will be hired or the new equipment won't be purchased; cutting staff is usually the last choice.

The pension plan is a real attraction in this job. As a firefighter, you could retire at age 50, after 25 years of service, and live quite adequately on half pay.

The only dark side of the career picture is the difficulty of getting hired in the first place, a problem caused by projected low levels of local government spending in the years ahead. The Bureau of Labor Statistics forecasts much lower than average growth for this occupation, with an increase in new job openings of only nine percent between now and 1995.

MONEY: Starting salaries for full-time firefighters average just under $16,200 per year. According to the International Association of Fire Fighters, the national average minimum and maximum salaries in the field are as follows. Firefighters: $17,130-$21,196; lieutenants: $22,543-$23,894; captains: $24,211-$25,828. Salaries are highest in the West, lowest in the South. The nation's biggest cities pay best too—including Los Angeles, New York, San Francisco, Dallas, Houston and Detroit. The high maximum for fire captains in most parts of the country is $45,000 and up.

LIFESTYLE: "There are nine-hour days and fifteen-hour nights," Bates explains. "There's an eight-day week and a twenty-five-day month." If that sounds confusing now, it isn't after the firemen get used to it. You might work the day shift on Monday and Tuesday, take Wednesday and Thursday off, then go in Thursday and Friday nights for 15 hours each. After that, you'd be off until Tuesday. Some firefighters, who have suburban houses far from the fire station, actually may work their entire 48-hour week in two days.

"You can go to the beach during the week or go shopping on weekdays when the stores aren't crowded," points out Bates. "I like it."

And when you and your true love are introduced at parties, expect a little old-fashioned hero worship from guests of both sexes. Unlike police officers, their fellow public servants, firemen have kept their image clean. (Although, in all fairness to the police departments of America, it's a mental stretch to imagine how a fireman might "go bad.") "Usually, people are impressed with the fact that you're a fireman," Bates admits.

WHAT IT TAKES: Firefighting is no career for a lone wolf. Being a good team player in this job can mean the difference between life and death—your own, as well as those of the people you're there to save. You need physical endurance, mental alertness, mechanical aptitude (hose, ladders, pumps and other firefighting equipment) and excellent judgment. At the moment, you do *not* need background in computer science. If you can't make decisions under stress, forget the whole thing.

Oh, yes, and you have to be very brave.

Only time will tell whether women will make real inroads in joining fire departments across the U.S. Meanwhile, if you can't get hired or if you'd rather see than be one, consider these alternatives. Work for the local firefighters' charity. Attend the local firemen's softball games during the summer. Put on your best face and make regular visits to the bar where your city's firemen hang out. ("We tend to be heavy drinkers," confesses Bates.)

EDUCATION: High school diploma. Learn how to play poker.

EARNINGS: $18,200 national median.

WORKSTYLE: An average 50-hour week, much of it spent on long shifts. Hazardous, stressful work with a real risk of injury or death.

DIRECT INTERACTION OPPORTUNITIES: Hanging around the fire-house—killing time, eating and sleeping together (so to speak).

FOR MORE CAREER INFORMATION: International Association of Fire Fighters, 1750 New York Avenue NW, Washington, DC 20006.

OPTOMETRIST

93% are men   7% are women

+ All the joys of being a doctor, but without death, disease or emergency calls.

− There are no problems. This is the perfect career.

"Mom, I'm so happy! I'm getting married, and he's an optometrist."

"That's nice, honey. I think it's important to look on the bright side of things, too."

Because almost no one in America outside the vision care field seems to be able to remember the differences between optometrists, opticians, ophthalmologists, oculists and occultists, you might as well become one of them—just to help your relatives keep things straight.

It's really very simple. If you're having headaches and think you might need glasses, you make an appointment with an *optometrist*—he tests your vision. If you were right and you need corrective lenses, he'll write a prescription for glasses or contacts.

You'll take that prescription to a dispensing *optician*, who will fill it just as a pharmacist fills a physician's prescription. He'll grind the lenses to specifications and help fit the resulting product.

On the other hand, if you were wrong and your headaches seem to be the result of some more serious vision problem, the optometrist will recommend that you see an *ophthalmologist*. This person is a physician, an M.D. specializing in injuries and diseases of the eye, who may prescribe drugs and/or perform surgery. Ophthalmologists were once called oculists (which was certainly a lot easier to spell).

Just as optometry seems to be the perfect career for a woman, an optometrist could be the perfect husband. He earns good money, can build a practice in any size community and has the prestige of being called doctor. Yet he doesn't have the emotional drain of dealing with the sick and dying every day. He can keep regular office hours, and will rarely be called in the middle of the night to do an emergency eye test. When you plan a romantic anniversary dinner, you can be sure that you won't be interrupted—at least not by a career demand.

Ideally, you'll meet this man while you're both in optometry school. That's not as easy as it used to be, however, because the percentage of women in colleges of optometry has skyrocketed from 2.5 percent in 1969-70 to 29.3 percent in 1982-83. In absolute numbers, that's a 16-fold increase, from 20 women students to 328. Women now make up 22 percent of the profession's graduating classes.

If you're looking forward to being one of the few women in a classroom filled with men, stay away from the State University of New York in New York City. Women make up more than 40 percent of the enrollment there. Instead, consider the three schools where female enrollment is lowest: Southern College of Optometry in Memphis, Tennessee; Northeastern State University in Tahlequah, Oklahoma; and the Illinois College of Optometry in Chicago (15-18.2 percent each).

If you're an adult female going back to school for a career change, we can only hope you're attracted to younger men. The mean age of optometry students is 22-25. However, at most schools the student age ranges up to the late 30s or older. At the University of California at Berkeley, the range is up to 50. And if father figures are your cup of tea, be patient: one out of three practicing optometrists is 55 or older.

After school, you may have to work harder to meet handsome fellow professionals. Six out of ten optometrists still work in solo practices. Group practice is a growing trend, however, so you might be able to team up with several other optometrists, which would also give you the freedom to specialize. A number of optometrists are going into multi-disciplinary practices or working on hospital staffs, too. In these cases, you will find yourself working with G.P.'s, dentists, obstetrician-gynecologists and other hospital employees every day. Most of the people in those careers are men, too.

Your patients could come from almost any group by age, sex and socioeconomics. Almost half of all Americans age 18-44 already wear corrective lenses of some kind. More than nine out of ten Americans over age 65 require corrective lenses. One out of every four students has significant reading deficiencies. Families with incomes below the poverty level have more and worse vision problems than families from other income groups. Studies show you'll probably do more than 1,200 visual diagnostic analyses each year. Of the 16 million or more Americans who now wear contact lenses, more than two out of three are women (most under age 45). But surely, out of all those people, one or two of your male clients just might be your type.

JOB SECURITY: You're needed. Studies show that we need 14.3 optometrists per 100,000 population (that's one doctor to every 7,000 people). At the moment we have only 9.8 optometrists per 100,000. And if we want to raise that ratio even to 12 per 100,000, we'd need 1,250 new optometrists graduating every year. With the nation's existing 15 colleges of optometry, we're a long way from achieving even that limited goal. Which means you're going into one of the few true professions that isn't suffering from a glut. (Just for the sake of comparison, please note: as of 1981, the U.S. had 185 physicians per 100,000 population.)

The Bureau of Labor Statistics predicts only an average increase (about 25 percent) in the number of "jobs" in optometry between now and 1995. The American Optometric Association sees a much larger increase, but new schools of optometry may be needed.

Those 15 colleges of optometry, by the way, are at the University of Alabama in Birmingham, the University of California in Berkeley, Ferris State College in Big Rapids, Michigan, the University of Houston, Illinois College of Optometry in Chicago, Indiana University in Bloomington, the University of Missouri in St. Louis, New England College of Optometry in Boston, Northeastern State University in Tahlequah, Oklahoma, Ohio State University in Columbus, Pacific University in Forest Grove, Oregon, Pennsylvania College of Optometry in Philadelphia, Southern California College of Optometry in Fullerton, Southern College of Optometry in Memphis, Tennessee and State University of New York's State College of Optometry in New York City.

MONEY: Even in the first year of practice, you'll probably be able to pay the rent and eat out—with a mean net income of $27,000, after the office rent, lab expenses and salaries are paid out. By the fifth year, you should be netting $42,000. And by the ninth year, you could be up to $55,000 net, the national mean for the entire profession. Optometrists make most lists of the ten highest-paid professions in the country.

LIFESTYLE: How wonderful to have the income and prestige of a doctor without giving up control of your own life! As an optometrist, you can set up normal office hours and keep them. Thus your personal life is your own. You can even live in a small city or town without sacrificing career success. Almost 40 percent of all optometrists practice in areas with populations of 25,000 or less.

WHAT IT TAKES: Because most optometrists, like physicians and dentists, run their own practices, you'll need good business skills and self-discipline. In addition to the scientific knowledge your formal education will provide, you'll need excellent judgment and the ability to assimilate many facts at once.

If you think you might prefer to become an ophthalmologist, see the section on Doctors, page 55. If you're interested in a career as an optician (63 percent male at last count), write the Opticians Association of America, 1250 Connecticut Avenue NW, Washington, DC 20036.

EDUCATION: Becoming a Doctor of Optometry is a four-year program after three or four years of college. State license required.

EARNINGS: $55,000 national mean after 9 years.

WORKSTYLE: Regular hours with a minimum of emergencies in a private office environment.

DIRECT INTERACTION OPPORTUNITIES: Group practice.

FOR MORE CAREER INFORMATION: American Optometric Association, 243 North Lindbergh Boulevard, St. Louis MO 63141.

8 Out of 10 Workers Are Men

> *"Ay, in the catalogue ye go for men."*
> WILLIAM SHAKESPEARE
> *Macbeth*

ARCHITECT

89% are men   11% are women

+ You're sure to live in a gorgeous home.

− It'll take both your salaries to build it.

> *"When you were given projects that left the choice of style up to you and you turned in one of your wild stunts— well, frankly your teachers passed you because they did not know what to make of it. But, when you were given an exercise in the historical styles, a Tudor chapel or a French opera house to design—and you turned in something that looked like a lot of boxes piled together without rhyme or reason—would you say it was an answer to an assignment or plain insubordination?"*
> *"It was insubordination," said Roark.*

When Ayn Rand created Howard Roark in her 1943 novel, *The Fountainhead*, she fashioned a character of such idealism that he would blow up his own building rather than see its design compromised. She also built him tall, strong and handsome.

If you want to meet a modern-day Howard Roark, we leave it up to you to test his principles and delve into his soul. But we *can* tell you a little about the average male architect in the 1980s.

He's 42 years old, more likely to be married than not (only 16 percent are single or divorced, but be patient), holds a bachelor's degree in architecture and has about 20 years of experience in the field. Chances are he's a project architect for a small firm—one with fewer than 20 employees—where he earns $40,500 a year.

His female counterpart has a slightly different profile. She is 35, less likely to be married (59 percent), less likely to have children and earns only $26,900 per year. She is more likely than the man to have a graduate degree in architecture, but that may be because she studied something nonarchitectural during her undergraduate years. Many have B. F. A.'s (Bachelor of Fine Arts degrees) instead. Female architects are more likely to work for larger firms—perhaps because the big companies are under pressure to hire both women and minorities.

If you want to make your career and social moves with the fewest number of fellow female architects in competition, stay away from California, New York and New England. Until recently, more than half of all women in the field worked in these states—and although the number of female architects is growing throughout the country, these are still the areas in which they're most populous.

If you want to go to architectural school with a classroom full of men, take the following schools off your list: the University of New Mexico, Princeton, University of Virginia, and Rice. They have the highest percentages of female enrollment in architecture.

JOB SECURITY: The occupational future looks good for architects. As one industry expert explains, "the building industry is tied directly to the oil industry." That's because energy helps produce the plastics, plywood and other materials used in construction. Architecture is not a huge field (about 84,000 strong now), but the Bureau of Labor Statistics expects that number to increase by 40 percent between now and 1995.

Careers are relatively stable, but not stagnant. Most architects work for four or more companies during their first 20 years. The business is strongly affected by the economy, however, so the unemployment line is certainly a possibility.

MONEY: The average architect earns more than the average insurance agent, accountant or interior designer—yet the field has a reputation (inside and out) for starvation incomes. More people are unhappy in the field because of earnings than for any other reason.

It's true that starting salaries (estimated at $14-$16,000 per year) are low for professionals with a minimum of five years of college behind them. And maybe an estimated national median income of $39,400 is nothing that J. Paul Getty would write home about, but it's well above what the average American earns. Although finances can be tough for budding entrepreneurs, the self-employed do best. Partners of large and even medium-sized firms generally earn $100,000 or more, and architects who make names for themselves probably won't suffer.

LIFESTYLE: If you can't cope with deadline pressures, choose another career. To keep a project on schedule, you'll probably find yourself working on weekends and/or into the wee hours of the morning.

Expect to live in or near a large city. New York, Chicago, Los Angeles, Boston and Washington, DC, still employ a big percentage of all U.S. architects, but several new areas are growing fast. Maybe you'll find yourself in Dallas-Fort Worth, in one of the growing cities in Florida or in Phoenix or some other part of the Southwest instead. When you entertain clients or co-workers at home, expect your hospitality to be judged—less for the cooking, however, than for the plate the food is served on and the room the food is served in.

WHAT IT TAKES: You have to be a designer, an engineer, a manager and a supervisor. It takes both artistic ability and the capacity to work with technical details. If you whip up great designs that don't conform to zoning or fire laws, you will find yourself with a fairly ordinary pink slip before long. And while you have to know how to work independently, being good with people is equally important. Your job is to satisfy the client, whether that's a newlywed couple building their first home or an industrial development company planning an entire shopping mall or office tower.

Advice from the experienced: don't fall so much in love with your own ideas that you can't incorporate the client's changes.

EDUCATION: A bachelor's degree (usually a five-year program, minimum) and/or a master's degree (one more year) in architecture. 20 percent of all male architects have advanced degrees; one-third of all women architects do.

EARNINGS: $39,400 estimated national mean.

WORKSTYLE: Days of meetings and construction inspections. Most architects travel as part of the job, but eventually it's always back to the drawing board.

AMBIANCE: Informal on most jobs, because the majority of architects work in small, friendly firms.

DIRECT INTERACTION OPPORTUNITIES: Putting your heads together when working on a team project. And then there are all those business trips.

FOR MORE CAREER INFORMATION: The American Institute of Architects, 1735 New York Avenue NW, Washington, DC 20006.

DOCTOR

84% are men   16% are women

+ Oh, admit it. The only thing better than being an M.D. is being one and being married to one, too.

− It's so awkward on invitations. Dr. and Dr., Drs., Dr. and Mrs., Dr. and Mr.?

"Obstetricians and gynecologists are flamboyant. Cardiac surgeons are prima donnas. Dermatologists are a varied lot. They're generally very scholarly, and probably not as tied to medicine as a way of life."

Dermatologists? "They don't have as many demands. Having fewer emergencies makes a difference," insists Dr. Albert Sagdon, a Washington, D.C. psychiatrist. "When you don't have to worry about your life being interrupted, you have a different life."

Sagdon admits that many different kinds of men and women become physicians today. What they all have in common, he believes, is above-average intelligence and a tendency to be "a bit obsessive."

Don't become a hospital administrator if you want to meet and marry a physician, he advises. The doctors and the administration have an inherently adversarial relationship. On the other end of the career scale, don't consider becoming the office secretary. The medical profession is so clubby that the "members," or professionals, believe no outsider truly can understand them. "He may date a medical secretary, but he'll marry a nurse," Sagdon observes.

If you took a survey of the occupations of physicians' wives, nurses would be very over-represented. "At that age when most people are choosing a mate, doctors have very little time for social life," Sagdon points out. "So they socialize with the people they work with. The nurse supports him through medical school, then you see a pretty high percentage of divorces right after school."

Doctors spend a lot of time with patients and with fellow physicians. And yes, doctors do marry doctors. "But it's tricky to have two prima donnas in one family," Sagdon wryly observes.

"Actually, the best way to meet a doctor is if your best friend's brother is a doctor," he concludes. "Some connection like that."

Going to medical school is recommended, nevertheless. You'll have prestige of your own, and he's less likely to divorce someone whose income is paying half the mortgage for the vacation house.

Medicine is not, however, a profession without problems.

1. *The costs of practice are sky-high.* According to one AMA study, the average medical student today graduates $24,000 in educational debt. New doctors have been known to take out $80,000 loans just to set up a suburban practice. One New York ophthalmologist we know bought a practice from a retiring doctor for $30,000, paid $8,000 for malpractice insurance, spent $10,000 for office equipment and prepared to pay $1700-a-month office rent. And that's considered the cheap way to go. (Malpractice insurance alone car cost physicians, in certain high-risk specialties such as obstetrics or neurosurgery, as much as $45,000 annually.)

2. *America has a glut of doctors.* This is nice for patients, because doctors have to compete for our business. Some have already given up scheduling two or three patients for the same office-appointment time slot. ("You can't overbook like an airline" says one doctor.) Others have established evening office hours for the convenience of working women and students. And a lot of the old paternalism and medical chauvinism are melting away.

No wonder, because doctors in private practice now have to

compete with health maintenance organizations, ambulatory surgical centers and shopping mall medical clinics that stay open seven days a week, 12-16 hours a day.

The most glutted states are Massachusetts, New York and Maryland, with 270 or more physicians per 100,000 population. Washington, D.C. has a ratio almost twice that high. If you want to go where you're most needed, set up a practice in Idaho, Mississippi, South Dakota or Wyoming. The ratios there are between 107 and 116 doctors per 100,000 citizens.

3. *Patients expect miracles.* If your great-grandfather got sick at the turn of the century, he pretty much had to accept fate. The doctor was there to attend and to ease the pain, but wasn't always expected to eliminate the source. Today's patients, says the A.M.A., believe that every injury can be repaired and every disease cured. With organ transplants and bypass surgery and new procedures coming into practice every day, the doctor's image in the late 1980s is just too good.

The message to new doctors may be: Don't reassure your patient that everything is going to be just fine. In the cases where it turns out not to be, he'll have you in malpractice court so fast your stethoscope will spin. In fact, the leading claims in malpractice suits are for bad treatment results, delay of needed treatment and misdiagnoses. But the second most common claim against doctors and hospitals, however, is *falling out of bed.*

JOB SECURITY: Once you get a practice established, you should be set for life. Become a P.C. (private corporation) and join the two-thirds of all physicians who make their livings from office practices and wise investments. Despite all the competition and big-city gluts, medicine is a fast-growing profession. There are now 479,000 practicing M.D.'s, and the Bureau of Labor Statistics foresees a need for 163,000 more (an above-average increase of 34 percent) between now and 1995. (Actually, there are only about 450,000 doctors. But the statistics come out higher because some of them hold more than one job, i.e. private practice and hospital staff simultaneously.)

MONEY: Here's the best part. After the hard years of medical school, you'll probably get $20,000 a year or so, plus the possibility of at least partial room and board, as a hospital resident. In the first year, you could start out as high as $46,800 (starting salaries for doctors at VA hospitals). As a working M.D., you'll net an average of $100,000 per year—more if you're a specialist.

Some of the highest-paying specialties (pathology, anesthesiology and radiology included) offer averages of $130,000 or more per year. According to a *Medical Economics* survey, neurosurgeons top the list of physicians in private practice with a net median of more than $147,000 per year. One out of 11 M.D.'s now nets more than $200,000 per year.

Unpleasant note: Female M.D.'s have a national net median income of only $57,190. Surveyors point out, however, that this may be because women physicians tend to be younger, newer in practice and more likely to devote some time to child care, thus limiting their earning hours.

LIFESTYLE: And here's the worst part. No matter how rich or important you are, you are owned by your work. The patient who goes into labor or has a heart attack or threatens suicide at 7:15 p.m. on Tuesday does not know that this is the night of your daughter's piano recital or the night you're finally using the theatre tickets you ordered months before. And even if they did know, it wouldn't change anything. Even worse, in a two-M.D. family, the odds are twice as high that you'll never have a romantic evening alone and that you'll age badly as a result of inadequate sleep. The average male physician works 60 hours per week.

No wonder entire publications (like *Diversion*) exist just to tell physicians where and how to get away from it all. It's good that you'll be able to afford to ski at Zermatt, buy a villa in Port Antonio and go scuba diving off Australia's Great Barrier Reef. You'll need the rest.

WHAT IT TAKES: About $50,000 for medical school, not to mention a sincere desire to help people. Many doctors may have gone into the profession for the money, but they wouldn't hold up long without some deeper motivation as well. You must have the ability to make fast decisions in emergencies, and you'll need a big helping of emotional stability to face the inevitable confrontations with mortality.

Bedside manner is more important than ever. You can take out ads if you want to, but personality is the most important marketing tool a doctor can have.

TRAINING: A bachelor's degree is necessary before entering four years of medical school. From there, you're most likely to take a three-year hospital residency. If you're going into a specialty, that can take another two to five years of advanced training and at least a couple of years of practice before taking the specialty board exams.

At last count, 126 U.S. colleges and universities offered the M.D. degree. Because of competition for admission, many would-be physicians choose to apply to a foreign medical school. About 20 percent of all M.D.'s in practice in the U.S. today have medical school diplomas from abroad. "That may be looked down on by some," one doctor explains, "but they figure it's a lot better than no medical degree at all."

EDUCATION: M.D. degree, normally a four-year program after college. Residency of at least three years. State license.

EARNINGS: $100,000 net national average.

WORKSTYLE: Long working days, irregular hours and great emotional demands.

DIRECT INTERACTION OPPORTUNITIES: The O.R., the E.R., the doctor's lounge. When a man hasn't slept in 24 hours, he's susceptible to suggestion. Make one.

FOR MORE CAREER INFORMATION: Office of Related Health Professions, American Medical Association, 535 North Dearborn Street, Chicago, IL 60610.

ENGINEERING TECHNICIAN

82% are men   18% are women

   + You'll work very closely with all those engineers.

   − You'll never get rich.

Q: What's the difference between an engineer and an engineering technician or technologist?

A: About $15,000 a year.

And three years of formal education.

   But a brochure distributed by the National Executive Committee for Guidance and approved by two professional engineering associations offers a more useful breakdown.

> *The engineer applies available scientific knowledge to plan, design, construct, operate and maintain complete technical devices and systems.*

> *The engineering technologist applies engineering knowledge to the solution of technical problems. He or she organizes the people, materials and equipment to construct, operate, maintain and manage technical engineering projects.*

If you're interested in engineering and in working intimately with all those male engineers, this is a faster way to enter the field than going to engineering school.

   In fact, what the engineering technician or technologist does all day may be your idea of what an engineer does for a living anyway. Typical duties include setting up experiments and calculating the results, often using computers; developing experimental equipment and models; doing drawings, sketches and some routine design work; preparing materials specifications, and devising tests to ensure product quality. Technicians also may function as field representatives or sales reps, passing along their expertise on installation and maintenance to the company's customers. Some become technical writers (see page 209).

It's a large industry, with about 855,000 people now working as either engineering or science technicians. Four out of five work in the private sector. You might find a job with a chemical, electrical equipment, machinery or aerospace company. Or you might work for an engineering, architectural or communication firm.

Some possible job specialties include the following.

• *Aeronautical Technology.* The engineers you work with may be designing and producing airplanes, rockets, guided missiles or even spacecraft. Your part in this might include preparing design layouts or models, doing lab tests or checking the accuracy of others' technical drawings or computations.

• *Air Conditioning, Heating and Refrigeration Technology:* Someone has to build a model of the new air conditioner. And someone has to create accurate installation instructions. You'll probably work exclusively in one product category—refrigeration, for instance.

• *Civil Engineering Technology.* While the engineers you work with are building a new highway or bridge, you might be drawing up materials specifications, working with the surveying team or estimating costs.

• *Electronics Technology.* Here, you could work on anything from home computers to radar systems to high-tech medical equipment. You may test, adjust and repair the equipment you work with. It's an asset here to understand the industry in which the equipment will be used.

• *Industrial Engineering Technology.* They used to call industrial engineers, "efficiency experts." Your work in this specialty could mean planning work flow, studying industrial safety or conducting time and motion studies.

• *Mechanical Engineering Technology.* You may make sketches and layouts of the tools and machines your company is designing. You'll also test experimental models and make recommendations for change. You could work in a specialized field like automotive technology.

• *Instrumentation Technology.* The title refers to complex measuring and control devices. You might help develop and design them for use in automated manufacturing, space exploration, oceanography, satellite communication, medical research or any number of other specialties.

JOB SECURITY: Your career as an engineering technician will be sensitive to the economy, just as careers are for the engineers themselves. The most recent Bureau of Labor Statistics projection was for "much faster than average" occupational growth between now and the 1990s. A number of technicians choose to go back to school, get their own engineering degrees and then move up into the professional ranks.

MONEY: According to the latest data, engineering technicians with two years of specialized education in the field receive average starting salaries of $11,600 per year. Those with a bachelor's degree in engineering technology earn more. Senior technicians in private industry average $22,300 per year. Technicians with Federal Government jobs average about $22,700.

LIFESTYLE: A career in engineering technology shouldn't take over your personal life. Engineers tend to be devoted workers, however. So if you're trying to impress one, working late might be a good start. When the two of you have settled down to live happily ever after, setting up an attractive, well-organized home office could insure togetherness.

WHAT IT TAKES: For starters, you'll need an aptitude for math and science—and a solid educational background in both. Technicians have to do detailed work, the kind that takes a certain amount of manual dexterity. This is not the career for undisciplined, unbridled creativity; accuracy matters.

Finally, you'll only be happy in this work if you like people. You're going to be part of an engineering team on your projects. And in the beginning, you're going to be closely supervised by the engineers or experienced technicians you report to. The closer he supervises, the better you look.

For more on engineers, see page 36.

EDUCATION: Two years of specialized training at a college or vocational school.

EARNINGS: $20,100 national average.

WORKSTYLE: Varies widely, depending on specialty.

DIRECT INTERACTION OPPORTUNITIES: Lots of teamwork and close supervision.

FOR MORE CAREER INFORMATION: Engineers Council for Professional Development, 345 East 47th Street, New York, NY 10017.

FINANCIAL PLANNER

85% are men   15% are women

+ With your combined financial savvy, the two of you ought to be able to retire early and sail around the world.

− When he buys you champagne and whispers in your ear, he may just be trying to sell you insurance.

Fall in love with a financial planner, and you'll probably be falling in love with an insurance agent or stockbroker too. This doesn't mean carefully scheduling your social life to keep two lovers from bumping into each other on the stairway; the financial planner is usually two, two, two men in one.

According to a membership survey by the International Association for Financial Planning, (I.A.F.P.), 74 percent of all planners hold insurance agents' licenses. And 58 percent hold Series 7 or Series 24 licenses from the National Association of Securities Dealers.

Financial planning is such a new career that, for many, it's still a sideline. And only a small percentage of today's planners went straight into the business after college. Most were in the securities, insurance, banking or even real estate field before making this career shift.

Wherever he came from, he's doing well. The average planner

earns $76,200 per year, and he's only 41. Chances are a little better than one in three that he holds a bachelor's degree (but not necessarily in a field that has anything to do with his work). Only 13 percent have M.B.A.'s, and another 10 percent have other advanced degrees. Almost 40 percent of financial planners have no college degree at all.

This may change drastically in the years ahead now that colleges and universities like Brigham Young, Drake, Georgia State and Golden Gate (in San Francisco and Los Angeles) offer bachelor's and/or master's degrees in the subject. Several other schools, including Adelphi, The American College (in Bryn Mawr, Pennsylvania) and at least three University of California campuses, offer financial planning certificate programs. But for now, the planner you meet may be a self-made man whose only degree is from the school of hard knocks (well-known, but no football team).

Women are outnumbered in America's financial planning offices, but we may catch up fast. The class that entered Denver's College for Financial Planning in 1983 was 23 percent female. The beauty of this career is that, even if your office someday becomes predominantly female, your client list probably won't.

The average financial planning client is just the kind of guy you'd love to spend your work day a desk's width away from. First of all, he *is* a he; about 68 percent of clients are male. He's about 43 and earns $80,335 per year. And when you're an established planner, you'll have an average of 133 clients to choose from.

Exactly what will you do for them? A new client fills out a lengthy financial questionnaire. This helps you determine his net worth, among other things, and set financial objectives. What he gets in return is a detailed financial plan, usually including a budget analysis, balance sheet and cash-flow statement. You may coordinate execution of the plan, and you may actually sell the products or services you recommend. The most popular investments are real estate tax shelters, followed by stocks and bonds, mutual funds, money market funds and IRAs.

JOB SECURITY: No one sees anything but enormous growth for the industry. "The need for financial planning is so high that we're not even scratching the surface at present," an I.A.F.P. officer told

National Underwriter, a trade publication. Because of inflation and tax-bracket creep, even middle-income earners now feel they need expert advice. And it seems they'd rather get it from one person, rather than visiting a banker plus an insurance agent, plus a stock-broker and so on.

Whether you're self-employed or with a financial planning firm, your income should be secure as long as you have good clients. Like other professionals, you'll build a practice with regular clients and often get new business from referrals. A number of large compa-nies—from Merrill Lynch to Sears—now offer financial planning services, offering you career opportunities in a more corporate en-vironment.

MONEY: We've already shared the good news about the average income you can expect as a planner. You're most likely to earn most of that from commissions, although you may work on a fee only, commission only or a combination fee-and-commission basis. Clients may pay fees of anywhere from $50 to $200 per hour. The cost of completed plans may range from $200 or so for a computerized printout to $2,000 for a customized detailed plan. A client with complex finances could pay as much as $30,000.

At least 15 percent of all planners earn $100,000 or more. An estimated 1.9 percent earn more than half a million per year.

LIFESTYLE: Whatever you want. The greatest number of planners live in California, Florida and the Northeastern cities, but the field is growing in all 50 states and in cities of all sizes.

WHAT IT TAKES: You don't have to be a kid with a hot new M.B.A. to get into financial planning today. In fact, maturity can be an asset—if only because you've had time to build a network of clients and contacts. You've also had some years of experience, working in or learning about money management, investments, insurance and tax planning. After all, if your clients don't have reason to believe you know your stuff, you won't have them as clients for long.

Good communication skills are important; you'll need to explain plans and write clearly. Attention to detail is a must. You'll need to be a saleswoman, if only to see yourself and your expertise. And you need to be able to work well with people, because your good relationships with professional advisors (accountants, brokers, lawyers, insurance agents and the like) are part of what you're selling.

GETTING HIRED: Large firms with financial planning departments may hire graduates straight from school. Many firms of all sizes, however, prefer to hire people with professional experience and contacts in related industries. I.A.F.P. suggests going into banking, accounting, insurance, securities or even law to prepare for a financial planning career.

One newspaper ad for a financial planner called for "experience in working with high net worth individuals... insurance, mutual funds, tax-advantaged products and a demonstrated ability to earn a six figure income." The president of a West Coast firm says opportunities are tremendous for people with "a good understanding of taxation, investments, cash flow, estate planning and the ability to integrate all that into financial planning."

EDUCATION: A college degree is necessary these days, ideally a bachelor's in financial planning or services. At the very least, get a business degree with courses in investments, taxes, financial planning and estate planning. To be taken seriously, get C.F.P. (certified financial planner) or other professional certification.

EARNINGS: $76,200 national average.

WORKSTYLE: Basically an office job with a 40-hour-and-up work week and at least an occasional evening or weekend client appointment. Some self-employed planners run their business from home.

DIRECT INTERACTION OPPORTUNITIES: Client meetings, consultations with financial advisors, day-to-day office contact.

FOR MORE CAREER INFORMATION: International Association for Financial Planning, 5775 Peachtree Dunwoody Road, Atlanta, GA 30342. The College for Financial Planning, 9725 Hampden Avenue, Suite 200, Denver, CO 80231.

FOREIGN SERVICE OFFICER

82% are men   18% are women

+ It's the ultimate glamor career, living abroad with perks galore.

− Remember the American Embassy take-over in Iran.

Representing America abroad has become risky business in the last few years. More than 100 foreign service officers have been killed in the line of duty. Five ambassadors are known to have been murdered since 1968. And if you get an assignment to El Salvador, you do not have the privilege of turning it down. When you sign up, you are agreeing to go anywhere in the world you're sent.

Yet for every new Foreign Service Officer candidate who packs up for his or her first overseas assignment, there are 50 who applied for the job and didn't make the grade. The pluses must make up for the risks.

There are the official receptions, lunches and cocktail parties, of course. In fact, one female officer's worst problem so far has been "spending a fortune on clothes."

No wardrobe allowance is part of the job (maybe because women in any number are new to the career, and men can always get away with a single tuxedo), but the Foreign Service seems to have thought of almost everything else.

Take housing. Even if you joined at the lowest possible job level (Level 9—perhaps a clerical employee or communications technician), you'd get a sizeable "quarters allowance" in many locations. In a hardship post like El Salvador, you'll get free government housing (almost half of all posts fall under the hardship classification). Even in Paris, perhaps the most desirable base of all, you'd get almost $10,000 per year to put toward your rent check. In Tokyo, it's $6100 for a Level 9 employee. In Buenos Aires, it's $16,000.

Then, in addition to your base salary, you may get a cost-of-living allowance. On top of that, you'll get a salary differential of up to 25 percent in hardship posts. Ethiopia, Pakistan, Afghanistan, Liberia and Upper Volta are among the 25 percent posts at the moment.

An assignment in Manama, Bahrain, will get you a 15 percent bonus. (It's on the Persian Gulf, just east of Saudi Arabia, and has an excellent paved road system.)

Every time you move to a new post, the U.S. government pays your moving expenses, of course. They'll ship your car to the new city and store or ship your furniture. And between every overseas assignment, they'll hand you a plane ticket and send you home for a six-week leave. Naturally, all your travel expenses are paid.

An unlikely combination of the search for adventure and for security draws people to the Foreign Service life. If you feel the pull, you'll probably like the men in the Foreign Service. The career has a reputation for being restricted to Ivy League men with preppy backgrounds, and there are plenty of those types around. In one recent study of 201 new F.S.O.'s, 45 were graduates of Ivy League schools (Yale, Harvard and so on). The largest group, 22, were from Georgetown University in Washington, D.C. Of course, you'll find top people from state universities too—in an assortment of geographical backgrounds, races, colors and creeds.

The average new Junior Officer is 31 years old, although you can now join up as late as age 60. The average Class 2 officer is 38-40; the average Class 1 officer is 43-45. He's a well-educated man. More than half of all recent appointees have master's degrees. More than one in ten has a law degree. Six percent have Ph.D.'s. Almost half of the new officers speak at least one foreign language; seven percent are fluent in two or more. And if he can't chat in French, Spanish or some foreign tongue now, he'll be able to by the end of training.

The Foreign Service seems to encourage you to meet and marry a fellow officer. When you do, they make every effort to give you "tandem assignments"—which means moving to and working in the same city. If that's impossible, you'll either have to endure the strains of a commuter marriage for a while, or one of you will have to go on unpaid leave until a tandem assignment is available.

As of 1981, there were 180 "tandem" couples. One woman, who married a fellow officer after five years on the job, got joint assignments with her husband in Pakistan and India, then chose to go on leave when she was pregnant. They have two small children now, are both back at work and are managing quite nicely, thank you.

You may end up in any number of jobs at any of America's more

than 230 embassies and consulates, in any of more than 140 nations.
• *Administrative Affairs*. Includes personnel, security, information systems, general services and the budget and fiscal areas. This area offers plenty of variety. You might develop new computer techniques, negotiate with customs officials or coordinate an overseas trip for the President.
• *Consular Affairs*. This means issuing visas. It also means representing America to U.S. travelers abroad, especially in time of need.
• *Economic Affairs*. Negotiating agreements and presenting U.S. economic positions to foreign officials.
• *Political Affairs*. Analyzing and reporting on any political matters that affect U.S. interests. Because political officers may specialize in a certain area of the world, this is a great place for former Asian studies, Latin American studies or similar majors. This is one of the most desirable work areas, because most ambassadors come from political affairs.

JOB SECURITY: You have four years to "learn the business" and prove yourself in the field. If you make it, and nine out of ten do, you're granted tenure. Then you practically have to be convicted of espionage to lose your job.

MONEY: Most Junior Officer candidates start at Level 5 or 6 (the equivalent of Civil Service Grades 9 and 8), with salaries of $19,740-$22,531. Income at Level 5 can go up to $33,000. If you have considerable work experience, you might join at Level 4 and a starting salary of almost $28,000. Senior Foreign Service Officers earn approximatly $61,000-$72,000. Chiefs of missions earn $68,700-$86,200. Remember the perks, too. Base salary is only a part of the overall package.

LIFESTYLE: Go to see "The Year of Living Dangerously" as research (or even just to look at Mel Gibson for two hours). Foreign Service-type Sigourney Weaver's social life appears to consist of lazy afternoons having drinks at poolside, rock 'n' roll parties attended primarily by journalists and other working Americans plus rather sedate formal parties. And this was just prior to the 1965 coup in Indonesia.
If you're based in a world capital like London or Paris, your

personal life is your own. Otherwise, the whole world may often seem to be watching and you may hear the words "be discreet" more often than you would like to.

And when you aren't on the move, pulling up roots for a transfer to a new post, someone else always is. Plan on attending a lot of farewell parties.

WHAT IT TAKES: The State Department booklet refers to "uncommon commitments...occasional hardships...a firm dedication to public service." Consular officers have to be sensitive to people and to foreign cultures. At the same time they exercise tact, they have to be tough decision-makers. Accurate political and cultural perceptions are high on the list of a good economic officer's skills. Perseverance is particularly important for Political Affairs officers, while topnotch management skills are crucial for Administrative Affairs officers.

Writing ability is important since the Foreign Service relies on reports from the field. And above all, being flexible is a key to getting things done in every Foreign Service job. This career is no game. After all, little errors can have big international consequences.

GETTING HIRED: This is the hard part. In 1982, almost 17,000 men and women applied to take the Foreign Service four-hour written exam given annually. More than 14,000 flunked. (Of course, if at first you don't succeed, you can take the test as many times as you'd like, until you either pass or give up.)

The way it normally goes, about 2000 of the 2600 or so left will be eliminated from consideration during the day-long oral exam. It's not even that there are right or wrong answers at this stage; would-be officers are judged on how they handle themselves, instead. Another 100 or more will be eliminated by either the physical or security check—or will give up and take jobs with international corporations during the 18 months this process usually takes, from start to finish.

Eventually, one in 50 of the original applicants will become Foreign Service Officers. Today, one out of three new trainees is female.

TRAINING: You'll start with a 12-week training period, a process that has changed in character in recent years. Not so long ago, new officers learned about the service's traditions, ethics, organization and job duties by sitting through lecture after lecture. Today, you're just as likely to find yourself role-playing (you have to help a young American who's been jailed on drug charges in an enactment that seems to have been lifted straight from *Midnight Express*) and simulated crises (the embassy is under siege and you may be taken hostage).

There are six and a half weeks of general training, followed by five-and-a-half weeks of consular training. You'll attend seminars in which you'll simulate every aspect of an embassy's operation. And if you aren't already proficient in at least one foreign language, additional training to make you fluent can take up to five-and-a-half months. Training in areas like policy-making and negotiating comes much later, after you've gotten tenure.

No matter what area of operations you're going into, you'll spend your first six months on the job as a consul. Do not expect Paris or Rome as an initial assignment. You're more likely to go to, as a *New York Times Magazine* writer described it, "yet another climactic hellhole that will stretch body and soul and family relationships to the breaking point." So is the Foreign Service really a glamor job? Its offerings can range from great luxury to great danger. And to some people, both are just two forms of the same thing: work as peak experience.

EDUCATION: Bachelor's degree minimum; preferred majors include political science, international relations, economics, languages and law.

EARNINGS: The equivalent of Civil Service Grades 5-15. $19,740-$27,806 starting salaries for Junior Officers. Maximum: $86,200 plus all those special allowances.

WORKSTYLE: Every job is different, but your work will be your life. You're likely to spend 60 percent of your career working abroad, making a move every two to four years.

DIRECT INTERACTION OPPORTUNITIES: All those official parties. All those unofficial get-togethers. All those Ivy League men.

FOR MORE CAREER INFORMATION: U.S. Department of State, Recruitment Division, P.O. Box 9317, Rosslyn Station, Arlington, VA 22209.

GEOLOGIST/GEOPHYSICIST

86% are men   14% are women

+ You'll get a really nice, down-to-earth kind of guy.

− You know what they say about nice guys.

The brochure's title is *Women Exploring The Earth*. Inside, five women's photos appear alongside profiles of their backgrounds and geoscience careers. Three have become successful with only bachelor's degrees (one each in math, physics and geophysics) working in offshore exploration operations, telecommunications and computer-enhanced seismic data. One, a soil engineer who holds both bachelor's and master's degrees in geophysics, has worked in Iran and on the Alaskan pipeline. The fifth, with a B.A. in geology and an M.S. in geophysics, has made an international career, interpreting data for a large oil company with global interests. She works and lives in Singapore with her husband, a fellow geophysicist she met back in the U.S.

The Society of Exploration Geophysicists didn't have to search high and low to find five outstanding women geoscientists to feature in their career brochure. By 1982, almost one out of four U.S. geology graduates was a woman, while 23 percent of all the master's degrees in geology went to women, as did about 18 percent of all Ph.D.'s in the field. In physics, the figures were slightly lower— from seven to 14 percent of all degree-holders were female.

What this means is that a woman geoscientist is no longer an oddity. She is, however, almost sure to find herself surrounded by men—nice men—in her profession.

"The geologists were your basic earthy-type people," former geology major Joanna Bellamy recalls. "They weren't flashy. They
weren't showy. They were all very smart, very interested in their
environment, very nice people. And they were very social. They
always liked to drink a few beers, socialize, talk shop."

According to working geoscientists, they still do.

"Maybe one of the reasons geologists and geophysicists have that
kind of camaraderie is that there haven't been any women on the
job to intrude on that male clubhouse atmosphere" believes one
woman. "And really, what other kind of man would major in earth
science?"

Oh, the kind of man who wants to finally determine what happened to the dinosaurs 65 million years ago. The kind whose work
might save lives the next time Mount St. Helens erupts or when
the next big California earthquake strikes. The kind who may some
day teach us all about the relationship between the ocean and cli-
matic variability.

Still, if you lined up ten geologists and geophysicists along your
living room wall, at least four of them would be working for oil and
gas companies. Another would be employed by a service company
involved in oil and gas exploration. Still another would be a Federal
government employee, probably with the Bureau of Mines or with
the U.S. Geological Survey.

"Most of the students that I went to school with ended up working
for major oil companies," Bellamy confirms. And how do these highly-
principled Earth Day-types feel about having sold out to big business?

"That's a funny thing," she says. "Most of them aren't there so
much to make money. I don't think most of them think in terms of
'I'm working for a big, bad oil company.' They just think 'I'm there
to do a job, to find oil wells.' I mean, do you relate it to world crises?
I don't know if they've even thought about it."

Whether you decide to work for an oil company or not, the trick
in the geosciences is to keep the job titles straight. The Bureau of
Labor Statistics' *Occupational Outlook Handbook* finally gave up in
1985 and began reporting on geologists and geophysicists as one job
classification, noting that the two fields are "closely related."

If you become a geologist, you'll "study the composition, structure and history of the earth's crust." You may try to find out how various rocks were formed and what has happened to them throughout history.

If you become a geophysicist, your work will be a little broader in some ways and a little more specialized in others. In addition to the earth's surface and internal composition, your areas of expertise might include the earth's atmosphere and its various forces: magnetic, electrical and gravitational fields. To study those areas, you'll need the very specific tools and principles of math and physics.

The term refers to either career: geology or geophysics.

There are, however, a dozen or more other scientific occupations that fall into one or both of these fields, many of them with familiar-sounding names. *Seismologists*, who study earthquakes, are geoscientists. So are *paleontologists*, the men and women who study fossils found in geological formations. *Geodesists* study the earth's gravitational field, often using satellites to map the earth's surface. *Astronomers* or *space scientists* are considered geophysicists. *Oceanographers* are geoscientists, although they can confuse the issue further by specializing and calling themselves *physical oceanographers, marine meteorologists, marine geophysicists, marine chemists* or *marine biologists*. And then there are the *hydrologists, tectonophysicists, volcanologists, petrologists, geochemists, planetologists, mineralogists* and even *meteorologists*.

Despite all the possibilities, women in the field have concentrated on one area: teaching. In an early 1980s statement, the American Geological Institute (A.G.I.) pointed out that 52 percent of all women geoscientists held academic jobs. Overall, the academic world accounted for only 21 percent of all jobs in the field.

"Teaching is not the best choice for a couple of reasons," says one female geologist. "A, it's very tough to find a job. And B, you're going to meet a lot more men working for an oil company. The money is better in petroleum geology too."

One reason women may have stayed away from the industry's nonteaching jobs, A.G.I. points out, may be the career's reputation for ruggedness. Given a choice between a job site in the Indonesian jungle or an air-conditioned classroom in New Haven or Ann Arbor, working conditions can be a deciding factor.

"Although the field aspects of geoscience are often over-emphasized as rugged, physically strenuous work conducted under primitive living and working conditions, women should not be deterred," A.G.I. urges. "In most cases, these stories are exaggerated. Many women have already demonstrated their ability to perform in the field and underground in the mines. While field work should be considered a basic part of a working geoscientist's function, many geologists work almost exclusively in the office and laboratory."

JOB SECURITY: It's been called a boom-or-bust career. The remainder of the 20th century, however, promises only a modest geoscience boom. According to the Bureau of Labor Statistics, there will be approximately 60,000 geologist's jobs by 1995. That's a thoroughly average increase of 24 percent.

Our future needs as a society are expected to create many jobs, as geoscientists will be needed to search for critical minerals and sources of fresh water. They will be called on to solve serious environmental problems, such as hazardous waste disposal. And they will be needed to locate additional energy supplies. An estimated 90 percent of all money currently spent on geophysical exploration is devoted to the oil and gas industries.

MONEY: You might start at $23,800 (the national average starting salary) with a bachelor's degree, $29,000 with a master's. The national median for geologists and geophysicists in all kinds of jobs is about $33,000. Federal government jobs average about the same for geologists, with a slightly higher average ($35,200) for geophysicists. Starting salaries for Federal government employees in this field can range from $13,000 or so with a bachelor's degree to almost $30,000 for Ph.D. holders.

LIFESTYLE: If you grew up in the farm country of Wisconsin or in the middle of New York City and can't bear the thought of moving away from your hometown, don't even consider geoscience as a career. About two-thirds of all geologists work in Texas, California, Louisiana, Colorado and Oklahoma. The greatest number of geophysicists work on the Gulf Coast, in the western or southwestern

U.S. or overseas. You may find yourself working on an oil rig, relocating to the Far East or even settling down in suburban comfort near Houston or New Orleans.

WHAT IT TAKES: A geoscientist should enjoy "working on a puzzle from which half the pieces are missing," says A.G.I. You'll need the ability to work as part of a team, good adaptability to different peoples and cultures, and physical stamina for the field work that can be a big part of the job.

Your educational background should have given you a strong foundation in math, including differential and integral calculus. Computer programming also has become a near-must.

The job calls for "accurate observation followed by objective reasoning." If you're the perfect geoscientific couple, you'll be curious and analytical. You'll be keen observers who notice details and can visualize things in three dimensions. And when this guy buys you a diamond, you'll both know exactly what it's worth.

EDUCATION: Master's degree in geology or geophysics recommended for all but the lowliest jobs these days. You may need a Ph.D. for a research career.

EARNINGS: $33,000 national median.

WORKSTYLE: Combination of office, lab and field work. Travel and possible work in remote locations come with the job.

DIRECT INTERACTION OPPORTUNITIES: En route to and from the field in the helicopter or the jeep. All sorts of team work.

FOR MORE CAREER INFORMATION: Society of Exploration Geophysicists, P.O. Box 702740, Tulsa, OK 74170-2740; American Geological Institute, Box 10031, Lamar University Station, Beaumont, TX 77710.

LAWYER

84% are men   16% are women

+ Attorneys make excellent money and are never intimidated by landlords.

− They're very hard to divorce.

It has never been this book's intention to advocate a lengthy and expensive education for the sole purpose of finding a man. Unfortunately, there are those who are way ahead of us on the meeting-men-through-work issue. And they don't necessarily agree.

"Lawyers are marrying other lawyers in their firms all the time, especially now that there are more young women attorneys," observes a New Yorker in her twenties. "My friend Teri spent all this time in law school. But as soon as she hooked her honey, she threw away her degree."

The "honey" in question was not an elderly, silver-haired partner, but a fellow attorney in his late 20s. Rumors from paradise are that he's a little surprised by his new wife's early retirement, having assumed that the two of them would enjoy a healthy two-paycheck household income and the concomitant lifestyle. But she refuses to go back to work, her friend reports.

Some might consider this a dishonest approach to courtship and marriage, akin to claiming to be an oil company heiress when in fact you can barely pay the gas bill. Miss Manners would not approve.

And the new groom was not Teri's first office romance. "This one went out with a lot of guys in her firm," the friend continues. "She was *not* hard to get."

What kind of man was she courting? "Lawyers are intelligent and they make good money, but they're also egotistical," summarizes the ex-wife of a tax attorney. "At the office, people treat you like you're God. That has to have an effect on you. You expect to be God at home too." She will allow, however, that attorneys come in behind doctors in that respect.

Is a specialty required? "For some kinds of attorneys, life is one long negotiation, which is great if you enjoy a good argument," she says. "Lots of criminal lawyers have a performer's mentality. But the trouble with tax lawyers is not that they're attorneys; it's that they're accountants at heart." This woman should know. Every time she bought pantyhose, her first husband would make some quick calculations and announce just how long she'd had to work to earn the after-tax money to pay for them.

Almost half of all law students today are women. Sitting in an auditorium of 57 male and 43 female students, you may not come to think of law as a man's field. Things will be clearer when you take your first job.

After deciding to join the rush to law school, your next decision is your specialty. If it's money you're after, study labor law. That's the most lucrative specialty nationwide, followed by insurance law, taxation, negligence-defendant, real property, corporate and business law.

The honor of taking home the smallest paycheck in the law profession belongs to the criminal attorney. Of course, think of the people you'll meet—judges, journalists, felons—when making all those courtroom appearances. Add to the low-paying list all legal aid, public defender and most patent law jobs.

In general, divorce lawyers aren't among the highest-paid specialists. In big cities, however, they can bill $100-$300 per hour—which normally adds up to about $5,000 per attorney per divorce.

When choosing an employer, going with a large firm (100 attorneys or more) can mean an equally large income. Back in 1980, a national survey showed that partners at big firms had a median income of more than $193,000.

• *Computer law* is a fast-growing specialty to be considered. The need for legal expertise in this area had become apparent by 1983. At that time, more than 3,500 computer-related cases were in the courts, yet the nation's leading computer litigation people knew of not a single college course in computer law. The situation has subsequently changed drastically. Law schools have begun to offer study that focuses on "the use of computers as a legal aid, the protection of computer software as intellectual property, contracting for computer services and government regulation of computers" (as outlined in a St. John's University law school syllabus).

Many computer cases center on old-fashioned contract disputes. Others have to do with "pirating," such as the famous case in which IBM accused two Japanese companies and several individuals of conspiring to steal confidential computer data (IBM vs. Hitachi, Mitsubishi et al.). Even if you can't yet get a degree in computer law, you'll need to be expert in areas such as the uniform commercial code and Federal copyright, patent and trade secrets laws.

• *Space law* is even newer and just as wide open to new attorneys as its name implies. At the moment, law firms handling aerospace cases primarily do work concerning the legal aspects of communications satellites. If the forecasters are right, however, the use of private space shuttles will soon open up the area and will create a new generation of billionaires. All of whom will need lawyers.

There are few precedents in this specialty, but at least ten schools already offer courses in space law. Among them: Yale, Southern Methodist, Northwestern, Columbia, Fordham, Georgetown and Notre Dame.

• *Divorce law* isn't new, but it's still growing. And when you represent the wronged husbands, you're constantly meeting soon-to-be-very-available men.

Job Security: The well-documented job-market glut of men and women with law degrees continues, with one lawyer for every 418 U.S. citizens. In litigious Washington, D.C., there is one attorney to every 25 residents. The best opportunities for opening and building a practice might be in one of the five states where only one attorney is at work for every 700 or more people: Alabama, Arkansas, West Virginia and both North and South Carolina.

According to one survey, corporate attorneys are facing heavy unemployment, and mergers, acquisitions and all manner of business consolidations are the culprits. In fact, finding and keeping a salaried law position or opening a new practice has become so difficult that it's no longer unusual for new graduates to put their law degrees to work in another field entirely. You might decide to work in trust administration or another area of banking, in labor relations, government or real estate.

Despite all these troubles, law is one of the faster-growing occupations in America. The Bureau of Labor Statistics expects us to be keeping 624,000 lawyers in business by 1995, an above-average increase in the number of jobs of 34 percent.

MONEY: In the early 1980s, young lawyers were being offered such high starting salaries by private firms that an outcry arose from the public sector. Stop paying them so much, the plea went, or we'll never get any of them to come and work for us. An attorney with Skadden, Arps (one of New York's largest law firms), however, pointed out that he had lived better on his 1948 starting salary of $3600 than new attorneys could manage on $40,000 a year today.

In 1983, the average starting salary for an attorney in private industry was $28,000. The national average salary for all lawyers was $52,000. The average for highly experienced attorneys in private industry was almost $85,000. Chief legal officers of corporations have a median income of just over $94,000. Corporate compensation is highest in the north central and northeastern states, where the median for that job is over $100,000.

LIFESTYLE: The average attorney is a 38-year-old man who works upwards of 50 hours a week and spends at least one Saturday a month in the office. By some accounts, he spends the rest of his weekend time driving his BMW to and from his country house.

In a two-attorney family, you may not eat every dinner together. But you'll be able to afford the very best take-out cuisine.

WHAT IT TAKES: Are you the sort of person that friends always come to when a big problem needs solving? Do the people you know tell you their most profound secrets, because they feel sure you'll understand and try to help? The ideal attorney is the kind of person who inspires that kind of confidence and trust, not only in her clients but in judges, juries and associates. The job also calls for a person who has perseverance, integrity, topnotch reasoning abilities and a strong sense of responsibility. But then law school usually weeds out those who don't.

EDUCATION: J.D. (juris doctor) or LL.B. (bachelor of law) degree, usually a three-year program after three or four years of college. Before beginning practice, you also have to pass the bar exam in your state. An advanced law degree is a good idea, if you plan to specialize, teach or do research.

EARNINGS: $52,000 national average.

WORKSTYLE: Long hours and considerable pressure. Schedules are more structured in salaried jobs, more flexible in solo practice. Travel likely.

DIRECT INTERACTION OPPORTUNITIES: Late-night work preparing big cases, business trips in teams.

FOR MORE CAREER INFORMATION: American Bar Association, Information Services, 1155 East 60th Street, Chicago, IL 60637.

PHOTOGRAPHER

80% are men   20% are women

+ It worked for Linda McCartney.

− The best career opportunities right now are jobs taking pictures of viruses.

When Linda Eastman was an assistant at *Town & Country* magazine, she knew how to network. Invited to a press party for the Rolling Stones, she took her camera along—and promptly decided that she was a photographer. She presented a photo she'd taken of Brian Jones to one of the group's business associates, Peter Brown. As a thank you, Brown invited her to a London club (she was in town on assignment), where he introduced her to Paul McCartney. Linda fell madly in love.

After "the cute Beatle" had broken up with his longtime girlfriend Jane Asher, Linda and her camera turned up at an Apple Records press conference. She slipped Paul her phone number. They went out. They were married on March 12, 1969.

It doesn't always work that way, as in the case of Ron Galella, the photographer who pursued Jacqueline Onassis so relentlessly that she won a court order to keep him at a distance. Literally.

But photography definitely can be a way to meet men: models, photographic subjects, journalists and fellow photographers. We asked a former sports magazine editor some questions about his co-workers.

Fringe Benefits: "What kind of man becomes a photographer?"

Editor: "Aggressive, entrepreneurial, hustling. The pull-yourself-up-by-your-bootstraps type. But they're intellectual in the sense that they live in the intellect, more than reality. They analyze. They project."

FB: "Who do male photographers date?"

Ed: "Hertz counter girls."

FB: "OK. But what *kind* of person?"

Ed: "You have to be a good listener to date a photographer. To hear about how wonderful he is and how exciting his life is."

FB: "Do they date fashion models?"

Ed: "The dumber ones."

FB: "What else have you noticed about the photographers you've known?"

Ed: "To a man they are married. And to a man, they are cheating on their wives."

FB: "Who do they marry?"

Ed: "Nice girls who deserve better."

Hmm.

Luckily for photographers, not everyone is such a cynic. Still, when one public relations woman tried to draw a profile of photographers by reflecting on the many she'd known and worked with, the result wasn't altogether flattering. "The one thing they all had in common, come to think of it," she said, "is that they all were constantly flirting with me. But on the two occasions that I decided to respond in any way, they both backed off fast.

"Once, on a two-day shoot, this one photographer just came on to me every minute of the day. He was Italian, about 30 and very short but very sexy. At the end of the two days—about the time that I was thinking, 'Oh, why not?', he announced that he had a beautiful wife and a beautiful baby on the way." Later, thinking it over, the PR rep decided she'd been of interest only because there hadn't been a $150-an-hour model to make eyes at. They'd been photographing luggage, instead.

Even photographers themselves seem compelled to throw in a few unkind words. "Commercial photographers are probably very analytical, very precise, very detailed, very pedantic," says a photography major, now working as a waiter, who limits his camera work to weekends and his personal vision. "If you're an abstract photographer, you're much more an artist, more spontaneous. If you're a documentary photographer, you just want to know more about life."

As a commercial photographer, you'll have a greater chance of meeting the hunks from the head sheets of top modeling agencies. Remember, Tom Selleck started as a model.

Even as a mild-mannered portrait photographer, however, you can do all sorts of close-ups with interesting clients. If you specialize in executive portraits, you'll meet the most successful men in town. If you specialize in head shots for aspiring actors, you'll meet some of the handsomest and most intense. No matter who you're shooting, you'll be the one who gets to say, "Move your head just a touch to the left. That's beautiful. Now give me a little smile. Right. The sexy one. Oh, that's it. Hold that, and keep thinking whatever you're thinking. Oh, what big muscles you have." It works every time.

JOB SECURITY: It's a competitive field, to begin with. Currently, the Bureau of Labor Statistics predicts photography will experience lower than average occupational growth (18 percent in new jobs) between now and the mid-1990s. For the self-employed, this can mean a constant struggle to win and hold on to regular clients. If you're looking specifically for a newspaper job, however, freelancing could be a good start. Just start turning up at news events (a politician's visit to your city or a championship sports playoff, for example), shoot away, then peddle your photos to the newspaper editors who hire.

Your best bets: a job with the police or other law enforcement group or one with a medical or scientific group. These are the fastest-growing specialties, although aiming your lens medically or forensically—at skin eruptions or murder evidence—may not be your idea of photography as a glamor career. To break in, get specific training in ultraviolet and infrared photography and other technical skills required for these very specialized jobs.

Your worst bet (because of both competition and projected slow job growth): photojournalism.

MONEY: Richard Avedon and Francesco Scavullo may be wealthy men, but not all photographers are. Beginning newspaper photographers' salaries range from $9,000 to about $36,000; the national average for those with four to five years experience is $24,960. Salaries are about the same in private industry. Scientific photographers do particularly well, with a national average of more than $33,000.

In a Newspaper Guild report on 139 papers, *New York Times* photographers came out on top with a top minimum salary of $46,020 ($885 per week) after two years. Papers like the *Detroit Free Press* and *Sacramento Union* were in the middle, at about $31,200 (about $600 per week) after four to six years. The lowest top minimums were $14,811 ($284.83 per week) at the *Morgantown Dominion-Post* and $14,560 ($280 per week) at the *Chattanooga Times*, both after four years of employment.

Then there are the non-news photographers who do well in cities like New York and Los Angeles. Shooting an ad for a consumer magazine can pay more than $3,000 per day. High-fashion photographers are the highest-paid group, according to *The American Almanac of Jobs and Salaries*, while travel and product shot specialists come in second and third.

LIFESTYLE: It depends. As a portrait photographer, your weekdays may be spent indoors in the relative peace and quiet of the studio. Then you may cover weddings and other events on weekends. If you're a sports photographer, you may be on the road a good deal of the time and risk getting hit by wild pitches. If you're a fashion photographer, you may work half the time in your studio, the other half on location halfway around the world. Medical and law enforcement specialists may have the closest thing in the photography business to a standard 40-hour work week.

Despite the career's reputation as a haven of independent artists, nearly six out of ten photographers actually hold salaried jobs. Even then, you may be assigned to night or weekend work (especially on newspapers). News events have a tendency not to schedule themselves between 9 a.m. and 5 p.m., Monday through Friday. If there had been photographers to cover the colonists' first armed stand against the British, those who didn't make it to the village green by dawn would have missed the Battle of Lexington.

So your schedule isn't always yours to choose. Unlike doctors, however, you'll often have plenty of advance notice before working at odd hours. And the chance to travel may make up for a lot.

WHAT IT TAKES: Good eyesight and good color vision, for starters. Photographers need creativity and the artistic ability for good composition, and at the same time need an aptitude for nitty-gritty details. Patience is a virtue in this career, whether you're waiting for babies and dogs to strike the right pose or holding still until the quarterback leaps in the air after his touchdown. When Charles finally kisses Diana on the balcony, there's no time to reset your shutter speed and F-stop, so if you haven't been waiting patiently, you'll miss the shot.

EDUCATION: No formal requirements, but college always helps. About 75 schools now offer bachelor's degrees in photography. Many others teach it in the journalism or communication department.

EARNINGS: $24,000-$25,000 national average.

WORKSTYLE: Deadlines and constant demands from customers. The self-employed may have irregular work hours.

DIRECT INTERACTION OPPORTUNITIES: All the times when every photographer in town covers the same event. Private photo sessions with a wide variety of clients. Going over the contact sheets face-to-face in the studio.

FOR MORE CAREER INFORMATION: Professional Photographers of America, 1090 Executive Way, Des Plaines, IL 60018.

Even better, get in touch with local colleges and photography schools.

POLICE OFFICER

89% are men   11% are women

+ You can both retire before age 50 and start a new life.

− What if you don't look good in blue?

"Policemen are either rigid personality types or they're the kind who really enjoy adventure," says Anne Gregory Portland, a former West Coast police dispatcher. "But either way, they like to control people."

Perhaps many police officers show both traits. "They enjoy order, lots of order," she continues. "They're very much into seeing that everything is followed to the letter. But the addictive part of it is the excitement."

Portland isn't surprised by the occasional police department corruption scandal. "I really believe that there's a very fine line between criminals and police. Especially someone like a motorcycle patrolman—he could become a Hell's Angel. They like the power and the authority. They enjoy confrontations.

"It's like playing cops and robbers. You could be on either side. You see policemen that end up going bad, and people are always amazed. I'm *never* amazed. I think that that's what's very likely to happen. They like excitement so much that it doesn't really matter what they're doing."

Well, let's be fair. Who else but someone addicted to excitement would put his or her life on the line to protect a largely ungrateful populace? And for more comforting role models, there are always *Barney Miller* reruns and late-night TV showings of *Serpico*.

If you want to meet a policeman without carrying a gun yourself, a job in the police station records department or dispatch office could provide heavy interactions with the officers on duty. Portland recommends the night shift.

"We had a lot of policemen who would come down on their coffee break, but that would never happen on the day shift," she recalls. "They'd come in and write their reports at the station or the dispatch center." Then they'd hang around and talk.

If you have your eye on a particularly appealing cop, chances are you won't be the only one. It seems that many police departments have groupies of sorts. "There were several women who used to call all the time and say they had prowlers. The cops would say 'Oh, no. Not her again.' Apparently these frequent callers would always greet them at the door in a nightgown and invite them in for a cup of coffee so they could tell them about their problems." The officers in question never shared the details of those visits with Portland or her fellow dispatchers, but she has her suspicions.

Still, the simplest way to meet a policeman—and make a real career of your own—is to become a policewoman. Men and women do go out in patrol cars as teams these days. And thanks to equal employment opportunity pressure, most police departments have opened up all kinds of assignments to their women in blue.

If you work in a big city, you may be part of a department of hundreds of officers. For that reason, you're more likely to specialize. The greatest number of cops are assigned to patrol or traffic duty. Others may work exclusively in an area like accident prevention, firearms identification, communications or juvenile offenders. In very large cities, you might work with the mobile rescue team, mounted police, motorcycle police or other special unit. Or you might become a detective, an investigator who gathers facts and collects evidence for criminal cases.

In a small city or rural area, you'll probably do a little of everything. As the *Occupational Outlook Handbook* explains, you might investigate a housebreaking, give first aid to an accident victim and direct traffic near the scene of a fire—all in a typical day.

One other possible career is as a state police officer. Most often referred to as state troopers or highway patrol, these are the cops who take charge whenever there's a traffic accident. They're also the fine officers that you try to be polite to when they stop you for going 70 on a beautiful clear day on a practically empty highway. Do you know how much speeding tickets cost these days?

Job Security: There may be an outcry for more police protection, especially in big cities, but this isn't one of the fastest-growing occupations around. Hiring of police officers, like that of firefighters, is tied to local government spending. There are about 550,000 cops on the job now, and the Bureau of Labor Statistics projects an increase of only nine percent between now and 1995. That's about one-third the growth for the average occupation.

Still, it's a secure job once you get hired. The benefits are good, and many departments allow you to retire after only 20 years of service. That could mean a life of leisure for the two of you at age 45 or 50, or the possibility of going into a new career with a sizable pension to back you up.

MONEY: Few honest cops ever get rich. The average new police officer starts at $16,400 per year and earns a median income of $18,600 later on. Those who make it to police or detective sergeant earn a median of $22,600. The median salary for lieutenants is $25,500, with an average maximum of just under $28,100.

LIFESTYLE: Most police officers have enough free time to lead normal family and social lives. Chances are, however, that people will always react to you with that same self-conscious barrier they put up for law enforcement types, ministers and IRS agents. No bother. Even when you're barbecuing in the back yard or making peanut butter sandwiches for the kids, you're a cop. It's part of you. Male cops, of course, have been known to take advantage of this awe when dealing with members of the opposite sex.

WHAT IT TAKES: This is a job with specific requirements. You have to be 21 or older, a U.S. citizen and meet department standards of height and weight. In addition to passing the written exam, you have to pass the physical. Strength, agility, stamina and good vision are necessary for police work.

Being "streetwise" doesn't hurt either, according to a veteran suburban New York policeman, because you're going to have to harden yourself in order to deal with the death and suffering you'll see. The job pace may be a little slower in small cities, he admits, but that just means you'll be exposed to harsh realities over a longer period of time. "After ten years on the force *anywhere*, there's almost nothing left to see."

GETTING HIRED: In some cities, little more than a high school diploma and an honest face could get you in the station house door. In others, college graduates are strongly preferred. To make yourself the ideal job candidate, get a bachelor's degree in law enforcement or police science. If that's impossible, at least take a course or two in these subjects at a junior college. Psychology, counseling and public administration courses can be helpful too.

If you live in Miami, New York, Los Angeles or another city with a large Spanish-speaking population, consider taking courses in the language. Being bilingual gives you a real edge in some departments. If you're not in good shape physically, take physical education courses or join a gym to build up strength before signing up for the police exams.

TRAINING: In small cities, your training may be informal on-the-job experience with a veteran officer. In larger cities, there are more formal training programs. You may sit in a classroom to learn about subjects like constitutional law, civil rights and accident investigation. But you'll get hands-on experience for training in areas like traffic control, firearms, first aid and self-defense.

EDUCATION: High school diploma minimum. Some college training gives you an edge in getting hired.

EARNINGS: $18,600 national median.

WORKSTYLE: Normally a 40-hour week, but that may include night or weekend duty. A much higher risk of injury than in the average occupation.

DIRECT INTERACTION OPPORTUNITIES: A patrol car for two. Shooting the breeze at the station house. Maybe even a team undercover assignment.

FOR MORE CAREER INFORMATION: Get in touch with your local police department or with the civil service commission in your city.

SURVEYOR

88% are men   12% are women

+ He's sensible, serious and down to earth.

− He's sensible, serious and down to earth.

Imagine yourself working as a surveyor. Just you and a team of five or six men, carrying the instuments and equipment out onto the land you're going to survey, conducting serious scientific work in wide-open spaces.

Most surveys are carried out by a survey party who measure distances, directions, and elevations of points, lines and contours on the earth's surface. A typical survey party is headed by a party chief, working with anywhere from one to six assistants and helpers. The instrument assistants are those who adjust and operate the surveying instruments.

Of course, field surveys won't take up all of your work days. "It's a small part of the surveyor's work," explains real estate broker Margaret Maxell. "Most of their work is done in the courthouse—looking up deeds, other surveys and tax maps. And they draw these intricate maps."

Perhaps that's why surveyors, cartographers (mapmakers) and geodesists share a common professional association. It's all related and has been since the Babylonians did the world's first known land surveys 3,000 years or so ago.

The Egyptians thought enough of their rich Nile valley to develop their own system of surveying and protect the boundaries and property lines there. Ptolemy (a second century A.D. ruler) invented the system of latitude and longitude.

Yet all these years later, surveying is still not an exact science. Because it's based on boundary law, established by numerous common-law precedents, all land owners have to rely on the surveyor's logic, good judgment and integrity as well as his technical skills.

Maxell describes the surveyors she works with as "nice guys, down to earth, sensible, quite serious and not terribly talkative." She points out that even this seemingly old-fashioned occupation has been transformed by high-tech. "They work with laser beams when they do their surveying. It's the new thing. They shoot the beam and that does the measuring."

You'll meet men with varying levels of formal education in this career. And if you decide to go into it, you'll have the same options.

If you're 18 years old or simply never went beyond high school, for instance, you still could get a job as an assistant on a surveying team. Ideally, you would at least have taken the important courses in high school—lots of math (algebra, geometry, trigonometry), drafting, mechanical drawing and computer science.

Or you might choose to get formal education in surveying at a junior college, community college, technical school or vocational school. One-year, two-year and three-year programs are offered. Having completed one of these programs (or having gotten an official associate's degree in surveying), you probably could start as an instrument assistant.

You'll be most marketable, however, if you have a college degree. A few colleges and universities offer bachelor's degrees in surveying. If that isn't an available option, at least take several courses in surveying while getting a bachelor's degree in a related subject.

The idea is to move up the ranks to survey party chief and finally to licensed surveyor. It generally takes five to 12 years of surveying experience to qualify for licensing. With a college degree, however, you might be able to take the state licensing exam after only two to four years of work experience. Licensing is a must, because surveyors can be held legally responsible for their work.

Chances are you'll work for an engineering or architectural firm. Almost half of all surveyors do. Another 25 percent work for local, state and Federal government agencies. Many land surveying specialists are self-employed.

• *Land surveying* is primarily concerned with determining boundaries and areas of real property. A land survey may mark public lands divided into townships, ranges and sections. Maps may show both natural and man-made features.

• *Engineering surveying* is done for the study and selection of sites for engineered construction. That includes buildings, bridges, highways, streets and utilities.

• *Geodetic control surveying* involves measurements required "to determine the positions of monumented ground points in networks or routes covering the earth's surface." We'll take the word of the American Congress on Surveying and Mapping that this is so.

JOB SECURITY: Here's a confusing job market picture. On the surface, prospects for surveyors look excellent. The Bureau of Labor Statistics forecasts above-average occupational growth (43 percent) between now and 1995. But a good deal of that growth will just be making up for jobs lost during the 1981-82 recession. In 1980, the occupation was about 52,000 jobs strong; by 1982, it was down to 40,000. The surveying field will always be affected by the economy and by declines or increases in construction activity.

There may be growth ahead, however. Professionals point out that the United States employs a very low ratio of surveyors to population, many fewer than in most European countries. As land values rise, as cultural development expands and as we continue to develop remote areas like Alaska, the need for absolutely accurate property and boundary surveys will grow too.

MONEY: If you found an entry-level surveying job right after high school, you'd be likely to earn only about $9,800 per year. If you'd taken the time to get even one year of formal training, that would increase to $10,650. If you'd gone to junior college and gotten an associate degree in surveying, you'd start as an instrument assistant at $11,950. Surveying technicians average just over $15,000 per year. The average income for all licensed land surveyors is $26,240 annually.

LIFESTYLE: Surveyors work in all parts of the country; therefore, so can you. Your work shouldn't affect your private life at all. The worst thing that can happen is that you might work late on beautiful summer days, when the weather is perfect for outdoor surveying.

WHAT IT TAKES: Let's start with the physical. You've got to be in good shape just to be able to carry your surveying equipment over hill and dale. You need good eyesight, hearing and coordination, because you may be communicating with other members of your survey party by hand signals or by shouting across great distances.

Can you do math quickly and accurately "in your head?" Your work in this career has to be accurate to 1/10,000th. Some surveys have to be even more precise. Surveying calls for a detail-oriented worker willing to check and recheck the work. Your drawings and calculations also have to be neat, orderly and easy to read.

If you think being absolutely precise is a waste of valuable time, this is not the job for you. If you admire fastidious work, you could be happy as a surveyor—and as a surveyor's wife.

EDUCATION: One to four years of formal training at a college or technical school. Licensing.

EARNINGS: $26,240 national average.

WORKSTYLE: Active, strenuous field work combined with courthouse research. Generally a 40-hour week.

DIRECT INTERACTION OPPORTUNITIES: Teamwork on the survey party.

FOR MORE CAREER INFORMATION: American Congress on Surveying and Mapping, 210 Little Falls Street, Falls Church, VA 22046.

7 Out Of 10 Workers Are Men

"But men are men; the best sometimes forget."
WILLIAM SHAKESPEARE
Othello

ADVERTISING

77% are men   23% are women

+ It's a glamor biz.

− You'll never again watch TV without thinking about work.

Account executive. The only acceptable position in advertising.
—LISA BIRNBACH ET AL.
The Official Preppy Handbook

Advertising is bigger business than ever. According to an *Advertising Age* estimate, there are about 8,000 ad agencies in the U.S., employing 100,000 people or so and spending roughly $85 billion a year to persuade us to change mouthwash brands, buy jeans with designer labels, fly the friendliest airline and so on.

If you go into the *account side* of advertising, you'll probably start as an account executive (A.E.) trainee or junior A.E. Then you'll work your way as far as possible up the ladder to A.E., then accounts supervisor, accounts manager and C.E.O. By the time you're a supervisor, you may also be a vice president.

The account person's most important responsibility is to keep the client happy. You are the agency's representative to the client, the liaison between the head of that fast food chain and the creative department employees who have prepared the new hamburger commercials. It's your job to know everything relevant to the client's product or service—the target markets, the competition, the sales patterns—and to convey it all to the account team. When it's time to present a new ad campaign to the client, you're in charge. And when it's time to actually execute the plans, the follow-through is your responsibility.

The agency's other side is the *creative department*, staffed primarily by copywriters and art directors. One of the coziest aspects of this work is that most writers and artists are paired off to work as a team. Talent is the most important prerequisite, but being able to write or design the cleverest print ads or TV commercials isn't necessarily the ticket to success. Too many agencies remember— and are wary of—the great campaigns that won all the awards but lost the account. When they remember the punch line but can't recall the name of the product, you're in trouble. (Quick: Did Mariette Hartley and James Garner do those commercials for Kodak or Polaroid?) Creating ads that *sell* the client's product or service is the goal.

A copywriter doesn't necessarily need a business degree (*somebody* has to hire the English majors), but should have taken at least a few advertising or marketing courses. Artists, logically enough, should have majored in art or gone to a visual arts school. For both careers, a portfolio containing samples of previous work is important.

Two other career possibilities: Consider going into *advertising sales*, where 52 percent of the work force is male. If your job is to sell ads in a sports magazine with a high percentage of male readers, for instance, you could spend your days working with the ad managers or representatives of male-oriented product companies. Or become a *media buyer*. The agency media department's job is to look at all the possible magazines, newspapers, TV shows, radio shows and other media in which clients' advertising can be placed. The goal for the buyer is to put budgets to best use by good negotiating and by choosing the media that will best deliver the specific audience the client wants to reach.

JOB SECURITY: Getting hired by an ad agency is a competitive prospect. Keeping the job can be even more challenging. When the agency loses an important account, the entire team working on it can be fired as a result. The bright side is that reputations travel fast within the industry. Finding a new job with a new agency normally won't take long if you're any good.

MONEY: Starting salaries can range from $10,000 to about $25,000. For a glamor industry with a big-money reputation, advertising doesn't pay quite as well as some might think. Account executives earn a national median of $30,500, according to *Adweek's* 1984 salary survey. The median for copywriters is $28,300 and for art directors, $30,000. As you move up, you can do much better, however. Accounts supervisors average $54,000 and the heads of creative departments make $65,000 per year. If you really want to make it big, you'll probably have to start your own agency.

Salaries can go to $100,000 and up in big-city agencies. The highest-paid metropolitan area, also according to *Adweek*, is New York with a median income of $44,000 for all advertising people in agencies, business/industry and the media. The Big Apple is followed in order by Chicago, Los Angeles, Dallas, Atlanta and San Francisco.

LIFESTYLE: We don't know why, but ad people like to party. Maybe their own campaigns inspire them to have beer parties, beach weekends, fast cars, and good friends who all look like models. On the few occasions you don't have to work late, you, too, can get a tan and serve International Coffees at your mountain cabin.

WHAT IT TAKES: Interest, imagination, initiative, energy and a competitive instinct are the requirements for a good AE, suggests one book on the subject. Being organized is another must.

GETTING HIRED: Beginners in advertising can feel a little like ingenues trying to break into the movies. When you send your resumé to the big agencies, you can be sure it will join a few hundred others in a large pile on somebody's desk. One thing that can make yours stand out is related work experience. If you can, get a summer job in the ad department of your local newspaper, TV or radio station. Take any kind of volunteer job or internship at an ad agency. Lower your sights and learn to type. (Almost 42 percent of the women in advertising today say they got their starts with a secretarial or clerical job.) If all else fails, take any job that involves selling and personal contact. And never, never go into an interview without being able to name at least three of the agency's major accounts.

If you're a career changer hoping to enter advertising later in life, much of the same advice holds true. Your best move, however, is to take advantage of the kind of work you've been doing until now. If you've been working as a computer programmer, for instance, present yourself to an ad agency that has one or more computer industry accounts. If you've been a hairdresser, approach agencies that do the ads for hair care, cosmetics and other beauty industry companies. To keep up-to-date on which agencies handle which accounts, read *Ad-Age* and the advertising columns in metropolitan newspapers like *The New York Times*.

EDUCATION: You're nowhere in advertising without a college degree. Business degrees are preferred; an MBA is ideal. At least one-third of all agency employees have gone to graduate school.

EARNINGS: $30,500 national median for A.E.'s; $28,300 for copywriters and $30,000 for art directors.

WORKSTYLE: Working late to meet media deadlines and to prepare client presentations comes with the territory. But so do travel, expense account lunches and an occasional taping with the latest celebrity spokesperson. If you can't learn to live with pressure, don't even consider the business.

DIRECT INTERACTION OPPORTUNITIES: All of the above. Plus, there's no greater excuse for a party, a friendly hug, or hanging out after work, than working together on an important presentation, then landing the account. Losing an account can also present opportunities for commiseration and mutual comforting.

FOR MORE CAREER INFORMATION: American Association of Advertising Agencies, 666 Third Avenue, New York, NY 10017.

CHEMIST

77% are men   23% are women

+ He's an educated man with an analytical mind and a quick wit.

− He may kick you out of your own kitchen.

If you hate to cook, marry a chemist.

Laura Champion, whose husband and father are chemists, claims they're both wizards in the kitchen. "My husband is a marvelous cook, and I attribute this to his being a chemist who no longer has access to a laboratory—because he's risen so far in management," she explains. "In a very real sense, my father was in the same pickle. And he, too, liked to cook.

"They understand about mixtures, temperatures, the whys of what's going on—why corn starch or flour thickens with water over heat. I don't know why.

"My father would focus on a particular thing—like crêpes—to get it exactly right. My husband likes to focus on sauces. Also, the presentation of a meal is very important to him."

Similarities between the two important men in her life extend beyond the culinary. "They have very similar senses of humor," she notes. "They both have an analytical ability to understand quickly the humor in a situation, to capsulize it and say in very few words what's funny. It's not the kind of guffaw you get from a Mel Brooks movie. It's more an admiration for the cleverness of the thinking."

Fall in love with a chemist, and you're equally apt to get a young man as a more mature one. Forty-six percent of all working chemists today are under 40.

Exactly what would you do all day in this career? Recent B.S. chemistry graduates explained their jobs to the American Chemical Society (A.C.S.) student affiliate newsletter in these words.

• *Organic Chemist, Eli Lilley and Company:* "I work with a Ph.D. research scientist who provides practical and theoretical instruction and support. We are presently examining the chemistry of a compound with promising medicinal activity. . . . I synthesize analogues of the compound to assess the effect that a particular structural change has on its pharmacological profile."

• *Spectroscopist, General Refractories:* "I determine the chemical content of various materials by using x-ray flourescence spectroscopy, x-ray diffraction spectroscopy and emission spectroscopy. The chemical content is needed to provide routine quality control, in handling customer complaints, to develop new materials and processes, and to investigate a competitor's product."

• *Laboratory Analyst, Upjohn Company:* "Each product manufacturing process must be documented. I therefore analyze the major ingredients in a large number of products. Besides the actual analytical work, I collect samples during the manufacturing process, do developmental work on the assays... used to analyze the ingredients, and I write the technical reports concerning the analysis and assemble the necessary materials for the final product validation documentation for F.D.A. inspection."

• *Research Chemist, Armstrong World Industries:* "I was hired to operate an excimer laser... and to conduct research using the laser as a tool. Currently, I'm conducting research that involves photo-polymerization initiated by laser light and the analysis of exotherms produced by the polymerization reaction."

• *Supervisor, Crime Laboratories, Department of Public Safety:* "I receive evidence to analyze from law enforcement officers and then submit an official report of the results to the officers and prosecuting attorney. If needed, I testify in court about the results. Types of evidence analyzed include drugs, blood alcohols, blood stains and broken glass."

• *Quality Assurance Chemist, Fasson:* "Fasson manufactures pressure-sensitive adhesives. I run tests, with the help of a technician, on the raw materials to determine if they meet our quality standards. In the lab I use a gas chromatograph, a refractometer, a viscometer, a pH meter and a surface tensiometer."

When experienced chemists looked back on their education in an A.C.S. survey, the college training they'd found most useful was in writing and public speaking. That topped the number two category: calculus, linear algebra and statistics. The studies that had proved least helpful were in geochemistry.

The most important undergradute courses for you to take, according to the same survey, are organic chemistry, analytical chemistry, physical chemistry and inorganic chemistry. The most important nonchemistry subjects: writing, public speaking and computer science.

JOB SECURITY: In 1984, only 1.7 percent of all A.C.S. members were unemployed. Unemployment was lowest in government jobs and teaching. Once you pass the hurdle of getting that first job after college, the job market looks fine. The Bureau of Labor Statistics predicts average occupational growth (22 percent), bringing the total number of chemists' jobs to 109,000 by 1995. The greatest number of jobs are expected to be in private industry.

MONEY: Chemists with brand-new bachelor's degrees start at an average of $21,000 per year; with a master's, $23,800; and with a Ph.D., $32,600. According to the College Placement Council's 1985 report, chemical engineers with bachelor's degrees are given average starting salary offers of $28,488. That's the second highest of all occupations, topped only by petroleum engineers.

Female chemists tend to start off doing as well financially as men. An A.C.S. survey showed that the median starting salary for a woman with a B.S. is $20,000, the same as for men. Both male and female Ph.D.'s taking jobs in private industry start at $35,000.

As time goes on, the earnings gap can widen considerably. Experienced female chemists seem to do best as Ph.D.'s in private industry and government jobs. Their median salaries there are $46,100 and $41,000 respectively, compared to $50,400 and $44,700 for men in similar positions.

The national median salary for all chemists is $38,000; for Ph.D. chemists, $42,000.

The highest-paid chemists are the 6 percent who work for petroleum companies. Their mean salaries are $40,600 with a B.S.; $46,100 with an M.S.; and $55,100 with a Ph.D. You'll also come out on top if you specialize in environmental chemistry ($51,000 median for Ph.D.'s), working your way into general management ($60,000 median for Ph.D.'s) and supervising 100 or more subordinates ($80,000 median).

The lowest-paid chemists are those specializing in biochemistry and those in basic research. In every area of the field, chemists with Ph.D.'s earn more than those with master's, and those with master's earn more than those with only bachelor's degrees.

LIFESTYLE: The good life in a city or suburban home—you should have both the income and the free time to enjoy it. You're even allowed to be a little eccentric if you'd like. All that formal education—and the fact that most corporate types still stand in awe of "real scientists"—allows you to get ahead without fitting into the corporate mold too predictably.

WHAT IT TAKES: Do you like working with your hands? You're sure to be doing just that, building scientific apparatus and doing experiments throughout much of your career. You'll also need imagination, an inquisitive mind, perserverance, attention to detail and the ability to work independently.

If you're interested in meeting chemists rather than becoming a chemist yourself, see the section on science technician, page 158.

EDUCATION: Bachelor's degree in chemistry minimum. Ph.D. necessary for many jobs.

EARNINGS: $38,000 national median.

WORKSTYLE: Regular work schedule in offices and/or labs. Possible exposure to safety or health hazards.

DIRECT INTERACTION OPPORTUNITIES: A microscope, a tensiometer or a spectroscope for two?

FOR MORE CAREER INFORMATION: American Chemical Society, 1155 16th Street NW, Washington, D.C. 20036.

COLLEGE TEACHER

73% are men   27% are women

+ Campus life after tenure can be sweet.

− You haven't seen "corporate politics" until you enter the groves of academe. And you haven't seen "corporate sabotage" until you look at today's freshman women.

The concept of the absent-minded professor may not be far off, according to former Ivy League administrator Hal Bridges. "Most of the people in college teaching are remarkably cerebral," he says. "They spend a lot of their time thinking. But they're also involved in some bizarre corporate politics that would make a shake-up at IBM look like small potatoes."

What would make anyone want such a career? Tenure, says the dictionary, is "permanent status, especially on a faculty after a period of trial." For college professors, it means working for six years at one school and then, if granted tenure, being set for life. Those who don't get tenure have to move on to another school and start all over again.

"College teaching also is a remarkably comfortable existence," adds Bridges. "Teachers often don't know that Harvard is a corporation just like Bendix. Of course, Bendix doesn't throw you out after six years. But then they don't make you a vice president for life—irrevocably—either."

The kind of man you meet in college teaching may be determined more by his field of expertise than by the fact that he's on a college or university faculty. "A law professor is probably more like a lawyer than anything else," Bridges believes, "and an English teacher is more like a writer. At the 'B. School,' you naturally find business types."

In fact, America's campuses may offer a greater variety of men than almost any other work setting. You may find a pipe-smoking, leather-patches-on-the-sleeves intellectual who'll argue Veblens' theories of the leisure class while savoring V.S.O.P. cognac in a book-lined room. Or you could end up with a marketing professor whose hero is Lee Iacocca.

Instructors are lowest on the totem pole. From there, you'll move up to assistant professor, associate professor and finally full professor—if and when you're lucky.

JOB SECURITY: The best and the worst, thanks to the tenure system.

For teachers entering the field in the 1980s, talking about tenure is a little like reaching for the moon. College teaching is one of the few American occupations which is actually expected to decline in the near future. There are 744,000 college and university teaching jobs now, but the Bureau of Labor Statistics predicts that, by 1995, there will be only 633,000. That's a 15 percent decrease [rate of negative growth].

The reasons are simple enough. The last of the Baby Boom generation got their college diplomas in the early 1980s; subsequent enrollments are expected to decline. Adults returning to school have held up enrollment statistics in many areas, but few colleges and universities are hiring. In fact, when retirement time comes for today's professors, some will be replaced and some won't.

MONEY: All teaching has a reputation for dooming its professionals to a life of genteel poverty. Considering the years of formal education required to get started, incomes aren't impressive. Some end up doing well, however.

The money you earn in college teaching depends not only on your job level, but on what you teach and where. The American Association of University Professors divides institutions of higher learning into several categories. At a Class I school, for instance, the average salary for all faculty members is $34,830. This category includes nonspecialized universities that grant a minimum of 30 doctorates in at least three programs. Princeton is a Category I school; so is the University of Alabama.

At a Class IIA school, the average salary for all faculty members is $29,770. These are comprehensive schools with some post-baccalaureate education, but no significant work at the doctoral level. Smith College falls into Class IIA; so does Bemidji State University in Minnesota.

Class III consists of two-year institutions—junior colleges and the like. The average salary in this category is $24,550.

Not surprisingly, the highest salaries overall are for full professors at Class I institutions ($49,880 average). But don't be a snob. You can still do well at a junior or community college. Full professors at the two-year schools average $32,880, which is a little higher than the average for associate professors back at the fancy Class I campuses—and more than $3,000 a year higher than the earnings of associate professors at Class IIA schools.

In terms of geography, New England schools pay best ($49,210 for professors; $32,880 overall average); Middle Atlantic and Pacific Coast colleges are close behind.

If you want to be a rich professor and/or find one, you might make a choice by department. Law professors do best, with an average salary of $45,420 nationwide. And then there's the West Point option: professors at military academies come in second with an average of $42,780. Graduate engineering professors take third place at $42,530 average. The same three subjects come out on top for salaries of teachers at all other levels, too.

The poorest college professors overall? Those in divinity schools. At a baccalaureate level, they average only $18,540.

Another way to assure yourself of good money is to hunt men and jobs at the highest-paying universities. Of 2,000 institutions surveyed by A.A.U.P., more than two dozen pay their full professors an average of $50,000 per year or more. They are:

Harvard University	Rockefeller University
Stanford University	Claremont Graduate School
Yale University	University of Santa Clara
Georgetown University	University of Chicago
Princeton University	Southern California
Massachusetts Institute of Technology	University of Pennsylvania
Wellesley College	Johns Hopkins University
Columbia University	Carnegie-Mellon University

University of California (4 campuses)
State University of New York (4 campuses)

And a couple of unexpected names:
Fashion Institute of Technology (New York)
South Texas College of Law

Of course, as in most careers, women don't get paid as well as men do. The mere handful of colleges that pay female full professors average salaries of $50,000 or more have familiar names: Harvard, Yale, Princeton, Wellesley and Stanford. Duke University may deserve special applause as the only U.S. college that pays its female professors a higher average salary ($52,600) than its male counterparts ($49,000). But then it may be because the North Carolina school has 276 men and only eight women at full professor level.

This study doesn't include medical schools, by the way, where even some associate professors can average $50,000 or more per year.

LIFESTYLE: Even when a campus is right in the middle of a big city, it takes on an atmosphere all its own. Imagine a lifetime of strolling to work and back across a grassy quadrangle in a little intellectual haven that's always filled with youth and promise—the proverbial Ivory Tower. Even in the middle of nowhere, intellectual pursuit goes on at colleges and universities of all sizes. Yes, faculty and administration politics may infringe on your personal life, but it's a small price to pay if this is your preferred milieu. For the darker side, think of the reality depicted in *Who's Afraid of Virginia Woolf?*

WHAT IT TAKES: What could be more important for teaching than good communication skills? Intellectual honesty, an analytical mind and an openness to new ideas are crucial traits, too. No one has given a name to the quality that enables faculty members to deal with the constant jockeying for position and the rivalry that exists on every campus on this planet, but you'll need plenty of it.

EDUCATION: You might get started with only a master's degree in your subject. But if you expect to stay active in this field at all, much less get promoted, a doctorate is an absolute necessity.

EARNINGS: $30,960 national average (including all job ranks and institutional categories).

WORKSTYLE: Flexible schedules, possible variety of work (classroom teaching, research, administration) and a strong likelihood of three months off every summer. Junior colleges may have heavier classloads, but they also can get you away from the publish-or-perish syndrome of high-pressure institutions.

DIRECT INTERACTION OPPORTUNITIES: Innumerable, from department meetings to faculty parties.

FOR MORE CAREER INFORMATION: American Association of University Professors, One Dupont Circle NW, Suite 500, Washington, DC 20036.

Note: If you have a particular educational subject in mind, the professional association for that career field may be able to provide specific information on college teaching opportunities.

INSURANCE SALES

74% are men   26% are women

+ If he should die before you do, your purchasing power will give new meaning to the words "rich widow."

– Until then, no one will want to talk to you at parties.

"If you walked in on a group of insurance salesmen at a convention, they'd look like a whole bunch of stockbrokers—but not dressed as well.

"They go into it because the opportunities are presumably limitless," continues Leigh Ravell, the ex-wife of a suburban New York insurance man. She admits that some of the industry's superstars make hundreds of thousands per year. "But the national average is somewhere in the mid-twenties. So figure how many are making practically nothing." An insurance salesman is also the kind of man, she points out, who would like to be self-employed but doesn't necessarily want to take all the risks that accompany such freedom.

"They're conservative and serious," she summarizes. "They take their jobs *very* seriously. This man really believes in the value of insurance—don't make jokes about it." But then you won't have to, she admits. Everyone else will.

"It's difficult at parties," Ravell says, in all seriousness. "When they hear that your husband sells insurance, you will see the entire group of people shift to the other side of the room. They all go look to talk to anyone else—even to a lawyer."

There are definite advantages to life with an insurance salesman, however, Ravell is happy to admit. "They're out at night a lot, so you don't have to make dinner every night. It's great for the working woman to be able to come home and have two hours to herself just to wind down. It's also great if you're the type of woman who doesn't want to deal with numbers. He'll handle the banking, the insurance, everything, for you."

Of course, if you're an insurance agent, too, and your husband hates paperwork, you'll be able to endear yourself to him by handling it all. Or you could take turns: this year, you'll do it all; next year, I will.

Allison Johns is one of those insurance salespeople who believes in her work. "I consider myself very different from the typical person in this field. The typical person will come in to make a lot of money, so I guess you'd have to call them ambitious, aggressive. I'm much more for the caring aspect of the work, for helping people. I don't know if I'm being idealistic, but I'm still hoping my ship will come in from working that way."

Johns, who came to insurance sales from investments, notes that her co-workers include former physical therapists, teachers, sales clerks and musicians. "These are people looking to make money because, in the positions they were in, they didn't have much of a chance to do that. And these are definitely very hard-working people. There's no salary at all; income is based on your own efforts. The people who aren't hard working are weeded out very early on."

She also sees insurance salespeople as detailed, meticulous and "married to their careers." The people who seem to succeed at it, she observes, are those who put the same kind of time and energy into their work that most people would rather devote to a personal relationship.

If you decide to go into insurance sales, your first decision is what kind of insurance to sell. You may specialize in selling life insurance, health insurance or in selling policies to insure people's homes, cars, business or households (property/liability or casualty insurance). Or you may become a "multiline" agent, offering your customers policies in all of the above categories.

Your second decision is how to work. The most secure arrangement is to apply for a full-time job as an agent for one insurance company. The alternative is to work as a broker, an independent salesperson who offers policies from several different companies. The latter provides greater freedom, greater opportunity and much less security than the former. All you have to do to get started is approach the various insurance companies and sell yourself. About one out of four insurance salespeople is self-employed.

JOB SECURITY: Insurance may not be the most glamorous business in the world, but it's one of the most stable. Even when times are hard, most people find a way to keep up the premiums on the car, the house and life itself. The Bureau of Labor Statistics forecasts a 25 percent increase in the number of agents' jobs during the coming decade. That's only about average growth, but this is a large industry: about 451,000 jobs by 1995.

The positive side is that Baby Boomers have reached their security-conscious, insurance-buying years. The negative side is that the increasing availability of group policies means fewer sales per agent, plus computers make it possible for an insurance company to maintain sales with fewer agents, and a trend toward "multiline" agents means that one broker representing several insurance carriers can fill all of a customer's insurance needs.

Mixed blessing: Insurance sales has a turnover rate that may amaze and astound you. According to one estimate, about 90 percent of the women and men who enter the field give it up after less than two years. This may not be the most promising statistic you've ever heard, but it means that there is always room being made for new agents.

MONEY: If you work for a company that pays its new agents a fixed salary during training, you're likely to start at about $1,200 per month or $14,400 per year. Later, you may work on a commission-only or salary-and-commission basis. After five years' experience, Mr. or Ms. National Average Life Insurance Agent earns about $35,000 (national median). Thousands of successful agents or brokers earn $50,000 or more—and a number earn more than $100,000. Make it to the top as an executive Vice President for a large insurance company, and your yearly paycheck could top $200,000.

LIFESTYLE: Whether you're an agent or broker, you'll be setting your own schedule. That probably means making evening and weekend appointments to see clients, which may preclude regular cozy family dinners. Your friends always will suspect your motives ("Is she really listening to what I'm saying because she's interested? Or is she just softening me up for a hard sales pitch?"). To avoid these problems, try establishing lasting friendships with other insurance salespeople—at least they'll know you aren't trying to sell them a policy.

WHAT IT TAKES: You'll need the enthusiasm, initiative, self-confidence and general communication skills that lead to sales. Then you'll need the self-discipline and time management skills to get things done.

Insurance sales is the kind of career people switch into after getting business experience in other fields. So find yourself a former actor or race car driver who's gone into insurance, and make the most of your near-miss schedules.

EDUCATION: High school graduates get hired, but a college degree is preferred. Many colleges now offer special degree programs in insurance.

EARNINGS: $35,000 national median after five years.

WORKSTYLE: Flexible hours and lots of local travel. Your time probably will be divided between sales calls and in-office paperwork.

DIRECT INTERACTION OPPORTUNITIES: You may be on the road all alone, but since continuing education is a fact of life in insurance sales, you'll meet fellow agents at conferences, conventions and seminars.

FOR MORE CAREER INFORMATION: The National Association of Life Underwriters, 1922 F Street NW, Washington, DC 20006 (for information on life insurance careers); Insurance Information Institute, 110 William Street, New York, NY 10038 (for information on careers in property-liability insurance).

MUSICIAN

72% are men   28% are women

+ You'll have loads of free time.

– You'll spend a lot of it with your friendly neighborhood unemployment clerk.

"Musicians tend to make fabulous lovers," boasts Don Taylor, a Princeton-educated composer and organist in his 30s. "Being a musician is, in its way, a very physical thing. I know fourteen different ways to push a piano/organ key eight millimeters. I find, when it comes to touching... that stands me in very good stead."

Musicians are performers, he points out, but not in the same way as actors. "Musicians don't have the same investment in their personalities that actors do. I don't think actors really care about Shakespeare. They care about who they are, their part. Musicians care about Mozart."

They also are attentive, patient and self-sufficient. Perhaps because they've always spent so much solitary time practicing, musicians must learn early in life to feel at home with him or herself.

"Some appear to be recluses at times," says Dean Sweeney, an oboist based in Rhode Island. "We get all wrapped up in things. Some musicians won't eat for days at a time when they're working on a competition.

"I feel we're a little more sensitive to people's feelings," he adds. "You have to be, if you're going to be any good at performing or understanding the music. The guy who wrote it had a special thing in mind. He may have been torn up inside, or very happy inside. If you don't understand that, you cannot perform it."

Understanding it doesn't always mean feeling it, however, Taylor points out. In fact, some of the most moving concert performances are performed "in cold blood," he believes.

"It's something I think the public greatly misunderstands," says Taylor. "In order to make a Mahler symphony sound as though everybody is about to burst into tears, they have to be as far from bursting into tears as possible. That is very hard work."

Classical musicians and popular musicians look upon each other with a certain class consciousness. "Popular musicians seem to be very different," says a classically-trained Boston keyboard musician. "Because of the way popular musicians work, personality is paramount. It doesn't matter if you can sing or play or not. It's what you look like and project.

"I think of popular musicians as being much shallower, and many of them are amazingly insecure about what they're doing."

Every musician has reason to feel insecure. The field is so competitive that only 16 percent of all music graduates find work as orchestral players, concert artists or opera singers. A full 75 percent teach music, five percent hold management, administrative or technical jobs in the music industry and four percent have given up and gone to work in other fields entirely.

The trouble is that jobs teaching music are becoming very scarce, and those who love music are being encouraged to find alternatives. Schools like New York University and the Eastman School of Music at the University of Rochester are offering courses and degrees in the management and technical side of the music business. You can take a single course that trains you in dealing with agents and recording studio people, or you can now get a Master of Music Business degree.

JOB SECURITY: No such thing in the music business. But at least it's not a dying field. The Bureau of Labor Statistics says the career will enjoy about average growth (25 percent) between now and 1995. That will mean a total of 155,000 musicians working at any given time.

MONEY: Well, you could be one of the thousands of unemployed musicians who work only a few weeks a year and have to make ends meet with other jobs (in which case, you're probably listed with the Bureau of Labor Statistics as a waitress or a clerical worker instead) or you could end up like Paul McCartney, who's said to be worth $500 million.

Of all musicians who were on salary and worked full-time in 1982, the median income (union wages, of course) was $410 a week or $21,320 a year. If you were hired to play your instrument in a recording session, you'd get a minimum of $170 for a three-hour session. If you had a contract with a local club or played in the orchestra for the local ballet company, you'd be paid a minimum of $10–$25 per hour.

If you were a member of a symphony orchestra, working for scale, you'd earn $326 to $780 per week, depending on geography. The highest-paying symphony jobs are in Chicago, Boston, Cleveland, Philadelphia, Los Angeles, San Francisco and New York City. Some of the lowest symphony pay scales apply in Louisville, Syracuse, Honolulu and throughout Alabama and Florida.

Classified ads for symphony orchestra members in a 1985 issue of *International Musician* included the following: Milwaukee Symphony Orchestra, second assistant principal viola and second violin section, 46-week season, five-week paid vacation, $30,000 minimum; San Francisco Symphony, second oboe, nine weeks paid vacation, $45,360 minimum; Omaha Symphony and Omaha Symphony Chamber Orchestra, associate, bass and horn, $12,992 minimum.

Then there are the popular musicians. Ringo Starr was paid a weekly salary of 25 British pounds when he first joined the Beatles. That translated to about $50 when the exchange rate was good. Today it would be about $30. Prince earned at least $17 million from his *Purple Rain* album. The words "feast or famine" come to mind.

LIFESTYLE: Well, you'll probably work nights, weekends and holidays and spend a lot of time on the road. But that shouldn't matter if the man you love is working right beside you. You're most likely to live in one of the centers of the entertainment and recording business, such as New York, Los Angeles, Chicago, Nashville, Miami or New Orleans. You'll get used to insecurity.

WHAT IT TAKES: Talent, as they say, is only a start. You'll need the confidence and stage presence to get up in front of an audience time after time. You'll need the self-discipline to go on studying and practicing, even when it looks as though you'll never make another penny in this career. You'll need a tough hide to take no for an answer more often than not. Finally, you'll need the physical stamina to survive a musician's schedule and lifestyle.

GETTING HIRED: You may send in a resumé like every other kind of job-seeker, but you may be asked to send in a resumé tape as well. Instead of an interview, you'll be called in for an audition. Knowing somebody helps, as it does in any industry, so making friends with the boys in the band is a good idea—whether they're the local city symphony or the opening act for Duran Duran.

EDUCATION: Musical training at a college, a conservatory or through private study.

EARNINGS: $21,320 national median (for full-time salaried musicians).

WORKSTYLE: Irregular, erratic and emotionally draining, with the possibility of heavy travel. The term "one-night stand" originally didn't have a thing to do with love or sex, you know.

DIRECT INTERACTION OPPORTUNITIES: Making beautiful music together. Rehearsing beautiful music together. Partying after making beautiful music together.

FOR MORE CAREER INFORMATION: American Federation of Musicians, 1500 Broadway, New York, NY 10036.

PHARMACIST

71% are men   29% are women

+ You can open a mom-and-pop drugstore and run your own lives.

− Free pharmaceuticals/medication (yield not to temptation).

By the time today's female pharmacy students graduate, one out of four is already married—or at least engaged—to a fellow pharmacist. Perhaps, surmises a Texas-based assistant professor of pharmacy administration, that's why the number of husband-and-wife teams in this business is proliferating so.

Trade publications still like to refer to the field as "the previously all-male profession of pharmacy." If today's pharmacy school enrollments are any indication, however, that's changing as dramatically as the previously all-male professions of medicine and law. By 1982, a full half (50.1 percent) of all U.S. pharmacy students were female. If these young women are having such good luck socially as the assistant professor of pharmacy administration claims, just think of the opportunities when they get out into the work force where male pharmacists still outnumber them 2.5 to one.

Statistically, you're more likely to meet an older pharmacist than a younger one. But that's only because you're likely to be such a young woman yourself. Almost 56 percent of all female pharmacists are under 40 today, and one-third of all pharmacists under 30 are women.

It's a far cry from the old days, which weren't so long ago. An Iowa-based female pharmacist, class of 1968, recalls having only three women classmates out of a class of 60 or 65 in pharmacy school.

She never found sexism a problem, but a Wisconsin pharmacist, who got her B.S. in pharmacy 20 years earlier, definitely did. "Back in the 1940s, the pharmacy school deans felt women would never complete the course or wouldn't go into practice," she remembers. "The deans felt the cost of educating a pharmacist was so high that it was unproductive to admit females. Instead, they tried to channel women into other disciplines, such as English." She beat the system, however, and today she operates six pharmacies with five partners— all male.

At the same time that the number of women in pharmacy increases dramatically, lots of other things about the profession are changing. For one thing, projections indicate that 10–20 years from now our image of the pharmacist as a small business owner and independent professional will just be nostalgia. Instead of going into community pharmacy, more and more new pharmacists are taking jobs with hospitals, while a small but growing percentage goes to work for pharmaceutical manufacturers. Of those who do go into community practice, the greatest number are taking jobs with large drug chains rather than independent drugstores. Almost one out of four pharmacists still own his or her own business, but you can look for that to change as well. As a profession pharmacy seems to be winning new respect. The idea that "any damn fool could prescribe," as a California pharmacist once put it, has gone by the wayside. In the 1980s, there are so many different drugs with so many possible side effects and interactions that it takes a person devoted to that field to know what she or he is doing.

Medical schools, the pharmacists point out, usually give future physicians only a single course in pharmacology. Then, when the doctors go into practice, they may be influenced more by drug company ads and salespeople than by a full knowledge of the way drugs work. Pharmacists are the real experts in this particular area of health care, and patients finally may be realizing that.

JOB SECURITY: The job market looks good for new pharmacists, as far as the eye can see. In a survey of pharmacy school deans, a majority predicted that jobs will be readily available for new graduates. The Bureau of Labor Statistics forecasts a 27 percent increase in the number of jobs between now and 1995 (that's average occupational growth).

If you see a newspaper article on the pharmaceutical companies' new financial woes, don't worry. It's true that some of the big U.S. companies aren't showing the dramatic growth in profits that they'd enjoyed until 1983 or so, but it doesn't mean that the pharmacist's career is in trouble; it only means that the U.S. has started importing a lot of prescription drugs (an increase of 34 percent in 1984 alone). The percentage of generic drugs that we buy has also increased.

MONEY: Take a hospital job out West, if income is your top priority. While the national average income for all pharmacists is approximately $29,000–$32,000, the average for hospital-based pharmacists is $30,000–$34,500. And hospital-based pharmacists in the Western part of the U.S. have the highest average earnings of all: a base salary of $37,000. Chain drug stores pay second best, and independents offer the lowest earnings. Bonus: there are more women in pharmacy management at hospitals than in any other work setting.

As for starting salaries, pharmacy school deans project that most new pharmacists will be earning $25,000 and up after only a year in the work force.

Maybe money can't buy happiness, but a professional survey showed that the highly-paid hospital-based pharmacists are also the happiest people in the field. A full 50 percent frequently leave work with a sense of accomplishment, and 51 percent would choose pharmacy as a career, even if they had it to do over again. That's compared to only 40–44 percent of all other pharmacists.

LIFESTYLE: There's no unusual connection, for good or bad, between the pharmacist and her private life. In retail operations, the pharmacist is a respected member of the community. In clinical settings, she's a professional respected for her area of special expertise.

WHAT IT TAKES: Basically, a good pharmacist needs all the attributes of a Boy or Girl Scout. It takes good judgment, dependability, accuracy, neatness, orderliness and cleanliness. The need to check and recheck your work can't be overstated. The consequences, should you make a mistake, could be life-threatening to your customers. Finally, with drug abuse being what it is, the pharmacist's ethics have to be above reproach. Handing out controlled substances without filing that triplicate form (or whatever your state demands) could be the end of a beautiful career.

EDUCATION: B.S. in pharmacy or B. Pharm. (bachelor of pharmacy), normally a five-year program. Depending on your educational background, it will take six or seven years to get a Pharm.D. (doctor of pharmacy). State license required.

EARNINGS: $29,400–$32,400 national average.

WORKSTYLE: The average male pharmacist works 47.1 hours per week, including overtime. For reasons unknown, female pharmacists average only 45 hours per week. Work conditions are fine, sort of a mini-lab. The only real drawback: you'll spend a lot of time on your feet.

DIRECT INTERACTION OPPORTUNITIES: The usual workday contact—better in a hospital or clinic setting than in a community drugstore.

FOR MORE CAREER INFORMATION: American Pharmaceutical Association, 2215 Constitution Avenue NW, Washington, DC 20037.

PRODUCT MANAGER

77% are men   23% are women

+ You're both in the fast lane to the top of the corporate ladder.

− You'll probably work nights. And no greater competitive egos will have been seen since Farrah Fawcett met Ryan O'Neal.

What's funny about being a product manager? Getting serious over which bathroom tissue is the softest, for one thing. Referring to toilet paper as bathroom tissue, for another.

Why would you want to become a product manager? So you can say things like "The market is very segmented," and "the color of the box can mean the difference between success and failure in today's marketplace." Or as Peter Drucker said, "the aim of marketing is to make selling superfluous." If you know your consumer well enough, he explained, the product or service will sell itself.

What kind of man will you meet on marketing row?

"Very aggressive, impressed with himself and with his M.B.A.," says one woman who works for a consumer products company (but not in marketing).

"They tend to be very competitive, very aggressive, very male and not very moral," believes one man in personnel. "If your job is to market a product, there's an inherent moral problem—an obfuscation of what's true. I'm not saying they're all suspect. I know there are bad priests and good product managers. But I'd keep my eye on him."

"Marketing is the most creative job in the corporation," claims a senior product manager, stretching out on the sun deck in his Westhampton summer house.

Most corporate observers will agree on one fact: Marketing is what modern American business is all about. The marketing department is the nucleus of any consumer-oriented corporation. And it's where an awful lot of tomorrow's C.E.O.'s may be incubating.

Broadly defined, marketing means selling. But most corporate marketing departments are staffed not by sales people but by product managers who handle one or several brands, treating each as if it were a small business. As a product manager, you're ultimately responsible for that brand's packaging, price strategy, distribution, advertising, promotion, public relations and sales forecasting. Your work begins when someone says, "Hey, don't we need a new shampoo for oily hair?" and continues through post-sales consumer service until someone decides to take the product off the market.

And products don't get from inventory to shelf as fast as most consumers may think. After extensive market research, there may be actual test markets (specially-selected cities in which the product is sold and advertised before being put into national distribution). After the electric toothbrush was developed, it was four years before it was brought into full-scale distribution. For instant coffee, it took 22 years!

The marketing process is easiest to understand in terms of consumer product companies like Bristol-Myers or Colgate-Palmolive. Some of the newest and fastest-growing opportunities, however, are in financial services and high-tech companies. A new savings account program is now marketed very much like a shampoo.

If you can do it, take your first job at Procter & Gamble, the undisputed king of the industry. Because they almost always promote from within, it's practically impossible to get hired there later in your career.

P&G marketing experience is the corporate equivalent of an Ivy League degree. It means a lot on your resumé when you go looking for subsequent jobs. Even more important for our nefarious purposes, however, is the unusual number of close personal ties among employees that seem to develop there. At alumni meetings (How many companies do you know where old cronies get together on a regular basis?), outsiders have observed that a surprising number of former co-workers come back as married couples.

JOB SECURITY: The demand for marketing managers started to shoot up just as the economy began to recover in 1982. By 1983, it had reached an all-time high. Brand management is not the world's most secure occupation, but it's far from the worst; many companies tend to move product managers around, from product to product, more often than moving them out. Your biggest risk of getting fired is when a new management team moves in.

MONEY: And now for the good news. Assistant product managers (the entry-level for most) can earn $30,000–$40,000 in some cities. Senior marketing people can make $80,000 a year and much more. The national average for all product managers isn't astronomical (just under $40,000), but it doesn't tell the whole story. One marketing consultant in California charges $2,000 a day for what he calls, "common sense and logic."

LIFESTYLE: Nowadays people see product managers as the ultimate Yuppies. You'll probably be based in a big city, dress well, live tastefully and stylishly, and sooner or later you'll stop thinking that leaving the office at 7 p.m. constitutes working late.

WHAT IT TAKES: At least once a year, you'll write marketing plans — a comprehensive and detailed document (easily 100 pages) outlining everything you plan for each of your brands during the coming year. It takes an orderly, logical and analytical mind to complete such a task (or to want to). It takes creativity, and it takes the ability to work as part of a unit. Even though you have a great deal of decision-making power, most of the people who have to carry out your plans aren't your employees. They're your peers or near-peers in other departments, so we can only hope you listened in all those management classes and people-skills' sessions.

GETTING HIRED: Most marketing-wise companies recruit at business schools. So get into the best MBA program in your city, even if you're going back to school part-time at age 40; then, make friends at the placement office. On-campus interviewers can only meet a limited number of students, so you'll need a friend in the placement office to get interviews with all the hottest companies. In a few companies, a field sales job can lead to marketing as well. Either way, knowing as much as you can about the company's products or services will give you an edge in the job search.

EDUCATION: A college degree, preferably in marketing, is a must. And two degrees are better than one, especially when one of them is an MBA.

EARNINGS: $38,437 national average.

WORKSTYLE: Long hours, plenty of pressure, lots of projects to coordinate. Worst week: once a year, when marketing plans are due.

DIRECT INTERACTION OPPORTUNITIES: Late-night work leading to drinks after hours. Business trips are great if you're accompanied. If you're alone, you're probably en route to see the regional sales people. Don't forget the opportunities to meet and work with your counterparts at ad agencies and other "suppliers."

FOR MORE CAREER INFORMATION: American Marketing Association, 250 South Wacker Drive, Chicago, IL 60606.

PURCHASING MANAGER

76% are men   24% are women

+ Suppliers will take you to lunch, buy you expensive presents, do almost anything to sell their product.

− Temptation and guilt. The jury's still out on the difference between common business practice and graft.

Purchasing is a good place for college dropouts who enjoy wielding real power, a management consultant once suggested.

The confusing part about meeting a man in purchasing is just how much the field has changed in recent years. Purchasing used to have two images, both of them bad. One was a humdrum little department of no importance. The men there just filled orders and made routine checks of prices, suppliers and inventories. The second was of a corrupt little department, filled with greedy agents and managers taking kickbacks and supplier gifts as valuable as Caribbean cruises and cars. We're not sure about the latter, but the former is a far cry from today's reality.

It all started the last time America's economy went down the tubes. With inflation, recession and the energy crisis, corporate attitudes toward the long-ignored purchasing department changed. That "penny saved"—in buying the raw materials that make up products—felt more like a dollar earned. Suddenly, purchasing management was a dynamic career opportunity, and a great place to prove your worth (literally) to the corporation.

Today, all that new blood is mingling with older purchasing department types and you might meet any kind of man in this field. Nevertheless, we'll try to draw an accurate portrait.

"It takes a certain breed to mold a career out of purchasing," a newspaper reporter wrote in 1982. "Unlike their natural foes—the bubbly sales people—buyers tend to be self-effacing, stony, skeptical, rational. Yet they wield great power." As an industry expert observed, the suppliers don't actually get down on their knees in front of purchasing managers—unless it will get the order.

Your purchasing department paramour may not fit your usual

image of a corporate executive. He's unlikely to have an M.B.A., for instance. In fact, more than 40 percent don't have college degrees at all. The six out of ten so endowed studied anything from liberal arts to engineering.

This composite purchasing executive is 43 years old, has been in the field for 13 years and earns $34,900. If you're looking for someone with a higher average income, go directly to Stamford, Connecticut ($43,100); New York City ($42,100); Houston ($39,600); or Newark, New Jersey ($38,000)—the highest-paying cities for this specialty. Do not, whatever you do, move to Providence, Rhode Island—a wonderful small city on many other counts, but the lowest paying for purchasing specialists.

One industry survey also takes a look at the "$100,000 Club," responding members of which earn at least six figures. The average member of this exclusive club is older (56), has a college degree, has worked in purchasing for two decades, has a staff of 141 subordinates and earns $117,700 per year. He's most likely to work for a giant company—one with sales of $1 billion or more—most likely an electrical equipment manufacturer. He could work in almost any region of the country, but is apt to come from the Great Lakes area. All the members of the $100,000 Club are men. So far.

Women in purchasing, like women in almost all careers, don't do as well financially or in terms of career growth. The average female respondent to the same survey is 38 years old, has been in the field eight years, has only one subordinate and earns only $23,700.

A University of Michigan study, however, reveals what may be some of the reasons. Women tend to come into the purchasing department at lower levels. About twice as many women as men started out as clerks or expediters. Their educational levels are lower too; more than seven out of ten women in purchasing have no college degrees.

More women than men work in government and educational purchasing, so these may not be the areas in which to look for a date. On the other hand, men outnumber women by 20 percent in industrial purchasing departments. Forget meeting men at professional development activities; you'll find the audience or classroom filled with women. However, both sexes seem to join professional associations about equally.

When you go into purchasing, your job is to spend other people's money for a living. And your goal is to get the best possible price, so your company's finished products can be sold for the greatest profit. (If you've considered going into retail buying, that's a different career altogether—because the process primarily is *reselling*. See the section on Buyers, page 165).

In purchasing, you won't normally make snap decisions. When a really big purchase is coming up, you may meet for months as part of a committee to talk with vendors and examine alternatives.

One of the newest trends in the field is "just-in-time" purchasing, a Japanese method now being tried out by some U.S. companies. Instead of storing months of raw materials inventory, the Japanese buy only enough to keep production lines running for weeks at a time. Because of the reduced overhead and other expenses, Japan's cost of delivering goods to the production floor have been 30–50 percent lower than ours.

Medical purchasing can be a high-paying specialty, and you don't have to be a doctor or a biomedical engineer to do it well. One female purchasing executive who recently bought $45 million in lab supplies and equipment from a single vendor was a Middle Eastern history major in college.

JOB SECURITY: Average occupational growth (a 27 percent increase in new jobs) lies ahead for purchasing, according to Bureau of Labor Statistics projections. The career seems relatively stable and secure.

MONEY: Starting salaries range from $12,000 to $20,000 or so. The highest salaries are in the petroleum industry and in purchasing capital goods. Average incomes are as follows: purchasing agents, $28,500; purchasing managers, $36,400; purchasing vice presidents, $57,400.

LIFESTYLE: When you leave the office at the end of the day (and you'll usually be able to do that on time), your private life is pretty much your own. If you do accept that yacht or that sports car from the eager suplier, you may have glamorous leisure hours, but be aware of any restrictions tied to accepting "gifts." Some companies are cracking down on the prices of gifts that can be accepted (no more than $25 at one Fortune 500 corporation) and are insisting that every time you accept a supplier lunch date, you have to take him out later to avoid being in his debt.

WHAT IT TAKES: If you're going to spend a lot of money responsibly, you need to be able to analyze technical data intelligently and work independently much of the time. Purchasing demands decision-making ability, negotiating skills and a memory for details. At least this means the man you'll meet in this career may remember your birthday and anniversary.

EDUCATION: An engineering degree, topped off by an M.B.A., is ideal for many purchasing jobs, particularly those in the petroleum industry and in manufacturing. Any business degree is a plus, however.

EARNINGS: $32,800 national average.

WORKSTYLE: A standard 35- to 40-hour office work week. Some travel is likely.

DIRECT INTERACTION OPPORTUNITIES: Meetings with members of the same committee; business trips.

FOR MORE CAREER INFORMATION: National Association of Purchasing Management, 496 Kinderkamack Road, P.O. Box 418, Oradell, NJ 07649.

STOCKBROKER

76% are men   24% are women

+ There's money in them thar hills.

− But can he talk about anything else?

"Stockbrokers are hyper-aggressive but smooth," says Thomas Atkinson, a Wall Street executive who has worked with many. "Unlike investment bankers, they can be unpolished. They're good-time types who slap you on the back. They're salesmen, remember. They have to be highly social. They have to be the sort of people who don't mind making a cold call; they live by them. They're not the least bit shy and they don't worry about whether or not they're wasting your time."

The average stockbroker, according to Atkinson, is an entrepreneurial type. He might like to own his own business and, in many ways, he is on his own. "Yes, they work in big firms, but essentially all they get from the firm is desk space and a telephone," he explains. "They work on commission and their compensation is very much the result of their own efforts. So they push."

Atkinson isn't even sure that male stockbrokers think about the personal sides of their lives during business hours. "They work like crazy in the office. They're very focused on work. I don't think they socialize in the office at all."

Of course, women in the securities business can develop the same single-mindedness. A 38-year-old female investment banker, profiled in *The New York Times Magazine*, admits that if she hadn't married at age 24, when the demands of her career were minimal, she probably wouldn't have married at all.

The beauty of the securities industry, however, is that it offers several unique occupations, each with a different workstyle. That means you should be able to find an investment career that suits your personality and talents, as well as the kind of man you could be happy with.

The *stockbroker*, also known as the account executive, registered representative or securities salesperson, has the most visible career in the business. He or she finds customers to buy securities or to have their assets managed by the broker's firm. The broker's job is the main focus of this career section. There are, after all, about 78,000 of them on the job today.

But then there are the aforementioned *investment bankers*. If you're looking for a man with a combination of polished Ivy League clubbiness and a killer's instinct for making a dollar, you've come to the right career. The investment banker's job is underwriting new securities. He's the deal maker who brings together people who have money and people who need it. And although this has been a very male profession, one leading university reports that about 25 percent of its graduates now going into the field are women.

If you marry an investment banker, don't expect to see much of him. With his long hours and heavy travel schedule, you may have to settle for saying good night to a photograph.

And if that isn't enough of a hectic, fast-paced lifestyle for you, consider becoming or falling in love with a *securities trader*. Many traders work right on the trading floor, buying and selling securities with their firm's money. They make money, often lots of it, on fluctuations in the marketplace. It's a short work day, but an intense one. How do they do it? More than one source insisted, "They're all on cocaine," but who believes idle gossip?

Securities analysts do the research on which the firm bases its investment decisions and recommendations. As recently as 20 years ago, many medium-sized firms didn't have research departments at all. Today, the analyst's job is growing and becoming more specialized. You might specialize in knowing everything there is to know about a particular industry—computers, perhaps, or chemicals. This could be a desk job or a traveling career, depending on where you work.

JOB SECURITY: Aye, here's the rub. When stock prices plummet, stockbrokers often take a powder. Between 1969 and 1974, when times were not their best in the securities industry, almost 20,000 registered representatives felt the sudden urge to change careers. That means one out of three American stockbrokers got out of the business fast.

If you're thinking in terms of a lifelong career, be prepared for some heavy storms; turnover is astronomical, even in the best of times. According to one estimate, 95 percent of those who go into the field call it quits within two years.

For now, the job market looks promising. The Bureau of Labor Statistics tells us to look for above-average occupational growth of 36 percent between now and 1995.

MONEY: For every career, there is a product—perhaps prescription drugs, clothing, steel, automobiles, paperback books or transportation services. In the securities industry, the product is money. And there seems to be plenty to go around.

Starting salaries for salespeople in training range from $10,800 to $14,400 per year, according to the latest *Occupational Outlook Handbook*. As far back as 1981, however, a representative of a New York City firm estimated the average training salary at $18,000 per year.

The national average income for stockbrokers handling individual investor accounts is over $60,000 a year, according to Bureau of Labor Statistics figures. Brokers who handle institutional accounts do much better, however. According to the same source, they average about $150,000 per year. According to the Securities Industry Association, brokers can earn from $20,000 to $200,000 per year, and their reported income indicates that most earn between $60,000 and $85,000.

Others in the securities industry do well. Investment bankers average $100,000 per year, but can literally make millions. Security analysts average $47,000, while senior analysts usually earn $100,000 and up. Traders average base salaries of $40,000–$70,000. If you add the bonuses that are usually given in these occupations, just about everybody is a financial success.

LIFESTYLE: Successful brokers are prone to saying things like, "Where else could I make a six-figure income and still get home every night for dinner?" It seems to be true. Here's a career in which you can probably afford a boat, a weekend house, a swimming pool, a splashy vacation—and the time to enjoy it all. Warning: the pressure *has* been known to get to some, however, and can lead to alcohol or drug abuse.

No, you don't have to live in New York. Wall Street-type jobs exist in virtually every U.S. city. Some of the bigger markets for your talents in this field include Los Angeles, Chicago, San Francisco, Denver, Dallas, Houston, Philadelphia, Boston and Atlanta.

WHAT IT TAKES: Good communication skills, good grooming, the ability to work independently and the ability to take rejection well are the traits most often mentioned. Sales or marketing experience is a near-must and motivation—being upbeat in a down-turned market.

TRAINING: Don't worry if you can't tell a stock from a bond. When you're hired, you'll be placed in a formal sales training program in order to learn everything you need to know. You'll then have to pass one or more licensing exams to get started.

GETTING HIRED: There's plenty of competition for those training slots. The Securities Industry Association estimates that for every broker trainee hired, there are as many as 50–100 applicants. Consider taking a job as a brokerage firm secretary; there's a crying need for them. Then type like mad, keep your ears open and look ambitious.

If you're 21 years old and reading this in your dorm room or off-campus apartment, don't get your hopes up. Most brokerage firms don't like to hire bright young things straight out of college. They'd rather let you simmer a little, get some business experience (preferably in sales) and develop a dash of maturity on somebody else's payroll.

For that reason, the average age of broker trainees is over 30. So who knows what kind of man you might find yourself training and working with? One firm found in its current training class a former dentist, an ex-secretary, a one-time veterinarian and a recent retiree starting his new career at age 58.

EDUCATION: College degree; a finance, business or economics major is preferable, but almost any educational background is acceptable.

EARNINGS: $60,000 per year national average, working on individual accounts; $150,000 working on institutional accounts.

WORKSTYLE: Fast-paced and frenetic office-based job.

DIRECT INTERACTION OPPORTUNITIES: It won't be easy to take his mind off dollars and cents during the business day. You'll have to stay late, and entice him out for drinks or dinner.

FOR MORE CAREER INFORMATION: Securities Industry Association, 120 Broadway, New York, NY 10271 (may offer a careers booklet for $1.00). For more detailed information on careers in the industry and on training programs, contact local brokerage firms directly.

SYSTEMS ANALYST

70% are men   30% are women

+ He's the businessman of the future.

− He'll never respect a woman who doesn't know COBOL.

In *Future Shock*, Alvin Toffler noted that the human animal's system of loyalties were changing—out of necessity. If you aren't going to join a company at age 21 and stay there until retirement, it seems foolish to develop a deep and profound loyalty to AT&T, IBM or The First National Bank of Peoria. If you're going to live in ten different cities during your lifetime, developing a hometown attachment to each is just going to upset you when you move on. So the thing to cherish and carry with you from place to place is your specialty, the work itself.

What does this mean for you? If you want a systems analyst or other computer type to be the father of your children, don't aspire to become the nation's leading expert in petrochemicals, transportation or high finance; crawl inside a computer yourself.

"A systems analyst will probably marry a female programmer," says financial executive James Dubose. "He won't marry a female bank vice president—she's too businessy. And most of these people identify with their technology, rather than with the business they work for. They don't think of themselves as being 'in finance' or 'in insurance.' They're inward-looking and really very clannish."

The systems analyst, Dubose points out, is a man or woman with great professional empathy. "The ideal one should see someone else's problems in systems terms, but relate to the other person in terms of their problems. He should not spout jargon to impress the other person with his knowledge."

Unfortunately, in Dubose's office at least, most don't meet the ideal. Members of the department have been known to stand around the elevator, speaking advanced computer-ese. "You're supposed to feel, 'Oh, I don't understand this jargon. I'm an outsider.'"

Many systems analysts start out as programmers, many hold the title programmer/analyst and still more don't quite understand the difference between the two. "One profession is not necessarily a stepping stone to the other," insists the president of a Massachusetts-based computer product development company. Nevertheless, many programmers took their jobs with definite hopes and plans for moving into systems analysis eventually.

- A *programmer* writes a set of instructions—called a program—telling the computer what to do.
- A *systems analyst* interviews computer users to find out their requirements and then designs appropriate computer systems. A system consists of many programs.
- A programmer studies what the computer can do for you.
- A systems analyst studies how it works.
- A systems analyst presents and sells his ideas and plans to management.
- A programmer "does lunch."

A systems analyst is a resource scheduler, one company president points out. "The computer is not just one device, but many," he explains. "You're responsible for setting up the computer in ways that it can be used most efficiently." For example, it might be using all of its writing power but not enough of its thinking power, or vice versa. A systems analyst is responsible for the overall system.

A career as systems analyst is far from a dead-end job. You may move up into M.I.S. (management of information systems). In some industries, that can mean top management, because operations and data processing are so closely linked. Banks and brokerage firms are two good examples.

JOB SECURITY: Now here's a rosy picture for you. The Bureau of Labor Statistics tells us that, between now and 1995, there will be an 85 percent increase in the number of systems analysts' jobs. That makes it the third-fastest-growing occupation in the country (surpassed only by legal assistant and computer service technician). And that will make a total of almost half a million people in this career.

Computer occupations are far more competitive than they used to be, but they're still growing like mad.

MONEY: If you went back to school for computer training and found your first job as a systems analyst, chances are you'd be offered about $23,000 in private industry. If you took a Federal government job, however, you might be offered only $15,600.

The experienced systems analyst working full-time earns an average of $28,080 in private industry. Lead systems analysts average just under $31,000. And the top ten percent of all working systems analysts earn more than $44,000 per year. Salaries in the Northeast and on the West Coast tend to be higher than in other parts of the country.

LIFESTYLE: If you love computers enough to make them your life's work, it's doubtful that you'll leave your work concerns at the office. In fact, it's doubtful that you'll ever leave the office.

This is strictly a personal choice, however. Systems analysts generally don't have the kinds of scheduling and business travel demands that interfere with home, family and recreation. Relax. You can live and work in virtually any part of the country, and in any modest style you choose. But you probably won't be rich.

WHAT IT TAKES: There are computer types, and, there are computer types. If you want a career in systems analysis, you'll need to be able to communicate well with people—with the programmers in their language, and with nonprogrammers too. You'll need the ability to concentrate and pay close attention to details. The career calls for some flexibility in workstyle; you may work independently at times, and as part of a team at others. If you hope to be promoted into M.I.S., develop your leadership skills early.

Lots of people (seven out of ten, in fact) switch into this career after having worked in another. That means you may be meeting older novices in the field. It also means you may find former Classics or English Lit majors here. You can be sure, however, that they've had formal education in computer science and that they're familiar with programming languages. Job candidates with M.B.A.s have a definite edge.

It also helps to fit into the corporate culture of the company to which you're applying. At Apple, they say, the average employee age is about 30 and the corporate Vice Presidents wear blue jeans;

at Intel, according to *The 100 Best Companies to Work For in America*, the company president wears an open shirt and a gold chain; while at IBM, where having a drink at lunch comes close to committing professional suicide, the atmosphere has been compared to that of the Marines.

For more on the kind of man you're likely to meet in the world of computers, see the Programmer section on page 154.

EDUCATION: Bachelor's degree, ideally in computer science.

EARNINGS: $28,080 national median.

WORKSTYLE: A standard 40-hour office week; some evening and weekend work possible.

DIRECT INTERACTION OPPORTUNITIES: Computer people just love to spend time with each other, working in teams at the office and socializing at the end of the work day. Expect lots of interfacing.

FOR MORE CAREER INFORMATION: Association for Systems Management, 24587 Bagley Road, Cleveland, OH 44138

6 Out of 10 Workers Are Men

"What a piece of work is a man!"
WILLIAM SHAKESPEARE
Hamlet

ASSOCIATION MANAGER

64% are men   36% are women

+ You can work in almost any field, representing almost any profession.

− You'll probably have to move to Washington, DC, New York City or Chicago.

He is a Protestant and a Republican, in his early 50s, with an average salary of $78,000 a year—the average association chief executive. If he is the man you want, go to work for one of the country's 19,000 national associations (or one of the hundreds of thousands of regional and local groups).

There's no end to the possibilities of association careers. You could work for the American Medical Association (one of the nation's oldest, founded in 1847) or the National Electric Sign Associates. You could take a job with a trade association (a group of companies in the same field or with similar interests) or a professional society (usually a group of individuals in the same occupation). Most associations fall into these categories, but about five percent are federations (associations of associations). All exist for one primary reason: to facilitate the exchange of information for the benefit of the membership.

You could work in one of the associations with hundreds of staff members each—the American Management Association, National Association of Securities Dealers or American Institute of Certified Public Accountants are examples. Or you could sign on with a smaller organization (the average is 24 employees—but with hundreds and thousands of members).

You can work in almost any management specialty. Most groups have departments devoted to public relations, research, meetings and conventions, finance, administration, membership, training and education. You don't necessarily have to be devoted to the field your association represents, (although one former accounting major, now with the American Dental Hygienists Association, does admit that he's started flossing more often). But the membership can be just as interesting socially as your co-workers.

Some of your best opportunities for meeting your constituency will come at convention time. About 95 percent of all state and national associations hold conventions. The average one lasts three days and draws 1,044 participants. Imagine working for an engineers' association and finding yourself in a hotel with a thousand engineers (940 of whom are likely to be male) for a three-day weekend.

Seminars and other continuing education events (offered by 73 percent of all associations) are another social opportunity. You might even consider going into the training and education side of association management to live out the fantasy of standing in front of a room of a hundred handsome lawyers or dentists or financial planners, all with their eyes on you.

First pick the kind of man you hope to meet. If he's a John Wayne type, shoot for a job at the National Rifle Association. Or send your resumé to the American Association of University Professors if you're turned on by the scholarly type.

The only limiting aspect to association management is location. More than a third of all the country's national associations are in these three cities: Washington, DC (3,100), New York (2,600) and Chicago (900). On the other hand, there's bound to be at least one association in the city nearest you; they do exist in all 50 states. The National Auctioneers' Association, for instance, is in Overland Park, Kansas. And the National Association of Legal Assistants is in Tulsa.

JOB SECURITY: Nonprofit associations tend not to fire people just because the industries they represent are having a bad year. In fact, serious industry concerns and/or economic downturns can make associations more important than ever. Lots of association managers end up moving into large companies in the industry they've represented, as well as into the government sector.

One thing that's for sure, it's a growing field. The number of national associations has doubled in the last two decades. And the average national association's income has tripled during the same period.

MONEY: Unfortunately, salaries haven't tripled. The average association employee's salary is just under $20,000. Department heads, however, can do better. Among the highest-paid titles and their average salaries are director of the Washington, DC office ($61,300), chief economist ($60,800) and government relations officer ($52,300). The lowest-paid specialties include convention and meeting director, membership director, personnel director and publications editor (all $33,000–$33,600 average). Perhaps not coincidentally, women outnumber men in three of the lowest-paying four.

In fact, women in association management tend to earn about sixty cents to the man's dollar earned (the national average for all jobs). One way to beat the system could be to get your Certified Association Executive (C.A.E.) certification by taking a written exam and documenting your experience. An industry survey reported in *Association Management* showed that C.A.E.'s have higher than average salaries.

LIFESTYLE: Association managers can lead relatively normal nine-to-five lives. You and your association-type husband may do a lot of business travel, particularly if you're in the meetings and convention area, or if one of you becomes chief executive. There can be deadline pressure and overtime, too—particularly at such crucial times as when final preparations are being made for an important bill that affects your group.

WHAT IT TAKES: Good communication skills—both oral and written—are a must. Association management is a people-oriented business. For anything but an entry-level job, some strong business and professional experience in your specialty is important. But one executive search consultant in the field insists that a service-oriented attitude is the most important prerequisite.

If you're not sure that this career is right for you, consider taking a volunteer job with a local association just to check it out. And if you're not sure in which management specialty you want to spend the rest of your days, look for a job with a small association. There, you'll be able to wear several hats, being responsible for several functions instead of just one.

EDUCATION: Any college degree is acceptable, but of course one in your management specialty is ideal. George Washington University is one of the few schools that now offer master's programs in association management.

EARNINGS: Average for all staff members is $19,788; department heads average $33,000–$61,300.

WORKSTYLE: A comfortable office job, with occasional overtime and deadline pressures. Considerable business travel in some jobs.

DIRECT INTERACTION OPPORTUNITIES: Interaction with members at conventions, seminars and classes. Plus the usual office tête-à-têtes.

FOR MORE CAREER INFORMATION: American Society of Association Executives, 1575 Eye Street NW, Washington, DC 20005.

BANKER

62% are men   38% are women

+ Working late at the office usually means staying till 5:01.

− In a world where there's a JC Penney National Bank, can anything about this changing field be predicted?

"There are bankers," says New York-based lending officer Sam Danielsen, "and there are people who work for banks. There's a big difference."

Bankers, Danielsen says, are bank-trained in credit and have the authority to lend money. People who simply work for banks, he explains, might be responsible for transferring funds between accounts and for letters of credit, but not for actually providing funds.

Danielsen sees two very different kinds of young men and women who go into bank training programs after college. One set is from the professional elite or, as he calls them, "trust fund babies." They've been recruited from the best colleges, and have a secure sense of social identity. They may choose banking because it's a good place to launch a social and business career, but also because the training programs are so highly regarded. Many trust fund babies leave banking after a few years to go into higher-paying fields.

The other set is the upwardly mobile group who are looking for the automatic respectability that comes with being a banker. "We're brought up to think of bankers and lawyers and stockbrokers as upper middle class," Danielsen points out. "The perception is that a banker is someone who is reliable, somebody you can count on, somebody who has a special place in society. A good number of people go into banking because of that. You get an automatic social identity, which means a lot to people who didn't have one before."

Of course, not every banker stays in the business out of class-consciousness. They also have to like what they're doing, and be well-suited to the career. "Most of them, because of their training, are not risk-takers," analyzes Danielsen, pointing out that they don't like to take risks in personal relationships either. "They tend to be, as a group, very conservative in dress and style. And they're aggressive. You wouldn't think it, but they are. Bankers now have goals they have to meet. So they're aggressive people, but they're looking for sure bets."

Southern-born writer Diane Wills, who has lived with a bank lending officer for two years, describes him as "accountable, dependable, very solid. A head-on-his-shoulders type." But Willis notices another side of him and his associates as well: "They're all very gregarious, very outgoing and open."

The advantages of spending the rest of your life with a banker? "He never has to work nights or weekends. And unless you work with him, you'll never have to set foot in a bank again." Or worry about being overdrawn. Or fret that the employer doesn't have a good enough savings plan. Some banks actually match every penny you save, adding it to your account as if a secret benefactor had taken you under his wing. So when you've saved $10,000 a total of $20,000 will actually have been deposited—plus the interest on all of it.

The trouble with trying to define the kind of man you're going to meet in banking is that the entire industry may be unrecognizeable five years from now. A University of Virginia M.B.A. once explained why he chose to become a lending officer and why the job is banking's natural route to the top. "Every corporate entity has something specific that it does, and lending money is what a bank does."

Well, it used to be. But deregulation, diversification and high-tech fever may be changing all that.

Ever since 1927 and the McFadden Act, banks have had to stay within their own state lines. One of the reasons that's changing is that people have looked at the Federal definition of a bank: "an institution that handles regular checking accounts and makes commercial loans." All a business has to do to become a "nonbank" is to drop one of those services. The usual choice is to stop making loans.

That's why companies like JC Penney, Sears Roebuck and Prudential Insurance can open their own banks and compete with traditional commercial banks for you, the customer. And Citicorp can open branches all over the country, and get away with it because they're "nonbanks"—they don't give loans at the interstate branches. On top of this trend, banks owned by holding companies have additional freedom. Holding companies aren't bound by all the laws that restrict interstate banking.

Now that insurance companies, brokerage houses and credit unions are competing with the neighborhood commercial bank, banks are branching out into other areas. Instead of sitting back politely in their bankers' suits and passive bankers' attitudes and waiting for customers to come to them, they're actively seeking out business. As one observer put it, "in the past, banks considered it impolite to try to take a customer from another bank." But it's a free market now and competition is fierce.

That's made great career opportunities for marketing people. New

M.B.A.'s who might have become product managers at Procter & Gamble (or who have been) now take banking jobs. What they get to market may be the bank's brokerage services or electronic funds transfers, as well as all those special-feature checking and savings accounts. As these people climb the corporate ladder, people may begin to say that marketing is what a bank is all about.

Information services executives are another group edging their way to the top. "Some of these electronic wizards have little or no background in credit/lending," an executive search expert told *Business Week's Guide to Careers*, "yet are on a beeline for the C.E.O.'s suite."

One of the nation's largest banks now regularly hires for a long list of jobs that didn't exist a decade ago. They include telecommunications lawyers, satellite communications specialists, electronic banking account officers, at-home banking salesmen and systems analysts (who do you think invented automatic teller machines?).

All these changes, could affect the kind of man you'll find in the banking industry. (For insights on computer and marketing types, see the sections on programmers, systems analysts and product managers, pages 154, 129 and 117, respectively.) One thing, however, hasn't changed. A man in the financial industry has a head start on financial success (and so do you, when you become a banker). According to an executive search firm survey of 300 top-paid executives in the U.S., more than 22 percent began their careers in finance.

JOB SECURITY: Banks have always been safe, secure places to work— but that may change as everything else about banking does. The good news is that jobs for bank officers and managers are expected to grow faster than the average occupation. By 1995, says the Bureau of Labor Statistics, there should be 617,000 jobs—an increase of 45 percent.

MONEY: Overall, salaries in banking aren't that impressive. The national average income of $24,000, however, is weighted by all the small banks in small cities, where incomes are low. Some officer trainees earn as much as 50 percent above average on their first jobs.

If you're joining a bank and you've got a bachelor's degree, you can expect to enter their training program at $13,200–$21,600. If you have a master's degree, expect a starting salary of $21,600–$34,800.

The top ten percent of all bank officers earn $46,800 and up. In large banks, the top officers in each department (trust, international, and so on) have salary ranges of $55,000–$90,000 per year. In small banks, those same jobs offer salaries ranging from only $25,000 to $35,000. Top executives in very large banks can earn $250,000–$800,000. Including bonuses, of course.

Expect a good employee benefits plan in banking. An American Bankers Association survey of 125 of the nation's largest commercial banks, for instance, revealed that 87 percent offer at least one form of Incentive Compensation Plan (I.C.P.). The larger the bank, the more likely they are to offer I.C.P.'s.

LIFESTYLE: Until the "new banking" has swept away the old images, you'll still be one of the most respectable and solid citizens in town.

Mr. and Ms. Bank Officer dress in the best conservative fashion, of course, and live in a conservative house. You'll see plenty of each other, thanks to "bankers' hours." Working late on a really rough day means leaving the office at six, instead of five.

WHAT IT TAKES: Without excellent judgment, you're sunk. If you can't look at the facts and figures and make an intelligent decision as to which individuals or companies are not likely to pay you back, you're not doing your job; don't forget, bad loan decisions can lead to default. You should be comfortable with details. Good communication skills and the ability to work independently are also important.

As banking evolves into a more aggressive industry, you may have to evolve in the same direction. "You have to go out and sell money," explains an officer in one New York bank, "just like a stockbroker sells stocks."

GETTING HIRED: The best way to get into a bank's formal training program is to be recruited right off campus. Go to the best school you can get into, then make friends with somebody in the placement office so you'll be sure to get an interview. But which school? According to *The Book of Bests*, the most impressive business degrees come from Harvard, Stanford, the University of Chicago, the University of Pennsylvania and Carnegie-Mellon, in that order. Also in the top ten: M.I.T., the University of California (Berkeley and Los Angeles campuses), the University of Michigan, and Columbia.

TRAINING: Most large banks have formal training programs that may last months or years. You may have a combination of classroom instruction and hands-on experience in the various areas of the bank. And although you don't have to enter knowing which specialty you're interested in, having a specific job goal doesn't hurt.

If you're considering a banking career, make your move soon. Women are gaining fast on the men in this career. According to the A.B.A., the number of women in the managerial and professional ranks has increased by 65 percent in the past decade.

EDUCATION: An M.B.A., preferably in finance, is a near-must. Your undergraduate degree could be in liberal arts, social sciences or business.

EARNINGS: $24,500 national average; big-city and big-bank officers can earn much more, however.

WORKSTYLE: Structured office work, usually in comfortable and pleasant surroundings. Only occasional overtime.

DIRECT INTERACTION OPPORTUNITIES: Formal training program. Meetings with staff or clients.

FOR MORE CAREER INFORMATION: American Bankers Association, 1120 Connecticut Avenue NW, Washington, DC 20036. National Association of Bank Women, 500 North Michigan Avenue, Chicago, IL 60611 (send $1.50 for career booklet).

BIOLOGICAL SCIENTIST

69% are men   31% are women

+ Maybe you'll learn how to clone Mel Gibson.

− After an 80-hour week, you'll be too tired to care.

"Everyone seems to be under 30 and jeans are the corporate uniform," one newspaper reporter observed at the Genetics Institute in Boston.

"Most of Dr. Olmstead's colleagues are under 35, and more than half have come from other countries," another reporter wrote of a computerized Merck, Sharp and Dohme plant in Rahway, New Jersey.

Another reporter also described a scientist in this field as one who "likes to wear tennis shoes with jeans to the office."

May we introduce the new scientist, a bit informal but dedicated to working fiendishly long hours and perhaps changing the world. "You give a young scientist a lab to run and responsibility for a project and he'll be happy," says a representative of one biotechnology firm.

These scientists are microbiologists, molecular biologists and plant molecular geneticists who work with biochemical engineers and chemists to turn the new life-science technologies into profits. Most are working for one of the 100 or so small companies that specialize in this new field.

"The difference is most noticeable culturally," says a former Bristol-Myers vice president who has worked in both large and small companies. Few Bristol-Myers executives wear jeans to work.

Then there are the biochip specialists. Described as "a small but influential group of physicists, genetic engineers, chemists, mathematicians and molecular biologists," their research efforts can seem like science fiction even to a generation raised on *Star Wars*.

• *Biochip 101, Lesson 1:* The biochip is an organic computer. With enough funding, we could have a working model of one by 1995 or so. The idea is to grow computer circuitry in biology labs—from living bacteria. Advantages include the following:

- The resulting computers could be incredibly small.
- These tiny super-computers would not have twice the memory of today's models, or even 100 times; they would have a capacity of 10 million times the memory of the most powerful computers that exist today.
- They could monitor your body chemistry and correct any imbalances they detect. If you'd suffered from chronic depression all your life, for instance, because your brain doesn't do quite what it's supposed to with norephinephrine, a biochip implant theoretically could cure you overnight. No more pills, no more therapists asking why you can't admit that you hate your parents.
- The next fireman you date could look a lot like R2D2. Robots with these supercomputers could take over all of society's most dangerous work, from fighting fires to defusing bombs.
- Silicon Valley would have to change its name, since future circuits could be made of organic proteins, not silicon.

Things start to get eerie at this point. These computers might be able to detect their own design flaws. They might be able to repair and replicate themselves.

Of course, not all biological scientists spend their work days splicing genes. The greatest number are working in specialties that have been around for some time.

Botanists, for instance, work with plants and their environments. *Microbiologists* investigate bacteria, viruses and other microscopic organisms. Those in medical specialties study the effects of antibiotics on bacteria, or the relationships between bacteria and disease. *Physiologists*, all of whom study the functions of plants or animals under various conditions, may specialize in reproduction, growth, respiration or in the physiology of a particular body system. *Zoologists*, of course, study animals.

Then there are the *pharmacologists, toxicologists* (see Chemist section, page 98), *anatomists, ecologists* and *embryologists*.

Real-life bionics, a related area, has become a $500 million business. The biggest-selling replacement parts for the human body are artifical joints, intraocular lenses, heart valves and blood vessels. The most impressive new product now, currently $50,000–$80,000 each, is the artificial heart. "Everything can be replaced eventually," say people in the industry, although they admit artificial nervous systems and brains may be tricky. Biological scientists, biomedical engineers and physicians all may work together on future developments.

You might end up working in any of these areas—and you might meet the perfect man, slaving over a mononucleotide. He's sure to be well-educated, sure to speak your language and almost sure to be filled with enthusiasm for his work.

One out of four biological scientists works in private industry. If you choose this route, you're most likely to find yourself on the payroll of a pharmaceutical, chemical, food or agricultural services company. You might also work for a nonprofit research organization, but fewer than one out of ten people in this field do so.

JOB SECURITY: The future looks strong throughout the biological sciences. The Bureau of Labor Statistics predicts above-average (35 percent) occupational growth. By 1995, they project, the number of jobs in the field will have increased to 71,000. The greatest number of jobs will be in the research and development departments of private industry.

MONEY: If you go to work in private industry with a bachelor's or master's degree, you're likely to be offered $16,500–$17,000 per year to start. Pay for Federal government jobs is apt to be slightly lower: approximately $13,400–$16,600 with a bachelor's degree; approximately $16,600—$20,300 with a master's. Starting salaries vary, depending on your academic record. If you have a Ph.D., however, the Federal government would hire you at about $24,500–$29,400. The average for all biological scientists in Federal government jobs is $31,900. According to industry estimates, private firms in biotechnology pay their Ph.D.'s an average of $50,000 per year.

LIFESTYLE: "I work as many as 80 hours a week and I love it," says a Boston-based Ph.D. "But it's a high-pressure place." Studies show that most biological scientists work normal office hours, but those in some of the most dynamic new fields virtually live at the office and lab—much as computer fanatics do.

More than one-fourth of biological scientists work for the Federal Government, almost half of them in the Department of Agriculture and the National Institute of Health. So there's a strong possibility of living in Washington, D.C., and developing a wonderful case of "Potomac Fever."

Genetic engineering/biotechnology companies are scattered across the U.S. Many of them, however, are in the Boston/Cambridge area, metropolitan New York/New Jersey, and Chicago. Northern California, Maryland and Pennsylvania are other possible future homes for you in this field.

WHAT IT TAKES: You may work independently, as part of a scientific team, or both—and you'll need the ability to do both. If your job involves field research, you'll also need physical strength and stamina to breeze through it.

GETTING HIRED: The dramatic growth and strong need for new scientists doesn't mean you can waltz in with a few A's in biology and be hired on the spot. The biotechnology experts are picky, and they can afford to be.

"There are relatively few people with the kind of skill we want," says one industry scientist. "It's hard to get the combination of experience in chemical engineering, microbiology and computers. . . . It's the person who has an overview and can stand above it all who is going to come out ahead." What they are looking for, he says, are intelligent, well-educated scientists with a combination of enthusiasm and stamina. Hundreds of resumés come into his office every week, but very few have what the company is looking for.

Your biggest advantage right now is being a woman. The industry believes the current situation indicates "a nationwide shortage of women in science" and is sending women employed in the field out to college campuses to explain what they do and to persuade female students to major in the sciences.

EDUCATION: Ph.D. required for most research jobs and for advancement. Master's degree sufficient for some applied research jobs.

EARNINGS: $31,900 and up national average.

WORKSTYLE: Regular hours in an office, lab, classroom or combination thereof. Field work in some jobs.

DIRECT INTERACTION OPPORTUNITIES: Teamwork.

FOR MORE CAREER INFORMATION: American Institute of Biological Sciences, 1401 Wilson Boulevard, Arlington, VA 22209.

ECONOMIST

60% are men   40% are women

- Everyone will blame you for the next recession, whenever it hits.

+ Economists say there isn't going to be another recession; at least, not until about 2020.

Maybe you *will* be able to own the big, sprawling house of your dreams, after all. Maybe you'll be able to manage the payments on a Jaguar with no trouble, eat out at good restaurants every night and treat yourself to the works (facial, manicure, pedicure, massage) once or twice a month at your favorite salon. Maybe you even can afford to have children.

A new age of prosperity is coming, say world economists. It's going to start some time in the 1990s and, by the time the year 2001 is upon us, we'll all be rolling in money.

It has something to do with 50-year-long economic waves (the ebb and flow of prosperity, recession, depression and recovery, in that order), or with capitalism correcting its excesses and shortcomings on a predictable schedule. The latter theory was proposed, not surprisingly, by a Russian economist. The last wave of recovery/prosperity began in the war years of the 1940s, with major developments in air transport, electronics, drugs and oil. Before that, there was *La Belle Epoque*, beginning in the mid-1890s and accompanied by such major developments as electricity, the telegraph, the telephone and the car. The great new fortunes of the coming turn-of-the-century boom will be made from biotechnology, microelectronics, telecommunications and nuclear energy, economists predict.

If any of this interests you beyond your own potential material gains, economics might be the field for you. But, is an economist your kind of man?

"The only economist I've ever known looked like a cross between Wallace Shawn and Albert Einstein," recalls a New Hampshire woman. "There was something about him that was a little like an absent-minded professor, but not quite. He was more like the character actor you'd pick to play the professor."

Yet, she points out, he was having an affair with a stunning blue-eyed blonde who was risking her formerly happy marriage to be with him.

"Economists, on the whole, are pretty serious people," summarized a college economics major who ended up going into another field. "But they have to be. This is not a subject you play around with. It's very difficult stuff, just to digest it. You have to have a very analytical mind and really understand graphs and trends. Even back in college, everybody in class was always very attentive to what was going on. I remember always having the feeling that these people were certainly into it more than I was. They were prepared to do a lot of work."

As a group, however, they don't always try as hard in other areas. Few economists will ever make the best dressed list, for one thing. Although a large percentage work in the same corporations that spawned the well-tailored dress-for-success look, some of them still dress as though they've just wandered in mistakenly from the nearest campus. "They don't have to fit the executive mold," the ex-economics major explains, "because economists aren't executive. They don't make decisions; they give *you* the information to make the decisions. They're the intellectuals, the forecasters in a corporation."

If you take a job as a business economist, your work will be much more practical than theoretical. Your goal will be to use the tools of economics to solve the business problems of the company you work for. That could mean predicting interest rates or forecasting the market for certain products and services. No company worth its salt today makes any major move—sales programs, acquisitions—without consulting its economists. Banks, insurance companies, manufacturing companies and securities industry firms are among the largest employers of business economists. If a top salary is your priority, apply for a securities industry job.

About half of all economists work in government jobs, from city governments to those in Federal agencies. As a government economist, one of your jobs might be to assess economic conditions on an international scale. And as new legislation is proposed or passed in other countries, you'd study and report on just how those new laws are likely to affect various aspects of our economy. You might specialize in an area such as finance, labor, agriculture, transportation or international trade.

No matter where you're employed, a big part of your work day will probably be spent doing research, either alone or as part of a team. When it's time to report your findings, you may do so in the form of a written report or newsletter. Or you may be called on to make speeches, either to executives of your own company, to outside audiences, or both. Of course, economists spend plenty of time in meetings, just as other business people do, as part of conducting their research and to share economic insights and input with their associates.

There's no question as to what you should major in to pursue this career: economics. In addition to the usual courses in macro- and micro-economics, however, you'll need an academic background in statistics, computer science, econometrics and monetary policy theory. To understand the world and the human beings you're making predictions about, you'll also need a broad background in subjects such as history, anthropology, science, psychology and sociology.

JOB SECURITY: Things could be much worse. There are 30,000 economists working today, and the Bureau of Labor Statistics forecasts a healthy average growth of 27 percent (up to a total of 38,000) by 1995.

Sidelight: In reality, there are about 45,000 working economists today. The additional 15,000 teach college economics. This, like other college faculty specialties, faces no job growth at all in the next decade. In fact, an actual decline in the number of teaching jobs is expected.

It's true that economists, like accountants, do well in almost all economic conditions. If times are good, organizations want expert advice on how to make the most of it. If times are bad, companies need even more help in knowing when they will improve and how to best ride out the storm.

MONEY: Business economists do much better than those working in other settings. Their national median in 1982 was $43,000. The national median for all economists during the same year was $30,200. The top 10 percent in the field earned $46,800 and up. Economics educators earn a national mean of about $21,700 to about $44,800, depending on job title and school. The average starting salary for economists is $18,500 a year.

LIFESTYLE: More economists work in New York City and in Washington, D.C., than in any other location, so be prepared for a fast-paced city life or a long commute. And if you do work in some other city, your business travel is likely to be to one or both of those cities.

Aside from business-related travel, you can keep your business life and personal life relatively separate. But when bad economic times hit again, be prepared for the people you meet at every get-together from church socials to black-tie cocktail parties to blame it all on you.

WHAT IT TAKES: The worst job candidate in economics is one who "is muddled and not self-disciplined," says a Connecticut-based economist, now a corporate vice president, or one who "skews all that he sees to fit, rather than being an objective observer of individual elements."

A lot of your time will be spent on data analysis, so you'll have to work accurately with details. Patience, persistence and a systematic approach to work are assets. Both writing reports and making speeches or presentations can be a part of your work, so communication skills are important, too.

Breaking into an economist's career calls for more than the average amount of formal education. A bachelor's degree might get you a job as a research assistant, but not easily. With a master's degree, you'll still face competition. At this level, there's little point in trying to compete for the limited number of teaching jobs. Instead, concentrate your job search on the business world. You'll do better there, especially if you have a good background in marketing and finance. Even Ph.D.'s will face competition for academic jobs. In business, industry and government, however, Ph.D. economists should find the job search smooth sailing.

EDUCATION: A master's in economics or an M.B.A. minimum for most jobs, a Ph.D. required for many.

EARNINGS: $30,200 national median.

WORKSTYLE: Deadlines, tight schedules, heavy workloads, some overtime and possible travel; structured office work schedules for most.

DIRECT INTERACTION OPPORTUNITIES: Working together on a research team.

FOR MORE CAREER INFORMATION: National Association of Business Economists, 28349 Chagrin Boulevard, Suite 201, Cleveland, OH 44122.

MARKET RESEARCHER

61% are men   39% are women

+ You and he will have the world psyched out.

− You'll never run the company.

"They were real materialists," says Nell Gary of the market research people she has known. "They had a real enthusiasm about things. Sort of a sense of *'Oh, wow! My entire life will change for the better if I can only have those Ralph Lauren sheets'*—or new wallpaper for the bathroom or whatever. I think that's why they were so fascinated with how advertising and promotion and packaging can control us."

But Rick Baldwin, a corporate publications manager, describes people in this career in almost exactly opposite terms. "A little bit aloof, a little bit superior, a little academic and very authoritative. At meetings, they always seem a little bit above the petty concerns of the brand management people. When they report on something it's in a tone of 'since you asked me, I'll tell you.' I think they see themselves as more objective than the rest of us.

"On the other hand," he continues, "they're very cynical about their work. The first time I asked somebody in market research for help in designing a questionnaire, he just raised an eyebrow and asked me, 'What do you want the answers to prove? We can design it to come out anyway you want.' If they're enthusiastic, they're hiding it well."

A cynic on the surface, with childlike wonder underneath? What a combination!

Market researchers have been called the "backseat drivers of business." Without their information about the needs and wants of the buying public, the sales and marketing departments of America wouldn't know which way to move.

The American Marketing Association has defined market research as "the systematic gathering, recording and analyzing of data about problems relating to the marketing of goods and services." The most commonly used tools of market research are surveys and interviews. These may be done by mail, by telephone or in person.

The in-person method is the most expensive, but it also can yield the fullest, most accurate information. If you were a part-time interviewer for a market research company, you might place yourself in a shopping mall for a day and stop shoppers to conduct the surveys on the spot. Do you ever buy frozen foods? Which brands do you buy? Do you believe food items contain the most nutrients when they're (a) frozen, (b) canned, (c) fresh, (d) makes no difference?

The focus group is another popular method of obtaining consumer information. If you owned a brewery, for instance, and wanted to introduce a beer target-marketed at women, you might hire a market research firm to find out what women look for in beer. The firm would gather a random group of perhaps eight to ten women in their offices and spend a morning in an informal roundtable discussion on the subject. These women might have been rounded up by word of mouth or they might have been recruited by classified ads.

Some of the questions that might be introduced into the discussion: If someone asked you to describe the typical beer drinker, how would you do that? If you do drink beer, what brand and how did you choose it? Would you feel more comfortable drinking beer from a can or a bottle? Information obtained from this focus group might be used to make decisions about product name, packaging, pricing, advertising, public relations, sales promotion and distribution.

The most ambitious kind of market research is the test market. In this case, a new product or service is introduced in only one or a few cities in order to determine reaction and acceptance—and to work out any problems that may arise. In a way, theatre producers do the same sort of thing: opening "out of town" in New Haven or Boston, working out the kinks and doing some rewriting there before bringing the finished product to Broadway for opening night.

In the case of a new laundry detergent or diet soft drink, the product might be introduced exclusively in such popular test markets as Denver and Syracuse, complete with local TV and newspaper advertising. Its success there determines whether or not the product will be introduced nationwide.

The trick, of course, is to find cities that mirror the entire country demographically. Theoretically, good results in a test market guarantees good results in full distribution. In 1982, the top 15 test market cities were listed (by industry estimate) as Albany-Schenectady, N.Y.; Charlotte, N.C.; Chicago; Dallas-Forth Worth, Tex.; Denver, Co.; Fort Wayne, Ind.; Houston, Tex.; Kansas City, Mo.; Minneapolis-St. Paul, Minn.; Peoria, Il.; Phoenix, Ariz.; Portland, Or.; "The Quad Cities" (Rock Island and Moline, Il., plus Davenport and Bettendorf, Ia.); Sacramento-Stockton, Ca.; and Syracuse, N.Y.

As a trainee, even with a college degree, you're likely to do some of the nitty-gritty work of market research: transcribing data and tabulating questionnaires and survey results. When you make junior analyst, you'll help conduct surveys and questionnaires and write reports on the results. When you've worked your way up to senior analyst, you'll be responsible for specific market research projects.

You may work for a manufacturing company's internal market research department, an ad agency, a television or radio station or for an independent market research firm. A.C. Nielsen (who gather and publish television's well-known Nielsen ratings), I.M.S. International, S.A.M.I. and Arbitron are among the largest.

Many old hands in this field recommend getting your start at a market research firm, even if your ultimate goal is a corporate job. "That way you'll have a complete understanding of the business," explains a state government market research executive who started his career with three years at an outside firm. "You'll learn the fundamentals of marketing research, how to design a questionnaire, how to use a computer, and you'll get to know media-gathering devices and which to use."

JOB SECURITY: The last forecast the Bureau of Labor Statistics made for market research specialists was for "better than average growth" between now and 1990. The number of jobs is sensitive to swings in the economy, however. A master's degree gives added job security, because it makes you more marketable on the next job search. Specializing in one of the economy's fastest-growing areas—perhaps doing research in banking, accounting or health care—is another plus.

MONEY: Trainees generally start out at $14,000–$17,000 per year. The average salary for all market research analysts is $24,130. Market research managers or supervisors average $32,950; market research directors, $41,360.

LIFESTYLE: Unless you work for a company which sees travel as a big part of your work, a career in market research should leave you free to enjoy your personal life. There are jobs in every part of the U.S., but the greatest number of market research people work in New York, Chicago and other big cities where major advertising agencies and manufacturing company headquarters are located.

WHAT IT TAKES: Creativity is the most important trait of an effective market research analyst. You start by analyzing the problem or project, but there's more than one way to research a market. You have to know a variety of techniques well and know how to choose the best one for each situation.

This career also calls for "an inquisitive mind, someone who is not afraid of the unknown," points out a Florida-based market research director. "There are times when you'll get answers you weren't expecting, and you have to be willing to accept them. There *is* a sense of adventure and discovery in marketing research, but you have to have an open mind more than anything else."

We haven't found one, but it's possible that not every man in the field is a cynic.

EDUCATION: Bachelor's degree, ideally in marketing, business, statistics or psychology. M.B.A. preferred.

EARNINGS: $24,130 national average.

WORKSTYLE: Basic office job, with long hours possible at deadline times; frequent travel in some jobs.

DIRECT INTERACTION OPPORTUNITIES: Putting your heads together to design a questionnaire, evaluate a focus group or plan a sampling program. Team business trips to check out test markets.

FOR MORE CAREER INFORMATION: American Marketing Association, 250 South Wacker Drive, Chicago, IL 60606.

COMPUTER PROGRAMMER

65% are men   35% are women

+ You can beat anyone at Pac-Man.

– One or both of you might become emotionally involved with your software.

Among the management set in California's Silicon Valley, there are at least four men for every woman.

Unfortunately, two of these four think polyester is a natural fiber, one wears adhesive tape on the bridge of his eyeglasses and the other is the nerd who was constantly asking you to dance in high school (only now he earns $75,000 a year). In the computer industry, when you hear that a certain bachelor hasn't spent a night in his own bed for months, it may mean only that he's shacked up with his terminal. Sleeping at the office is not unheard of in this world.

Single women who work in the computer industry are optimistic about the newer generation of the computer male, however. For one thing, they seem to come from a group who've developed social relationships with human beings as well as machines. For another, some of them are quite dashing.

But then the entire computer career picture is changing faster than you can purge a file from your floppy disk. As recently as 1981, *The New York Times* called the computer field "a seemingly infinite frontier" and quoted computer science experts as calling the shortage of qualified people "a national crisis." Just a year later, the editors ran an article on the field's tighter job market, quoting an employment agency president as saying, "There is something of a glut at the junior end of the market." By the fall of 1984, careers columnist Elizabeth M. Fowler had interviewed industry experts who saw slowed growth and reduced turnover. "What used to be a growth area for jobs," one career counselor related, "has probably reached maturity."

But all is not lost. Although there are already 266,000 Americans going to work every morning as programmers, the Bureau of Labor Statistics swears there will be a need for 205,000 more between now and 1995. That's a 77 percent increase, about three times greater than in the average career.

The only problem is that there has been a much bigger increase in the number of people qualified to take those jobs right out from under you. As recently as 1975, there were only 5,000 computer science graduates coming out of U.S. colleges. By 1982, that had jumped to more than 20,000—not counting the more than 5,000 master's degrees and Ph.D.'s in the subject. By the following fall, one out of three M.I.T. students who had declared a major had chosen computer science.

Just in case you've been out in orbit for the past 15 years or so, a programmer codes, tests and "debugs" (finds the errors and fixes them) programs based on specifications provided by a systems analyst or programmer/analyst. A program, defined to the point of oversimplicity, is like a recipe; it's a list of steps telling the computer what to do.

JOB SECURITY: If job security is what you want, go to work for IBM. They never lay off people; if your skills become obsolete, they'll retrain you instead. You can join the company country club for $5 a year. And they promise not to transfer you to a new city more than three times every decade. Unfortunately, you'll have to give up drinking (it's forbidden at certain social functions and frowned upon at lunch). But if you want to meet an extremely neat man who wears a dark suit, white shirt and striped tie every day, this is the place.

Job security was the last thought on most programmers' minds a few years ago. Programmers had a reputation for job-hopping, as they took advantage of their in-demand status by switching jobs regularly to increase their incomes quickly. These days, surveys show that the average turnover rate is one-third of what it was back in the good old days of 1981.

The best bet for job security is moving up the career ladder, with new skills and continuing education courses in both business and new technology. Some people are beginning to think programming is a dying art. So prepare yourself to be promoted to systems analyst, to M.I.S. (management information systems) or perhaps to a specialized job like E.D.P. (electronic data processing) auditor.

MONEY: The computer field may look lucrative to high school kids whose other choices are vocational school courses in auto mechanics or lifelong counter jobs at McDonald's. It is not, however, a get-rich-quick field for most. According to one personnel firm's survey, programmers average $24,000. The Bureau of Labor Statistics is in line with a median national income of $23,140. The top ten percent earn $35,000 and more. It's too bad that the job market looks better for applications programmers than for systems programmers; the latter tend to earn about 20 percent more.

There are possibilities of bigger money ahead. Directors of M.I.S. have median earnings of $65,400.

LIFESTYLE: When not hypnotized in front of their monitors, computer programmers are relatively normal people like everyone else. Choose this career, and you still can go out partying, go to the movies and even take vacations once or twice a year. But if you're both truly computer people, never underestimate the joys of a weekend at home—cuddling up in front of the Apple, eating popcorn and playing each other to the death at your latest video game creation.

WHAT IT TAKES: "It takes an orderly kind of mind," says the president of one computer consulting firm. "People who like to divide things into categories make good programmers." Patience, persistence and extreme accuracy are also important.

GETTING HIRED: Getting the first job in programming may be the biggest challenge of your career. Afterward, you should be able to move up relatively fast. Employers seem to be looking for entry-level people who can do more than read COBOL, FORTRAN or the other computer languages. They want you to have good communication skills in English, too, to know something about the industry you're applying to work in (insurance, banking, whatever) and to think of yourself as a businesswoman—not just a technical employee.

EDUCATION: At least a bachelor's degree in computer science. Additional education, especially in business, is a plus.

EARNINGS: About $24,000 national average.

WORKSTYLE: It's basically a 40-hour office work week but, if the computer is only available at night or on weekends, that's when you'll use it. Emergency calls are possible at any hour.

DIRECT INTERACTION OPPORTUNITIES: Sometimes a team of programmers will work on a project. And the employees of big computer companies do tend to socialize with each other.

FOR MORE CAREER INFORMATION: Computer and Business Equipment Manufacturers Association, 311 First St. NW, Washington, DC 20001 (*Computer Careers* booklet, $3).

SCIENCE TECHNICIAN

65% are men   35% are women

+ Here's a way to meet scientists without having to get a Ph.D.

− You do the experiment; he gets the Nobel Prize.

In black-and-white science fiction and horror movies, there was always a handsome young male scientist. And then there was a girl. Sometimes she was a scientist herself ("What? *You're* Doctor Ludwig? Doctor *Lee* Ludwig?"). Or she was the professor's daughter, there only to keep house and be company for her white-haired widowed father, the world's foremost expert on paleontology/arachnid mutations/the effects of atomic radiation on soft-shelled crabs.

The idea was just to put a woman in daily intimate contact with the handsome young scientist. All the better to allow the plot to develop. And all the better for the experimental creature to carry her off in his pincers/paws/scaly arms.

But now, even if it's just too radical for Hollywood, you can play the part of a beautiful young science technician instead, if a science career interests you, but not enough to dedicate the next decade to getting your Ph.D.

Science technicians, like engineering technicians (see page 60), do a lot of the work that we always imagined their bosses handled. If you become a technician, you'll conduct tests and experiments, measure and analyze the results and write up reports. And you could be working in this career just two years from now, even if you haven't seen a test tube up close since high school chemistry (of which you remember nothing).

Junior colleges, community colleges, vocational and technical schools offer two-year technician training programs. Some offer co-op programs, so that you could start working at the same time you attend classes. Some corporations offer on-the-job training, but formal education in the field will give you a much better chance of getting a job.

Just like a scientist, you'll have to choose a specialty. Possibilities include the following.

• *Agricultural Technicians* have careers in food production and processing, working side by side with agricultural scientists. Your tests might improve the yield and quality of food crops or increase a certain plant's resistance to disease or insects. Food technologists, who usually have a bachelor's degree in biology, chemistry, agriculture or even food technology itself), study the chemical, physical and biological nature of food to learn how to process, preserve and store it safely. If frozen food tastes better than it used to, we have food technologists to thank.

• *Biological Technicians* work primarily in labs and may choose any number of sub-specialties. As a microbiological technician, you'll study microorganisms and you might be involved in immunological research. If you take a job as a laboratory animal technician, you'll study and report on the lab animals' reactions to various substances. Working with biochemists, you might analyze biological substances (blood, drugs, food). With all the recent advances in biotechnology, this could be an exciting and rapidly changing career choice.

• *Chemical Technicians* work with both chemists and chemical engineers. In this job, you'll set up and do tests on products or processes being developed or improved by your company. You might specialize in a particular industry, such as pharmaceuticals.

• *Toxicology Technicians* are expected to be in great demand in the coming decades, as are toxicologists themselves. Toxicology is the science of poisons, their effects and their antidotes. And all you have to do is look back on the Union Carbide tragedy in Bhopal, India, to realize what a crucial area this is, particularly in the industrial chemical field. The goal: to safely produce and store industrial chemicals that are highly toxic.

JOB SECURITY: Job growth looks good, particularly in the biological sciences. Of course the need for scientists and science technicians are linked. Therefore, your best bets are in private industry, rather than in college or university settings where few new jobs will be created.

MONEY: Only limited information on the earnings of science technicians is reported by the Bureau of Labor Statistics. Life science technicians who work for the Federal government average $13,600 per year. Physical science technicians average $18,100. Given the government's tendency to undercut industry standards, it's likely that pay is higher in the private sector.

LIFESTYLE: Four out of five technicians work in private industry usually on the same work schedule as secretaries and personnel managers. Jobs are available throughout the country, so your career shouldn't dictate your choice of lifestyle in any noticeable way.

WHAT IT TAKES: Being a successful technician takes an aptitude for math and science, manual dexterity, attention to detail and a very high degree of accuracy. It's also important that you enjoy team work. You'll be part of a team composed of scientists, your fellow technicians and other skilled workers.

You'll work under very close supervision at first, of course. But how else were you going to get the handsome young scientist to notice you? (For more on scientists, see page 142.)

EDUCATION: Two-year program at college or technical school.

EARNINGS: $13,600–$18,100 national average in Federal government jobs.

WORKSTYLE: Usually a standard nine-to-five office job with time divided between lab or plant and office. Some safety or health hazards are possible.

DIRECT INTERACTION OPPORTUNITIES: Working side by side over a test tube.

FOR MORE CAREER INFORMATION: American Chemical Society, 1155 16th Street NW, Washington, DC 20036; American Institute of Biological Sciences, 1401 Wilson Boulevard, Arlington, VA 22209; American Society of Agronomy, 677 South Segoe Road, Madison, WI 53711; Institute of Food Technologies, 221 North La Salle Street, Chicago, IL 60601.

AT LEAST 5 OUT OF 10 WORKERS ARE MEN

"The lamps shone o'er fair women and brave men;
A thousand hearts beat happily."

LORD BYRON
Childe Harold

ACCOUNTANT

59% are men   41% are women

+ You'll know every income tax trick in the book.

− There's more to life than joint returns.

A woman we know joined a community theatre group a few years ago and met a handsome young C.P.A. He was bright (an undefeated *Jeopardy* champion who even had a photo of himself with Art Fleming on the living room wall) if a little less scintillating than Oscar Wilde. And he was a great kisser.

They dated hot and heavy from August to February. But he was not the great love of her life, so when they began to drift apart, she found it easy to accept the evolution of their relationship into that of pals. In March, she asked him to help her with her taxes. In April, he sent her a bill for $250. "Well, you called me so much for advice during the year," he explained. She contemplated sending him a bill of her own.

In the interest of objective journalism and fairness to the accounting profession, the same woman swears that one of the two best lovers she ever knew was an accountant. The other was a magazine editor. "He even looked a little bookish, like the stereotype of an accountant," she recalls. "But he was the Errol Flynn of his crowd. I'm told he fell in love with a prostitute—honestly!—after he divorced his first wife, and she liberated him somehow."

Whether the accountants you meet turn out to be more like Clark Kent or Superman, they're apt to be serious about their careers. In recent years, accounting has been called the nation's fastest-growing career field. The *New York Times* pronounced 1982 "the year of the accountant," and the Bureau of Labor Statistics is still predicting occupational growth at a rate faster than average (up 40 percent) between now and 1995.

When you look for your first job as an accountant, you have three choices. You can go into public, management or government accounting.

In a way, *public accountants* have the most glamorous specialty. These are the guys who, among other things, come into a corporation, check the company's figures and give their official approval to all the financial data printed in the annual report. They also count the votes for the Oscars—and are forced to be filmed wearing tuxedos and carrying briefcases for the amusement of the masses. One out of three accounting graduates goes into public accounting.

The cream of public accounting jobs is with one of the Big 8 firms: Arthur Anderson, Price Waterhouse, Coopers & Lybrand, Haskins and Sells, Arthur Young, Ernst & Ernst, Touche Ross, and Peat, Marwick, Mitchell. You'll be likely to find the cream of the male crop there too. If he doesn't make partner (and only one out of ten will ascend to this lofty position), however, he may decide to work for one of the firm's client companies instead.

That would make him a *management accountant*. And his job would be to handle the financial records of the company he works for. Two-thirds of all accountants have jobs like this—recording financial data, analyzing it and presenting it to management.

Government accountants work for the Internal Revenue Service, the General Accounting Office and elsewhere. Their jobs are to oversee government operations that are subject to funding constraints.

You and your true love may choose to specialize, perhaps in one of the fast-growing areas like auditing, tax accounting or computer fraud cases. One fast-track with special opportunities for meeting soon-to-be-available men is divorce work.

One out of two couples married since 1970 will end up in divorce court. New laws providing for equitable distribution of property are making divorce cases more complicated than ever. Divorce lawyers often hire accountants to provide tax information for judges or to work things out when the husband, wife or both were business owners. Part of your job will be testifying in court, so look your best and try to work with the attorneys who represent the husbands if you want to meet men.

JOB SECURITY: Losing your job is the last thing you should worry about. Accounting is a huge profession (with a work force of almost 900,000) and, next to bankruptcy law and undertaking, the most recession-proof of all. If a company needs accounting services when things are going well, it needs them even more when they're not.

MONEY: Maybe it's because of accountants' proximity to money, but they have a greater reputation for financial success than they deserve. New graduates start at an average of $16,000–$21,000, and the average experienced accountant earns $19,000–$56,000. Of course, chief financial officers at the largest companies earn $99,000–$162,000, according to a salary survey by Robert Half International. And the partners at one Big 8 firm averaged $115,000 in a recent year, while the chairman of the same firm earned more than $900,000. Accounting salaries appear to be highest in Alaska, Hawaii and Nevada. Because of the expertise that goes with the job, being a C.P.A. generally adds ten percent to the salary you can expect.

LIFESTYLE: You'll both have the time and money to live very comfortably, if you can just stop checking the price tags on every pleasure life has to offer.

WHAT IT TAKES: One female accountant describes the ideal job candidate as "a problem-solver; a person with a skeptical, logical and inquisitive mind who is willing to sit back, think, ask tough questions and then make sound judgments." Accounting takes accuracy, patience, integrity and an aptitude for math. But employers advise new accountants to learn about people and about the businesses they work for as well. Otherwise, you'll become known as a "numbers-cruncher," doomed to career mediocrity forever.

Women now account for 47 percent of all accounting graduates, according to the American Institute of Certified Public Accountants.

Even the public accounting firms now recruit four women to every six men. But that's still a promising ratio to meet kindred spirits.

EDUCATION: Either a bachelor's degree or an M.B.A. in accounting is a must, particularly for prestigious Big 8 jobs.

EARNINGS: National average $19,000–$56,000.

WORKSTYLE: A comfortable office job with structured schedules. Tax accountants can expect pressure and long hours during tax season.

DIRECT INTERACTION OPPORTUNITIES: On the job, both in the office and via clients.

FOR MORE CAREER INFORMATION: American Institute of Certified Public Accountants, 1211 Avenue of the Americas, New York, NY 10036; National Association of Accountants, 919 Third Avenue, New York, NY 10022.

BUYER

58% are men   42% are women

+ He'll dress like a *GQ* model.

− He'll always be in Hong Kong when you need him.

"I was in love with a buyer once," remembers copywriter Martha Perdue. "He was very insecure and very hotheaded, but he dressed well, and it *is* an exciting job. He got to travel all over the world.

"He was a buyer for a big sportswear company, and department store buyers would buy from him," Perdue explains. "So he would buy designs from all over the world, then they'd be made in Hong Kong or Taipei. Usually, he would travel with one other person— a woman who was another buyer, I think—and he would always go First Class."

Pressed for the man's good points, Perdue adds: "He was a good conversationalist, and he had a sense of humor."

Perdue describes the only other buyer in her past, an old friend from college, in different terms. "He was egotistical, but I guess that could have been based on insecurity. He was arrogant. And he was a real 'man's man,' the type of guy who was always slapping other guys on the back." She shudders. "He was a real rat. But he could carry on a conversation, too. And he dressed well, even in college." That man eventually left his buying job at Bloomingdale's to return to his Southern home city and the family law firm.

So if you're looking for a well-dressed, obnoxious man who will constantly be leaving town—run, do not walk, to the nearest department store and beg to be admitted to their buyer training program.

Of course not every buyer matches up with the type Perdue encountered. David Arthur, an office furniture manufacturing executive, has a completely different list of attributes to describe the buyers he works with. "When it comes to the men, they usually tend to be wheeler-dealers. 'Come on, Arthur. You guys can give me a break on that.' Getting a good price is their only goal." The women in the field fare no better. "They live in the suburbs, they're usually not married, they're anywhere from 25 to 35," he says. "They're usually frazzled, and never dress very well." (Curiouser and curiouser.)

Arthur likes to describe buyers in terms of what they are not: detail-oriented, diplomatic, well-informed. "Buyers in general, nine times out of ten, don't know very much about the products they're supposed to purchase," he observed. "They've just been instructed to buy whatever it is as cheaply as they can."

Reason tells us that buyers, deep-down, are really very nice people who simply need someone to tell their troubles to—maybe each other. Coming home to an empty apartment after a glamorous buying trip to Hong Kong or Milan can probably get depressing after a while.

Not so many years ago, getting into a big store's buyer trainee program was as easy as graduating from your nearest state university and typing up a resumé. History, English and elementary education majors found their way to the personnel offices of the nation's department stores.

There, they were put on respectable if unimpressive salaries, sent to classes in merchandising and store policy, then put on rotating sales assignments in various departments of the store "to learn the business." Even that part of the job could be glamorous. Dustin Hoffman might turn up one day browsing in crystal and china; a Kennedy the next day, charging away in resortwear.

When the training program was over, these perky young college graduates would be presented with the title of assistant buyer—where they'd learn the ropes from experienced buyers until they worked their way up.

The system continues to work the same way, except that attitudes toward liberal arts majors just aren't what they used to be. Today, most personnel interviewers put a lot more weight than they used to on seeing the words "B.A., Marketing" (or at least a long list of merchandising, marketing and purchasing courses) on your resumé.

The job and the challenge have not changed. Buy today what the public will want tomorrow. And in the exact quantity they'll want to buy. Refer to past sales patterns, market research reports and your own instincts to guess what next year's trends will be. Then get that merchandise for the best price and get it delivered on time.

To do all of this, you'll definitely be traveling—visiting manufacturers and attending trade shows. Do remember, however, that not every buyer spends her or his career in *haute couture*. You won't be invited to the fall collections in Paris if you're the buyer for a national hardware chain.

If you work in retail buying (as two out of three people in the field do), you'll purchase merchandise for resale to customers at the retail store or stores you work for. You might go into wholesale buying instead, making purchases from manufacturers, then selling to the buyers who work for retail stores.

JOB SECURITY: Retailing is a competitive business, so never expect to rest on your laurels for long. A good industry reputation for anticipating trends and making smart buys is your best job insurance.

The job market does look bright, thanks to America's overall population growth and our continuing love affair with material goods. The number of buyers' jobs is expected to increase by an above-average 30 percent between now and 1995, for a total of 332,000 jobs in all.

MONEY: Buyers generally don't get rich, except by moving out of the field and into top retail management. The national median income is just $17,300, according to the Bureau of Labor Statistics. According to another slightly more optimistic estimate, the national average is in the $20,000–$30,000 range.

Status isn't everything in this field. It may seem chic to work for the expensive little boutique in an exclusive suburb, but you'll probably earn more buying for a big discount chain like K-Mart—or going into the wholesale side of the business.

LIFESTYLE: Of course money isn't everything, either. You may earn no more than some secretaries you know. But they don't jet away on company-paid overseas buying trips—or buy merchandise for themselves at huge discounts. In the right department store job, for instance, you can be the best dressed woman in town, living in one of the most smashingly-decorated apartments (right down to the French cookware), and you can entertain your dates with tales of the funniest thing that happened on your last trip to Hong Kong, all at bargain rates.

Just keep this in mind for the future. When a single person travels a lot, it's glamorous. When two people in love travel a lot on business, they usually aren't getting on the same plane or traveling at the same time. Be prepared for separations, and learn to make the most of your reunions. You'll make good use of the fact that both champagne and chocolates can be purchased in most airport duty-free shops.

WHAT IT TAKES: You should be good at planning, decision-making and communication. If you once went to Las Vegas but only played the nickel slot machines, you may have the wrong mind-set for a buying career; a good buyer has to be willing to take risks.

EDUCATION: College training, preferably a bachelor's degree in marketing or purchasing.

EARNINGS: $17,300 national median.

WORKSTYLE: Fast-paced and pressured, with a good deal of travel.

DIRECT INTERACTION OPPORTUNITIES: Oh, those buying trips! Have you ever seen the Hong Kong skyline from the Star Ferry?

FOR MORE CAREER INFORMATION: Some general information on retailing careers is available from the National Mass Retailing Institute, 570 Seventh Avenue, New York, NY 10018. For more specific career guidance, get in touch with department stores, discount chains or other retail employers in your area.

EDITOR/REPORTER

54% are men   46% are women

+ He may have the loveable gruffness of a Lou Grant.

− He may have the faithfulness quotient of a Citizen Kane.

Working on a newspaper can be a wonderful way to start a romance, but it depends on the paper.

"Somebody much older and wiser once told me 'There are drinking papers and screwing papers,'" confides a Boston public relations woman. "The *Globe*, I'm told, is the latter."

An old-timer in New York verifies this as a national pattern. "The curse of the *Herald-Tribune* was drink," she recalls. "The curse of the *Times* is sex." Far be it from us to judge the relative value of the two, but keep in mind that the *Herald-Tribune* died in the early 1960s; the *Times* is still printing all the news that's fit.

All of this is hearsay, of course, but journalists do seem to find each other attractive partners. A former staff member of a now-defunct national magazine attributes the number of office affairs there to the publication's precarious financial situation. "We had a young staff, with an even mix of men and women. We felt under the gun, drawn together by the pressure. So we went out drinking a lot together." When it came time to go home after drinks, certain parties decided to share taxis—and a good deal more.

Still, staff members try to be discreet. One couple did a successful job until an editorial assistant noticed the woman in question washing out *two* coffee cups in the office kitchen. ("No woman today does that unless she's in love," the assistant concluded.) Today the two— he was a staff editor, she was head of research—are married, have two young sons and both are freelancing.

Which may prove that drinking publications can evolve into the— uh—other kind.

In terms of being surrounded by male co-workers, newspaper jobs are probably your best bet. According to Women in Communications Inc., only 35–40 percent of major newspaper reporting staffs are female. Over half of all magazine editors, on the other hand, are female. And book publishing, once known as a gentleman's business, is rapidly becoming a ladies' domain.

Other possible editorial jobs on a newspaper include copy editor, city editor, wire editor, department editor, correspondent, managing editor and critic. You might also go into advertising, promotion or circulation—but the business and editorial sides of the papers don't always see eye-to-eye about their relative importance.

As in many other fields, women may hold more jobs than ever before but we still aren't running the business. Although 30–40 percent of today's "hard-news" newspaper reporters are women, most of the lead stories are still being written by men. When re- searchers analyzed the nation's papers during a four-week period in the fall of 1984, *The New York Times* was the worst culprit—only 10 percent of its front-page stories had female bylines. *USA Today* did best, with 41.5 percent, followed by *The Boston Globe* and *The Atlanta Journal*.

Yes, 120 U.S. newspapers now have female managing editors, but most of these are small-circulation dailies. Overall, only 11 percent of the top editorial jobs—the policy-making newspaper jobs—are held by women. As one columnist observed, "There are more women in the Reagan Cabinet meetings than in most editorial meetings."

JOB SECURITY: Relax. If you work for a newspaper, you're a union member with all the job security that implies. Of course, there are

120 fewer daily newspapers today than there were in 1960, and some of the most respected dailies in the country have bitten the financial dust. Magazine work carries the same risk. Neither *Vogue* nor *U.S. News & World Report* is likely to go out of business any time soon, but be wary of new, special-interest and possibly under-financed publications. Although numerous new monthly magazines come into existence every year, periodical publishing has more spectacular failures per year than the average industry. The total number of magazines published has remained steady at around 4,000 for the past 25 years.

MONEY: Editor and reporters spend much of their careers feeling sorry for themselves because of their low paychecks. But things aren't quite as bad as they'd have you think. Starting newspaper salaries today may start at $9,100 per year (hardly enough to pay back your student loan), but go up to more than $38,000. The bigger and more prestigious the paper, the more money you're likely to earn.

The national median for full-time reporters is $19,760. The average for reporters with four to five years' experience is $25,636. Senior editors on major newspapers or magazines with nationwide circulations can earn $60,000 and more per year.

Some of the nation's top-paying newspapers are the *Chicago Sun-Times, Minneapolis Star & Tribune, St. Paul Dispatch, St. Louis Post-Dispatch, Denver Post, San Francisco Chronicle,* and all three New York City dailies (*Times, Post, Daily News*). Newspaper Guild "top minimums" for reporters at those papers range from $35,138 to $46,020 after two to six years.

Beginning salaries for magazine editors can be dismal too, but some people actually make money in this business. The national median for editors-in-chief of magazines of all kinds and sizes is $31,000. Senior editors on large-circulation consumer magazines average $57,000.

The situation in book publishing is similar. According to published estimates, acquisitions editors' salaries generally range from $25,000 to $50,000, and developmental editors normally earn $18,000 to $35,000, depending on the company and years of experience. Editorial directors, however, may earn $50,000–$65,000. And superstar editors, including those with their own imprints, often rate annual salaries of $100,000 and more. Starting salaries in book publishing are notoriously low, beginning at $10,000 at one company we know for the job of editorial assistant.

LIFE/WORK STYLE: Lifestyle and workstyle often begin to merge for editors and reporters. Magazine and newspaper people tend to socialize with each other and with the people who are their daytime business contacts. When you're invited to a midnight book party at this year's hottest disco, is it work or play? If you're assigned to cover the war, you can't go home at night and forget what you do for a living.

WHAT IT TAKES: In one scene from a *Lou Grant* episode, Robert Walden as Rossi asks a library employee for all the books and records on a particular subject. He needs this to check out a possible lead on a newspaper story he's working on. The male librarian listens, nods, then looks at Rossi sympathetically and says, "Boy, and I thought *I* had a lousy job!."

Only a fellow reporter or editor could think that was funny. Once you've learned how important it is to ask people how to spell their names (yes, even John Smith; it could be Jon Smythe), you're on the road to the kind of pickiness you'll need to be an accurate journalist.

It takes much more, of course. You'll need curiosity, persistence, initiative, resourcefulness and objectivity, among other things. Most important, you need the ability to present the facts clearly, succinctly and accurately; you must be a writer.

GETTING HIRED: Ever since *All The President's Men* showed moviegoers what heroes Woodward and Bernstein were in the Watergate investigation, the nation's journalism schools have been flooded with applicants—presumably hoping to bring down a future administration (or meet up with the likes of actors Redford and Hoffman). That single phenomenon had turned journalism into an even more competitive career than ever before.

One way to beat the competition and get an actual newspaper or magazine job is to work without pay to start. Internships (or any kind of summer job) give you real working experience in the field, and help you make your first contacts in the industry. Another edge is having a specialty. Even if it boxes you in a little, consider what you want to write about. If you choose political news, take a minor, a second degree or at least a few continuing education courses in political science and spend your summers working in Washington, D.C. If you want to be food editor, get some college training in home economics or go to the best culinary school you can find. Knowing your subject—and being able to prove that you do—is often the difference between being called in for a job interview and having your resumé promptly thrown into the "thanks, but no thanks" file.

Final hint: Be willing to work anywhere on any kind of paper, especially in the newspaper business. If a weekly paper in a small city or suburb beckons, go for it. A year from now, you'll have gained a good deal of practical experience. Plus you'll have clips (samples of your published work) to put into your portfolio for the next job-hunting round.

EDUCATION: A college degree in journalism or communications, preferably with a very specific major such as news-editorial journalism. A master's degree is a plus.

EARNINGS: $19,760 national median. The top ten percent in the field earn $36,400 and up. Top editors can earn much more.

WORKSTYLE: Deadlines are a constant fact of life in editorial work. This means pressure, a certain hectic atmosphere at times, and schedules that may include night and/or weekend work.

DIRECT INTERACTION OPPORTUNITIES: Journalists practically live together when covering a big story. Reporters and editors often team up with photographers on assignment, too. The traditional after-work drink, however, may be enough for getting to know your colleagues. Cities with big papers often have restaurants and bars where journalists and editors gather.

> **FOR MORE CAREER INFORMATION:** The Newspaper Guild, 1125 15th Street NW, Washington, DC 20005; Women in Communications Inc., P.O. Box 9561, Austin, TX 78766.

EDUCATION ADMINISTRATOR

56% are men   44% are women

+ He'd have to be a man who loves kids.

− He may grow to be a man who hates parents.

One group of parents doesn't want sex education taught in the school. Another insists on school prayer. A community action group wants all children under 12 fingerprinted in case they're lost or abducted, while another wants Judy Blume's novels removed from the library.

If one word describes the school administrator's job, it's diversity. The titles of the American Association of School Administrators' publications reveal just the kinds of issues you might deal with: *Stopping School Property Damage, Making the Grievance Process Work, Perspectives on Racial Minority and Women School Administrators, Work Stoppage Strategies, Changing School Mathematics: A Responsive Process, Teacher Competency: Problems and Solutions.*

"The kind of man who goes into school administration is not necessarily the same kind of man who goes into teaching," explains a principal's wife. "The administrator is more likely to be a political type. In a way, he's always campaigning." So if you've always been attracted to politicians but hate the thought of his constantly being away from home during campaigns, this may be the man for you.

Recent classified ads for superintendents' jobs across the country paint a clear picture of the experience and talents needed for the job. "Effective management, supervisory and executive skills" is the phrase seen most often. But there are others: "ability to implement an excellent instructional program," "public relations and communications skills," "strong financial and management skills," "multiracial experience," "a record of success in productive relationships with board, staff, students, community, effective communications, motivating staff, delegating responsibility" and "ability to create high expectations, ability to unify community behind schools." The salaries offered for these posts range from $35,000 to $75,000.

School districts looking for deputy, associate and assistant superintendents often asked for more specific kinds of background: "strong curriculum experience," "experience in finance and budget development," "thorough knowledge of laws and administrative rules pertaining to personnel and collective bargaining." Administrators at this level often handle only one particular area of operations.

Becoming a school administrator may not be the best way to meet another administrator, the principal's wife points out. "You'd be more likely to interact with a principal just by being a parent who works with the PTA or comes in to see about her child. Or by being a teacher. My husband deals with teachers every day."

Things may change slightly at the assistant superintendent level, however, when you might work in an office of several deputy assistant administrators plus specialists. Most administrators start as teachers, advance to principalships and then move up to district jobs that could lead to the superintendent's office.

All the way up the career ladder, administrators consider "style shifting" one of their most important abilities. "It just means being able to talk to a lot of different kinds of people, but in their own languages and in terms of their own values," one administrator explains. Parents, teachers, students, administrators, secretaries, aides, maintenance people and paraprofessionals are among the groups you might communicate with in an average week.

JOB SECURITY: Perhaps you've heard the word tenure? Once a school grants it, you've got a job for life. On the other hand, future job growth isn't impressive. The Bureau of Labor Statistics forecasts only a 15 percent increase in jobs between now and 1995, well below the average for all occupations.

MONEY: Whether you'll make money in this field depends on how ambitious and/or lucky you are. Assistant principals, the entry-level people in this field, average $27,419–$31,252, depending on whether they work for an elementary, junior high or high school. Principals average $32,451–$37,602. Assistant, deputy and associate superintendents average $42,194–$47,404. Superintendents themselves average $50,260.

Of course, the larger your school district, the more you're likely to earn. Administrative salaries are highest on the West Coast and in the Mid-Atlantic states; lowest in the Southeast.

LIFESTYLE: You'll need to be the epitome of propriety in your private life, of course. You're setting an example for the next generation, you know. And you won't be able to spend every night at home in front of the fire, due to the number of meetings involved with your work. Even if you don't get summers off (many administrators don't, even though their teachers do), the work load lightens at that time of year—and you can take advantage.

WHAT IT TAKES: Some of your most important assets will be self-confidence, leadership skills, managerial skills, communication skills, the ability to withstand criticism, and an extra helping of tact.

GETTING HIRED: The way to get started up the administrative ladder is to teach. You probably won't become a principal without several years of teaching experience. Other administrative jobs can be good routes to the top of the career ladder too. These include curriculum specialist, financial advisor, audiovisual director or head of special education.

EDUCATION: Master's degree in educational administration is usually a must for principals; a doctorate in the same subject is almost a necessity for those moving up to superintendent level. State certification required.

EARNINGS: $27,419–$50,260 national averages, for assistant elementary school principals to school superintendents respectively.

WORKSTYLE: Meetings, meetings, and more meetings, with a few that are downright confrontational. Otherwise, a fast-paced, office-based job.

DIRECT INTERACTION OPPORTUNITIES: All those meetings with teachers, parents, community leaders, local and state politicans.

FOR MORE CAREER INFORMATION: American Association of School Administrators, 1801 North Moore Street, Arlington, VA 22209.

HEALTH CARE ADMINISTRATOR

50% are men   50% are women

+ You get to meet doctors.

– They don't like being bossed around.

When Dustin Hoffman played *Tootsie*, his title character was a hospital administrator on a soap opera. And when one of the older physicians made advances, Tootsie got her first screen kiss. TV's *House Calls* starred Wayne Rogers as a physician and Lynn Redgrave as his hospital administrator; they were attracted to each other episode after episode. In the 1970s movie hit, *The Hospital*, George C. Scott played one of the old-line hospital administrators whose response to noisy demonstrators, questionable alternative treatments and a mysterious doctor-killer on the loose was to have a brief affair (literally in-office) with a patient's daughter.

If you choose a career as a hospital administrator, you too may have romantic adventures with physicians, patients and passers-by. On the other hand, doctors may not want a woman in a position to tell them what to do, so keep an eye out for wealthy patients in private rooms, too.

The term used most often to describe this occupation is hospital administrator, but it may have to be replaced soon by the more general "health care" or "health services" administrator. Three out of five jobs are still in hospitals, but that's rapidly changing. In the

1960s, nearly all graduates with health administration degrees took hospital jobs. Today only half do. Perhaps that's because there are about 2,500 new master's degree graduates each year and only about half that many jobs available in the nation's 7,000 or so hospitals.

The reasons are numerous. There's an enormous trend toward hospital mergers and toward their selling out to profit-oriented hospital conglomerates. Plus hospital care is going through its own recession. In 1984, admissions fell by four percent, which was the largest decrease on record. The average length of a patient's hospital stay dropped five percent to 6.7 days. And for the first time, admissions of patients over age 65 fell. The age of cost-consciousness had arrived.

There are plenty of other employers in the health care field, however. You might work at one of the nation's 22,000 nursing homes or one of the 10,000 clinics. Other choices include an alcohol or drug treatment center, an H.M.O. (health maintenance organization), a large group medical practice, a home for the emotionally disturbed or a public health agency.

Your job might not even involve administration in the way you'd expected. You might work for a government agency, analyzing regional needs for health care, you might work for a health insurance company, designing new types of coverage, or you might take a job with a hospital association as a lobbyist.

Doctors use to run the hospitals and clinics themselves. When someone decided that was a bad idea and that health care administration needed to be professionalized, the career grew like wildfire. New graduates found themselves hired into top jobs practically before the ink on their diplomas was dry. That too has changed.

"Would a new M.B.A. come out of graduate school and become vice president of AT&T?" asks a female chief administrator in New York. "The same thing holds true in hospitals. These are not play laboratories; they're real. Just because people have a degree doesn't mean they can come out and run these complex institutions."

During that boom for new administrators, you might have made it to a chief administrator's job in as little as five years. Today, surveys show that it takes most people nine to 15 years, if they get to the top at all.

On the way, you might manage a hospital department or floor

instead. Or you might handle all administration for a much smaller facility.

Once you reach the top, you may not even handle the day-to-day operation of the facility anymore. You'll be too busy speaking before civic groups and handling all the planning, budgeting and policy-making decisions. You'll have millions of dollars in equipment and facilities in your hand, as well as the professional lives and health care of hundreds of employees and patients.

JOB SECURITY: The Bureau of Labor Statistics sees substantial growth for this career. By 1995, they say, there will be 478,000 health care administrators' jobs. That's a far-above-average increase of 58 percent.

The only administrators who should be looking over their shoulders are those who work for hospitals. If the current trend continues, the big conglomerates could start closing down hospitals that aren't profitable. With our aging population, however, the need for health care won't be shut down; you're almost sure to be needed in another kind of health services facility.

MONEY: The average starting salary for a recent graduate with a master's degree in health administration is $24,500. Associate directors earn an average of $28,000 to $58,000, depending on the size of the hospital in which they work.

A rule of the hotel management business holds true for health care administrators as well. The money you make depends largely on how many beds you're in charge of. Hospital administrators earn an average of $37,000 at the smallest facilities (less than 100 beds), $57,500 (100–349 beds) and $85,000 (more than 1,000 beds). Salaries are generally lower in nursing and personal care homes.

LIFESTYLES: Many administrators, like so many physicians, accept medicine as a way of life, as more than just a career. Even if you're supposed to have a standard 40-hour office week, you're sure to find yourself working late at night and on weekends, either in cases of emergency or just because of heavy workload. Expect it to infringe on your personal life to some degree.

You're most likely to live and work in one of the large cities where the greatest number of health care facilities are found. You might end up in Atlanta, Boston, Chicago, Dallas, Denver, Houston, Los Angeles or New York. There are small-town jobs as well. If you marry a fellow administrator, however, or a doctor, you'll need a location in which jobs are available for both of you.

WHAT IT TAKES: Stamina and patience are the two prerequisites most often cited. You'll also need the ability and maturity to make decisions and take responsibility for them, good communication skills to deal with people on many levels, leadership ability and excellent judgment.

GETTING HIRED: Getting only a bachelor's degree in health care administration could get your resumé shifted to the bottom of the pile. Almost every job candidate has a master's or better.

At the moment, employees seem to prefer job candidates who have M.B.A.'s with concentrations in health administration. Career experts even suggest that you hang around school an extra year to get both a master's in health administration and an M.B.A. Master's degrees in personnel or public administration also are looked upon favorably right now. Most graduate programs will take two years. If you hope to make it to chief administrator someday, or if you plan to teach or do research, get started on a Ph.D.

Your chances of getting hired are greater at nursing homes than at hospitals. Your chances for advancement may be best at H.M.O.'s, because their expected growth in the 1990s is so high.

EDUCATION: Master's degree in health administration, M.P.A. (master's in public administration) or M.B.A. with concentration in health administration. Licensing required for nursing homes and some other long-term care jobs.

EARNINGS: $37,000–$85,000 national average.

WORKSTYLE: Long hours, emergency calls and the possibility of travel.

DIRECT INTERACTION OPPORTUNITIES: Your workday is meetings, meetings and more meetings.

FOR MORE CAREER INFORMATION: American College of Hospital Administrators, 840 North Lake Shore Drive, Chicago, IL 60611.

HOTEL MANAGER

59% are men   41% are women*

+ Think of it. Complimentary room service, maid service and a chocolate on your pillow at bedtime for the rest of your life.

− Hookers, union walkouts, overbookings, disgruntled guests and a six-day work week—and that's for the cushy spots.

"In my next life, I'm going to come back as the *wife* of a hotel manager," the Dutch-born manager of the Mark Hopkins told a San Francisco newspaper reporter.

And why not? If a hotel's general manager chooses to live in the hotel, he and his family probably will enjoy the following: a rent-free two- or three-bedroom suite, maid service (including clean, crisp sheets every day), laundry and dry cleaning service and free parking. When they're hungry, they can order room service (free) or eat "out" at one of the hotel's restaurants. If they'd prefer to cook in the apartment kitchen, no one has to go grocery shopping; one of them just picks up the phone and calls the hotel's purchasing department—or fills out a requisition—for anything that's needed.

There are a few drawbacks. The office may be just an elevator away, and that means you're always "at work." Most G.M.'s (general managers) start their day by eight a.m., end it at eight p.m. or so and then make rounds (like doctors) at least a couple of times before going to bed. You're always only a phone call or a beeper away from

---

* These figures represent all properties managers, including apartment buildings as well as hotels. According to industry estimates, it is roughly correct for hotel managers at all levels. The workforce of hotel general managers, however, is believed to be at least 98 percent male and two percent or less female. Of 140 or so general managers in forward-thinking New York City, for instance, two are women.

an emergency—which could mean anything from a walkout of union employees to a guest whose suite has been burglarized.

Lack of privacy is a constant problem. Hotel managers and their spouses admit that whenever there's a family quarrel, every employee knows about it. Plus you're always on display. Being perfectly dressed and groomed is a must, even if you're just popping out for a newspaper.

Many managers see advantages in raising children in this environment. Everyone on the staff becomes their friend. And they learn good manners very early in life.

What kind of man is the average hotel manager? "Very reserved, very polished, well-groomed and articulate," says manager Lisa Simmons.

"Charming is the word," adds Phil Tennant, a manager at the same hotel. "They're all diplomats. They have to be, because they're juggling employees and clients. I honestly don't know where they find time to date and find somebody to marry. The married ones I've known married people in the industry."

The two agree that women are making inroads in this previously all-male industry. Many department heads (sales, front office) are female. "But when you get into the upper echelon," Tennant points out, "they're few and far between".

Simmons feels certain she can move up to a general manager's job someday, but not just anywhere. "I wouldn't expect to become G.M. of the Waldorf or the Palace," she points out. "There's a certain image that a hotel manager portrays. You think of a hotel manager as being a European." Preferably silver-haired, titled and immaculately tailored.

But that's changing. "People are coming up the ranks through sales and marketing and going into management," Simmons explains. "You're getting a more outgoing, exuberant-type person, more people-oriented." And then, of course, there's Leona Helmsley. . . .

JOB SECURITY: You may be transferred from city to city and property to property, but the hotel business is not so volatile that you have to live in constant fear of being fired. Job growth looks good, too. Hotel managers hold almost 67,000 jobs now. With the average (23 percent) occupational growth predicted by the Bureau of Labor Statistics, that number should be up to 82,000 by 1995.

MONEY: If you get into a hotel company's training program, you're likely to start at $13,000–$18,000. The national average income for all hotel managers and assistants is $22,000. The top ten percent earn $36,000 or more.

How much will you make after you've worked your way up to general manager? That depends on whose figures you believe. The Bureau of Labor Statistics says $32,000 average, but ranging up to $65,000—plus a bonus of 5–25 percent of your annual salary. A placement officer at Cornell University's hotel school says $16,000–$31,000 at a small hotel (400 rooms or less), $22,000–$42,000 at a medium-sized hotel (400–700 rooms) and $34,000–$84,000 at a large hotel (up to 1000 rooms). Not to mention all the aforementioned freebies, bonuses and benefits.

LIFESTYLE: Gracious, elegant, maybe even a little formal, but your job is your life in the hotel business.

WHAT IT TAKES: The perfect hotel manager can solve problems day in and day out, organize and direct the work of his or her entire staff and concentrate on little details at the same time.

GETTING HIRED: There was a time when you could just start as a waitress, bellhop or summer desk clerk, then advance through the ranks. It doesn't work that way anymore. Taking a part-time or summer job in a hotel or restaurant while you're young is still a good idea—if only for making industry contacts—and the hotel personnel departments still like to see it on your resumé.

But these days the hotel industry takes management very seriously. The best way to get hired is to go back to school for a degree in hotel and restaurant administration, ideally a four-year degree, and wait for the college recruiters from the big hotel companies to come to your campus. About ten colleges now offer bachelor's degrees in the subject, and hundreds of junior colleges and technical schools offer hotel administration courses.

The important courses include hotel administration, accounting, economics, marketing, data processing, housekeeping, food service management, catering and hotel maintenance engineering. If you can prove you know something about computers, finance and labor relations, you're way ahead of the job candidates who can't.

Learn a foreign language, perhaps French or Spanish, if you ever want to work abroad. You'll need it too if you're applying to one of the international hotel chains now active in the U.S.

TRAINING: If you get into one of the hotel chains' management training programs, they'll teach you everything you need to know. In most cases, you'll undergo six to 15 months of intensive training, which involves a rotation through all the company's major departments.

You'll be learning how to schedule a hotel staff, order supplies, take inventory and check guests in and out. You'll also be taught how to plan and sell special functions, from business conferences to weddings. You may learn to develop weekend packages ("3 days and 2 nights, including champagne breakfast and a night at the theatre, only $199 per couple"), as well.

In most programs, you won't be asked to choose an area of specialization until near the end of your training. You might go into food and beverage, personnel, sales and marketing, rooms, accounting, conventions or catering. Those in the know advise you to go into food and beverage or sales and marketing if you want to get ahead. Both are considered very desirable experience for future G.M.'s.

If you see a man in the training class who interests you, make your move. This may be the last time the two of you will be based in the same city.

EDUCATION: Bachelor's degree in hotel and restaurant administration.

EARNINGS: $22,000 national average for all managers and assistant managers.

WORKSTYLE: Night and weekend work. Shift work. Hectic pace. Pressures. The possibility of being on call 24 hours a day.

DIRECT INTERACTION OPPORTUNITIES: When you live on location, anything is possible. But discretion is an absolute must.

FOR MORE CAREER INFORMATION: American Hotel and Motel Assocation, 888 Seventh Avenue, New York, NY 10106.

MEETING PLANNER

53% are men   47% are women

+ It's a growing new field with lots of travel.

− While everyone else takes a midnight swim, you'll be inside with the hotel staff reviewing the next day's menus.

Gena Strait still has the photos from her first national sales meeting. She remembers flying out to Phoenix on a plane with a dozen fellow headquarters executives. (Only a certain number of employees could take the same flight, lest a single crash wipe out an entire division of the Fortune 500 conglomerate.) She remembers being driven to the Arizona Biltmore and checking in twice: first at hotel reception, then at the company's conference desk to get her name tag and information packets. She remembers the bag of products and other goodies (a beautiful crystal decanter, for one thing) that she found in her room. And she remembers the last-day announcement that every person there would be receiving a tiny portable black-and-white TV as an additional gift. (They were mailed to everyone's homes.)

After the mornings of product presentations and speeches, there were always planned activities: a golf tournament, a tennis tournament, a combination trail ride/picnic and so on. One night's dinner was a Southwest barbecue buffet. And on the final night, two celebrities appeared: Lou Rawls, to entertain; and skating star Dorothy Hamill, just to say hello. She was starring in the commercials that year for one of the company's best-selling hair conditioners.

Strait also remembers the somewhat frazzled sales administration executive who was responsible for planning the entire conference. At the end he moaned, "Planning this thing is a full-time job."

Today, it is. Business finally took a realistic look at what an enormous job it is to organize arrangements for rooms, menus, air fare and other travel, speakers, entertainers, business programs, awards, audio-visual equipment, registrations, budgets, name tags, themes, parties and gifts. Even though many still hand the meeting planning function to an employee with other duties, the trend is toward full-time planning. And even the part-timers can console themselves with the knowledge that top management now is aware of their burden.

Although many meeting planners have come up from the secretarial ranks (handling all the nuts-and-bolts details is part of both jobs, thus a natural promotion), men still slightly dominate the field. When Mr. Average Meeting Planner strides toward you at the next conference, this is how you can recognize him (according to a survey by *Meeting News*). He'll be a 47-year-old college graduate with at least a $38,000 annual salary and nine years of experience in the field. He'll work for a corporation or an association, although there's a slim chance he could have an education or government job. The one place men heavily outnumber women is as corporate executives with some planning responsibilities (27.8 percent male to 6.2 percent female). The average woman in the field, however, is only 35 years old with just six years of planning experience. She's less likely to have a degree, and earns $12,000 less per year.

Of course, you don't have to limit your search for the perfect man to your fellow planners. You'll be meeting new people constantly, working with hotel executives, audio-visual experts and tourism people, to name a few. Your most fertile hunting grounds of all, however, may be the group that the industry awkwardly refers to as "attendees." Most meetings are small enough for you to get to meet and talk to people at some length. In fact, more than four out of ten business meetings have fewer than 100 attendees. More than six out of ten have 200 or fewer. Of course, you're in an ideal position to look over every man there, find out who that really handsome one is and come up with a convention-related excuse to approach him.

To maximize your choices, you may want to look for a job in which you'll handle several meetings per year. You could even become an independent meeting planner, signing contracts to handle meetings for various organizations. On salary or as consultants, meeting planners may handle any number of meeting categories: trade shows, educational seminars, sales meetings (national, regional or local) stockholder meetings, small management meetings or conventions with thousands of attendees.

If you're thinking of becoming an association meeting planner, see the section on Association Managers (page 133). But don't take a job with the American Association of Retired Persons unless you're seriously in the market for a father—or grandfather—figure. And the four million members of the Boy Scouts of America could be a dead end, too, except for the troop leaders.

JOB SECURITY: The Bureau of Labor Statistics doesn't include meeting planner in its *Occupational Outlook Handbook* and doesn't make a formal forecast about occupational growth. The future looks good, however, just in terms of the number of meetings and conventions held throughout the U.S. each year. According to the latest set of figures, the American business community spends more than $10 billion a year on meetings. And 75 million of us attend.

As the field grows, the only unknown is how the meeting planning business will fare during economic slumps. Will planners be let go, as fewer meetings are held? Or will meeting planners who can save the company a bundle, and still put on a good show, be more valuable than ever? The safest route now is to be one of the 50 percent of all M.P.'s who hold executive jobs in which meeting planning is only one facet.

MONEY: Those same multifunction executives take home the highest paychecks, too. Corporation executives who have meeting planning as one of their responsibilities average more than $44,500 per year. (Biggest employers: manufacturing, finance, insurance.) Association executives with the same arrangement average $32,108. Association meeting planners, whose exclusive responsibility is this specialty, average just over $28,600. And corporate meeting planners (those who do nothing but) have the lowest national average of all: exactly $26,854. Even planners who work for educational institutions— normally a low-paying area—do better, with an average of just over $27,900.

The bigger your meeting budget, the higher salary you'll be able to demand. Corporations tend to have considerably higher budgets than associations, because their meetings involve getting employees from one or more work locations to the meeting location—and paying their major expenses there. Therefore, budgets include air fare, hotel room charges and more. When an association sponsors a national meeting, it's usually each member's responsibility to get there and to pay (either personally or through the company each person represents) for hotels, meals and overall conference charges.

LIFESTYLE: Travel is the only part of a meeting planner's career that might affect your lifestyle, for better or worse. The morning-to-midnight schedules occur only right before and during the conference, which you may have planned for up to six months. At other times, you can get home in time for dinner, take weekends off and maintain normal personal relationships.

Warning: In a two-M.P. household, remember that you'll have to see each other through preconvention hysteria at least once a year— not at the same time, we hope! In fact, depending on the kind of jobs the two of you have, you might go through this once or twice a month. Maybe you ought to man-hunt among the conference delegates instead.

WHAT IT TAKES: "An infinite capacity for dealing with screw-ups," offers one female meeting planner. According to one successful planner, you should be a self-starter who functions well within budgets, a good negotiator and a topnotch hand-holder who gets along well with people. If you absolutely thrive on little details, on making lists and on getting everything and everybody around you organized, this is the career for you.

You might go straight into a meeting planner's job if you have past experience in the hotel, travel agency or convention bureau business. It could be tricky to find a college program in meeting planning; attend special seminars on the subject instead.

EDUCATION: No formal educational requirements, but a growing number of M.P.'s have college degrees. Ideal major: business administration.

EARNINGS: $30,679 national average.

WORKSTYLE: Annual or more frequent deadlines, pressure, travel, hectic pace, late to bed and early to rise during the meeting itself.

DIRECT INTERACTION OPPORTUNITIES: All that late-night work before and during the meetings, the party atmosphere on convention nights and all those attendees.

FOR MORE CAREER INFORMATION: Meeting Planners International, 3719 Roosevelt Boulevard, Middletown, OH 45042.

PERSONNEL MANAGER

54% are men   46% are women

+ He's a caring kind of guy.

− So was Machiavelli.

If you worked for the ROLM Corporation (a California-based PBX and minicomputer manufacturer), you might be able to take off all of next summer at full pay. You could sublet your apartment, turn twelve weeks' salary into travelers' checks, then roam the back roads and beaches of Europe, as carefree and careless as if you were sixteen again. Every ROLM employee gets a three-month sabbatical after six years' service (or a six-week sabbatical at double pay). And they're far from the country's only corporate employees who get sabbaticals or other rather dazzling fringe benefits.

If you worked for Johnson & Johnson, you'd have your own company fitness center in which to get thin, firm and gorgeous. If you worked for Polaroid, your employer would pay up to 80 percent of the costs to keep your children in a good day care center. If you went to work for Anheuser-Busch, you'd get two free cases of beer per month.

Keeping the workers happy is the name of the corporate game these days, particularly in terms of employee benefits and "perks." But that's only a small part of the change that's gone on in what used to be called the personnel department.

Look for the words "human resources management" (H.R.M.) on the office door today, but don't miss the meaning of the name.

> *Resource (ri-sors'; re'sors), n.*
> *1. any supply that will meet a need.*
> *2. any means of getting success or getting out of trouble.*

Human resources is all about using people to meet the company's needs. Yet the departments often are staffed by men and women who consider their powers of empathy second only to Mother Theresa's.

"These are very nice, humanistic people who were interested in the helping professions like social work and teaching, but wanted to go into a career where they could make good money," opines Henry Langdon, an Ivy League psychology graduate who chose not to work in corporate personnel. "These aren't the competitive, aggressive corporate types. Human resources is one of the careers where you're supposed to be above it all."

The current school of thought in H.R.M., says Langdon, is that "if you treat people well, you can make more money off them." He sometimes wonders, however, what would happen if a new study proved people would work harder or more efficiently if they were subjected to mental abuse or threatened with physical punishment. Would corporate America adopt these philosophies? And would sadists be drawn to human resources careers?

Happily, good treatment appears to make for productive workers. And as long as that theory holds water, America's personnel/H.R.M. departments will continue to attract the nice guys. Here you'll find the kind of man who's sure to have a framed photo of his smiling wife, children and family pet on the desk. Or if he's not married yet, you'll find pictures of his parents and/or his sister's kids. "If it's brooding male sexuality you want," says Langdon, "if it's Heathcliff you're after, this is not where to find him."

A study by the American Society for Training and Development (A.S.T.D.) drew this profile of the human resources development executive. He is a 41-year-old male with a master's degree and more than five years of experience in the field. He places family above personal achievement, professional achievement and money. He is equally likely to be a Republican, Democrat or independent. And 88 percent of the A.S.T.D. members said they believed in God.

Whether H.R.M. is a place for you to find a man at all is a little questionable. In recent years, it's been turning statistically into a woman's field. Although men still slightly dominate the managerial jobs in personnel and labor relations, women now outnumber men in the rank and file. Of all personnel, labor relations and training "specialists" employed today, the Bureau of Labor Statistics tell us, 55.5 percent are female.

There are, however, at least two reasons for giving H.R.M. a chance. First, it's changing rapidly, with new specialties like employee training and development winning new respect. U.S. employers now spend an estimated $32 billion on employee education and training. Second, it's the one department in which you could ostensibly interface with men from every other area of the company. If you have a certain kind of man in mind (a corporate lawyer, a computer type, a go-getter in marketing), you might even specialize in recruiting that kind of talent.

JOB SECURITY: Personnel's job market picture is just average, with a projected 23 percent growth for personnel specialists between now and 1995, according to the Bureau of Labor Statistics. But the field definitely can be sensitive to the economy. Personnel and human resources staffs often get slashed when times are hard, as do many service departments. Otherwise, however, this is a stable and secure career.

MONEY: It depends on the specialty you choose. According to one survey of Federal government personnel jobs, mediators and labor relations specialists do best, with national averages of about $45,500 and $33,100 respectively. The lowest paychecks went to specialists in personnel staffing, wage and salary administration, equal employment opportunity and employee relations (about $27,200–$28,800, respectively).

An American Society for Personnel Administration survey showed slightly lower figures. National median salaries ranged from $22,000 for wage and salary administrators to $27,000 for benefits planning analysts. The average salaries of personnel directors range from about $32,000 to $62,000.

Training and development generalists earn a median income of $28,490, according to A.S.T.D. Top training executives earn just over $41,000 on the average.

Personnel and human resources vice presidents in large companies can earn much more, of course. Salaries of $200,000 or more aren't unheard of. In companies with sales of $125 million or more, even those at the managerial level can earn as much as $100,000.

LIFESTYLE: Human resources wouldn't be very humane if it ate up all your time and energy, leaving nothing for family and friends. So it doesn't.

Chances are, you'll work a normal nine-to-five schedule most of the time. And it's practically your corporate obligation to lead a rich, warm and full home life with your personnel-manager husband and your 2.2 little beneficiaries. Business travel shouldn't be much of an intrusion, unless you specialize in college recruiting.

WHAT IT TAKES: You've got to like people, and be able to deal with all kinds. You may be interviewing a nervous 18-year-old clerical candidate at 10 a.m., then meeting with the chairman of the board at 11. Talking to both at their own levels is called "style-shifting," and it's an important skill.

A former personnel manager who has worked in publishing, retailing, insurance and the non-profit sector suggests another possibility. "Maybe everybody has it backward," she says. "Maybe people who *hate* people go into personnel. You have to get to know all the personal aspects of people's lives, to get into the closet, so to speak."

No matter what your inner motives are, you'll find that communication skills, emotional stability and a persuasive personality are real assets in this career.

Many people come into the personnel department from very different kinds of work, and some career development experts recommend just that. When it comes time to promote you into top human resources management, it's a real plus, they say, if you've had "line" experience, for example in sales.

EDUCATION: Bachelor's degree, preferably in business. A specific degree in personnel administration, labor relations or a related specialty is even better. Liberal arts graduates still can get hired, however.

EARNINGS: $22,000–$27,000 national median.

WORKSTYLE: A standard office job, with a 35- to 40-hour week. Longer hours in labor relations, particularly during contract negotiations.

DIRECT INTERACTION OPPORTUNITIES: In human resources, the most popular kind of meeting is one-on-one.

FOR MORE CAREER INFORMATION: American Society for Personnel Administration, 30 Park Drive, Berea, OH 44017.

PHYSICIAN ASSISTANT

59% are men   41% are women

+ You get to meet a lot of doctors.

– Nebulous future.

Q: What kind of man becomes a physician assistant?
A: A medic who served in Viet Nam.

At least that's how this new career was born just 20 years ago. In 1965, four former Army medical corpsmen took the first physician assistant training at Duke University. Today, there are more than 17,000 P.A.'s practicing across the U.S. Many are former corpsmen,

orderlies and nurse's aides. Most entrants into the field are not fresh
from school; the average age of a P.A. student is 28. Before entering
the program, two out of three already had a college degree.

The career would have solved a lot of problems for Mary Ellen
Walton. When the eldest daughter of television's fictional *Waltons*
began practicing as a nurse in the mountain country of Virginia, she
was frustrated by not being able to do enough to help her patients.
Her only choice was to go to medical school—not a particularly
popular solution for a woman just after World War II, and not an
easy option for one from a family whose kids still played in tree
swings made from tires. Today, Mary Ellen could have become a
P.A.

If the career has any public image problem, it's a matter of its
very nature being misunderstood. A P.A. is neither a nurse, nor
someone en route to becoming a doctor. A P.A. is not even a physician's or physicians' assistant. Those in the profession drop the
possessive to make a point.

"It's like the difference in publishing between an editorial assistant
and the assistant editor," one woman patiently explains. "Maybe it
would help if the public thought of us as 'assistant doctors.' We
handle the cases and the treatments that aren't so complex, the ones
where it's not necessary to bring in the boss."

Another P.A. compares her job to "being an old-fashioned country
doctor." During one day, she might work out a diet for a heart patient,
do a Pap smear, talk to a patient who wants to quit smoking and
give a baby an immunization shot.

From the patient's point of view, it makes sense. The last time
you came down with a flu bug, did you really need a woman or man
with 12 years of postgraduate education to verify it and write a
prescription for the appropriate antibiotic? Physician assistants in
13 states are authorized to write prescriptions under the supervision
of doctors.

From the doctor's point of view, it means productivity. With a
P.A. on staff at the office or clinic, more patients can be seen and
taken care of each day. The P.A.'s duties include taking medical
histories, making diagnoses (either independent or with the consulting physician), developing a treatment plan and explaining it to

the patient, ordering lab tests, performing certain therapeutic procedures and handling emergencies—from drug reactions to cardiac arrest. Studies show that a trained P.A. can take care of at least seven out of ten patients who show up at the average general practitioner's office on an average day.

As a physician assistant, you can choose to specialize. The trend in this career, as with physicians, is toward primary care specialties (general practice, family practice, internal medicine). Female P.A.'s dominate two specialties: obstetrics/gynecology (90 percent women) and pediatrics (64 percent). If you want to go where you're needed— and where you're more likely to meet male colleagues—consider surgical practice. A full 61 percent of surgical assistants are male. In surgical specialties, 69 percent of the P.A.'s are men.

JOB SECURITY: Although this career has experienced the kind of spectacular growth rarely seen these days outside the computer industry, its future is still something of a question mark. If many medical insurance plans refuse to cover visits to and treatments by a P.A., won't this stop patients from seeing them? If states continue to review and change laws about what a P.A. is and isn't allowed to do, won't that have a serious affect on employment? Does a doctor or hospital want to hire an employee when, at any moment, the kinds of work she or he can do could be changed drastically? And with a surplus of M.D.'s in many areas of the U.S., how many doctors striving to build new practices will want or can afford a physician assistant?

Physician assistants and their supporters are hoping and working for the best on the issues of medical insurance and state law. In September 1985, a bill that would call for employer reimbursement for P.A. care was introduced in the Senate. Some care in HMO's, rural health clinics and at home is already covered by government insurance.

Another one bright spot is that many new P.A.'s say they prefer to work in smaller cities and towns and in rural areas now underserved by physicians. A big percentage of P.A.'s claim to be happy to go where they're needed. And even with all the doubts clouding this new profession's future, the Bureau of Labor Statistics forecasts a healthy average occupational growth of 27 percent between now and 1995.

MONEY: Starting salaries average just over $20,000. The national average income for all P.A.'s is about $22,000. Salaries tend to be lowest in clinics; those P.A.'s who work at hospitals, health maintenance organizations and in private doctor offices generally earn more.

Earnings can go considerably higher, as a survey by the American Academy of Physician Assistants (A.A.P.A.) shows. More than 28 percent of its respondents earn $25,000–$30,000. Another 25 percent earn $30,000–$40,000. And an elite 6.1 percent earn more than $40,000 per year.

The low number (11.9 percent) of those surveyed who earn under $20,000 include physician assistants working less than a full schedule. At least eight percent of all P.A.'s are employed only part time.

LIFESTYLE: It depends on the work setting you choose. You're more likely to have a standard five-day, 40-hour work week at a clinic— a situation that allows you free evenings and weekends to live your own life. In a hospital, you may work 12- and 24-hour shifts. And even in private practice, your work may involve hospital rounds and work hours that are out of the ordinary.

In those cases, you'll make some of the personal sacrifices that M.D.'s make routinely. But on your salary, you probably won't be able to get away to the south of France or one of those secluded Caribbean resorts to make your own periodic recoveries (unless you've married the boss). On the other hand, if a lifestyle similar to a traditional country doctor's is the source of deep satisfaction you were looking for, you're probably not going to mind missing Carneval in Rio this year.

WHAT IT TAKES: You'll need a good bedside manner. Patients may feel they can talk to you a little more easily, just because you're not as intimidating as a doctor. You'll also need many qualities that a physician's career calls for: self-confidence, emotional stability, great conscientiousness and a willingness to study hard now and for the rest of your work life.

TRAINING: Although most educational programs are only two years long, you'll probably need some previous background in health-related subjects. At least two years of college science courses or some work experience as a nurse, orderly or health technician can go a long way toward getting you started.

After graduation, you'll take a national certifying exam. Every six years, your certification will expire. To be re-registered, you'll need at least 100 hours of continuing education approved by the A.A.P.A. or the American Medical Association.

EDUCATION: A two-year program in most cases. Some P.A. programs last four years. Certification requires continuing education throughout your career.

EARNINGS: $22,000 national average.

WORKSTYLE: Varies widely, depending on the work setting (clinic, hospital, private doctor's office). Can be almost as demanding as for physicians.

DIRECT INTERACTION OPPORTUNITIES: Consultations, formal and informal, in every work setting.

FOR MORE CAREER INFORMATION: American Academy of Physician Assistants, 1117 North 19th Street, Suite 300, Arlington, VA 22209.

PUBLIC RELATIONS

51% are men   49% are women

+ You'll eat well on expense account lunches.

− It's a life of constant temptation. Didn't you see *Days of Wine and Roses?*

There is a law about socializing in the public relations field, known as N.F.T.C., a Boston publicist explained. Which, politely defined, means "Never fraternize with the client."

"However, nobody ever said," she continues with a sly smile, "N.F.T.P." Which is to say, "Never fraternize with the press."

Public relations is a people business—and the women in P.R. have more than the average opportunity to meet a variety of men in their work. Whether you work in a corporate P.R. department, for an outside publicity firm or as a self-employed publicist, the social opportunities abound.

First, there are fellow publicists, of course—offering a certain amount of in-house opportunity. Then, as the lady in Boston pointed out, there is interaction with the press.

Your job in publicity is to convince the staffs of newspapers, magazines and broadcast stations to feature your client or employer ("Are you sure the *Tonight Show* doesn't want to do a segment on seaweed facials? It's very visual!"). And there's nothing wrong at all with dating the writers, editors and reporters you meet in the process.

You'll also work with a variety of "suppliers" in the process of producing brochures, press kits, press events (from serious conferences to gala parties) and even movies and videotapes. You'll probably interview and work with photographers, caterers, hairdressers, makeup artists, printers, graphic artists, hotel and restaurant banquet managers and movie types. If you're representing a male-oriented product, you may even have to interview dozens of male models before finding the right one. For the shooting, that is.

Rule of thumb: It is better to handle a male-dominated account than a female-dominated one. "When I worked for a cosmetic company, it was like belonging to a sorority," recalls a New York publicity manager. "The models were beautiful blonde 22-year-old girls, the hairdressers were gay men and all my co-workers were single women. The only place to meet a straight man was in the marketing department—and half of them looked down on P.R. too much to get something going."

If you fall for a P.R. man, what kind of guy are you going to get? "Two kinds of men go into P.R.," assesses a woman who's been in the field for 15 years. "One is the kind who would have been a salesman, but for the automatic prestige in this. He's the fast-talking 'have-I-got-a-story-for-you' type. The other is the disillusioned former editor or writer who feels he's sold out by taking a P.R. job. He's more likely to be a sensitive type, but he's also more likely to act out his frustrations by turning into an alcoholic or a womanizer."

Movie fans may recognize one or both descriptions as the character Jack Lemmon played in *Days of Wine and Roses* more than two decades ago. This P.R. man, whose responsibilities included procuring hookers for clients (probably not part of a typical job description nowadays), went downhill into alcoholism and took wife Lee Remick with him. We should point out, however, that the two characters did meet at the office!

JOB SECURITY: P.R. budgets go up and down with the economy, but it's a generally safe career within a corporation. At independent P.R. firms, it can be a different story. Just as in ad agencies, when a client resigns the account, all the people working on that account may be fired. The bright side: because P.R. is a people business, a good business reputation should get you rehired somewhere else pretty quickly.

MONEY: Lots of people leave journalism for this career because public relations pays so much better than editorial work. According to a survey by *P.R. Reporter*, the national median income is $44,000. The highest-paying organizations are utilities, industrials and consumer products companies, all with medians of about $51,000 per year. P.R. firms and other consulting jobs are right behind at $50,000 annually. Hospital P.R. ($34,500) is one of the lowest-paying specialties, as are jobs with state governments ($34,000).

Neither education nor geographical area seems to make a big difference in P.R. people's incomes. The median for those with only high school diplomas ($40,000) is only $4,500 per year less than for those with Ph.D.'s. Salaries in the West and Northeast are tops at $45,000, but the lowest-paid region, the South, offers a median of $42,000.

It does appear, however, that newly-hired P.R. people are earning more than some of the old hands. And the consensus is that it's their marketing and business educations that are valued by their employers.

LIFESTYLE: Many public relations jobs call for heavy business travel and socializing. That can mean, if the two of you are on different accounts, you'll probably be on different schedules too. At least you'll eat well—at expense account lunches, cocktail press parties and awards dinners. And don't forget entertaining the client at home.

WHAT IT TAKES: The people who hire new publicists often look for writing talent. You don't have to have a Pulitzer prize, but you do need to be able to whip up an effective press release to announce the latest news on your client.

According to one survey of P.R. firm chief executive officers, foreign language ability is listed as an important skill. That's because of the projected growth of multinational business in the years ahead.

Even more important, P.R. takes creative sales ability—and an ability to hear the word no and still keep trying. An experienced P.R. person is nowhere without her contacts—the editors and broadcasters she knows and can count on to at least consider her publicity ideas. That's a network that's built up over the years, so if you break up with a reporter from the *Times*, be civilized about it. You may need him later.

EDUCATION: A college degree definitely, but the people who hire disagree as to the ideal major. Some still advocate a bachelor's in journalism or communications. Others say business administration is preferred. Still others prefer a degree specifically in P.R.

EARNINGS: $44,000 national median.

WORKSTYLE: Deadlines, strange hours, travel and lots of people contact at all times.

AMBIANCE: Fast-paced and upbeat. P.R. also takes on the coloration of its related industry. Banking P.R. people tend to act and dress conservatively, for instance, while fashion P.R. people make Perry Ellis look passé. Hollywood P.R. people are, how shall we say, not completely down to earth.

DIRECT INTERACTION OPPORTUNITIES: Press parties, business trips, late-night office hours at deadline time.

FOR MORE CAREER INFORMATION: Public Relations Society of America, 845 Third Avenue, New York, NY 10022.

REAL ESTATE SALES

52% are men   48% are women

+ When a great place comes on the market, you'll see it first.

− If you specialize in residential, you spend your days with happy couples, gushing over bay windows and eat-in kitchens.

The character is a cliché by now: a housewife who's devoted the past ten or fifteen years to her family suddenly looks up and realizes that her kids are so busy with band practice and adolescent sexuality that they don't need her very much anymore. So she puts on a suit and a pair of high heels and begins showing houses as a part-time job. After all, what does she know better in life than her own neighborhood and the value of good closet space?

Real estate executives say the industry trend is away from such dabblers and part-timers, that a certain amount of dedication and formal education is more important in the 1980s real estate business than ever before. In fact, a college degree in real estate may soon be a must. Still, women dominate America's residential real estate force—the least lucrative branch of the business.

So why not go for the real opportunities? The men in this field aren't out showing split-levels; they're making commercial real estate deals. Instead of showing two-story Colonials and neo-Tudors with backyard pools, spend your days leasing office space, stores and entire apartment buildings instead.

"If one person takes a lease in a New York office building, the commission alone could be $200,000–$300,000," estimates Lise Khenelly, who recently married a Manhattan-based commercial real estate broker. "In his office, there are maybe twenty or thirty people. There are two women—who, by the way, are making a fortune—and they're about 28 years old. The rest are guys."

She sees her husband's co-workers as definite types, too. "They're 'guy' guys. They come to work in pin-striped suits, but they're not corporate types,' she explains. "They're aggressive and they're self-starters. In this business you have to be, because you're essentially making your own rules."

A passion for the good life seems to be part of the profile. "They go skiing in Switzerland," Khenelly reports. "They're into Rolls Royces. They're into gadgets. They're into living very well. They want to make money and retire by the time they're 35. It's a different mentality from the guy who wants to be chairman of the board of Gulf & Western."

Aside from office contact with your fellow agents and brokers in this career, you'll meet men through sales calls and possibly through "co-broking" arrangements with other real estate firms.

When you're handling commercial space, your clients are almost sure to be affluent executive types—business owners or at least high-level management. "It's a great excuse for just walking up and asking, 'Are you thinking of moving or expanding?'" reports one New York businesswoman. "It doesn't have to be the president of a huge conglomerate taking seven floors. It could be someone who needs a showroom of 2,500 feet. It could be a small ad agency. It could be a legal office. This career is a perfect excuse to talk to anybody who owns a restaurant or store."

One male real estate entrepreneur got his first client just by reading the business section of his morning newspaper. He saw a notice that two financial executives were leaving a large firm to start their own business. When he called to ask if they were looking for office space, he was the first real estate person to approach them— and he made the deal. A female agent or broker might use the same method, taking a personal interest when the executive's newspaper photo is appealing.

If you feel you'll only be happy in residential real estate, at least don't insist on handling suburban houses. Consider renting apartments (particularly sublets or short-term leases) or selling urban condos. That way, you might catch the male executive on a one-year relocation assignment in your city, or the newly-separated husband taking his first apartment after the break-up.

To find a field with an even better male-to-female ratio, work your way into real estate development. It means finding the site, making the deal, negotiating with contractors, approving budgets, overseeing construction on behalf of the owners and much more. Some of the few top women developers have come from work backgrounds as varied as architecture, Wall Street and the CIA. New York superstar developer Donald Trump's wife, now executive vice president for the Trump organization, was a model before she'd married Donald and became involved with the business.

JOB SECURITY: Economic downturns can do serious damage to the real estate business, but the commercial side in particular has been holding up well in recent years. Now the Bureau of Labor Statistics sees the career growing by a third (a 33 percent increase in the number of jobs) between now and 1995. Even residential business should be good, thanks to the growing number of baby boomers hitting home-buying age.

MONEY: Real estate may be a get-rich-quick career for some, but the first year or so can be a killer. Some firms pay beginners a salary (perhaps $200 a week or so) against commissions during the first year. Experienced people in the field often recommend that the beginner have another source of income during the first year—or move in with relatives.

Later, you're most likely to earn money from commissions only, and even when you're doing well, the business can be feast or famine. You may get a huge commission in January and not earn another penny for months. But you'll have the opportunity to meet a handsome financial planner, who can help teach you how to live this way.

The National Association of Realtors figures show that full-time real estate salespeople earn a median income of $18,000 per year, and women outnumber men 57 to 42 in this category. The median income for all brokers, a category in which men make up 66.6 percent of the work force, is $30,000 per year. As in most careers, the men out-earn the women too. In fact, more than one-third of male brokers earn more than $50,000 annually.

LIFESTYLE: If you specialize in dealing with wealthy clients, you'll be forced (poor baby) to emulate their luxurious lifestyles. So, if the top executives you need to see take long weekends during the summer, you can take Fridays off yourself. If they belong to certain country clubs and athletic clubs, the boss may insist on your joining too. And of course he'll pay the dues.

More tragedy: In this business of symbols and status, it'll also be an asset for you to dress well, take clients to fashionable restaurants and drive an expensive car.

WHAT IT TAKES: Your personal style is almost as important in real estate as your academic background and training. Tact, enthusiasm and a good memory for faces, names and details are among the traits employers look for.

GETTING STARTED: To become an agent, you'll need to take real estate courses at a local college or another educational institution, then pass a written exam for your state license. Most states require a minimum of 30 hours of classroom instruction. The procedure is the same for becoming a broker, except that most states require 90 hours of training and one to three years of experience in the field. In some states, having a college degree in real estate allows you to get a broker's license without the work experience. More than 1,000 U.S. colleges now offer courses in real estate.

The difference between the two jobs is simple. An agent can only show properties and get a verbal agreement for the sale; a broker has to close the deal. Brokers also can rent and manage properties, develop building projects and arrange for real estate loans and title searches.

Choose a specialty. In addition to residential or commercial real estate, you might work in industrial or farm-and-land brokerage, property management, land development or real estate appraising. In any specialty, your best start is working for an established broker.

The average broker you might work for is 48 years old (only 11 percent in this field are 35 or younger) and is sole or partial owner of the business. And if he doesn't turn you on, think of all the men you'll meet in the process of seeking out new properties. When you see a gorgeous guy in the lobby, just walk right up and say, "Excuse me. Do you happen to know who manages this building?" Go ahead. It's your job.

EDUCATION: Formal education in real estate (usually 30–90 hours minimum) plus state license. College degree in real estate preferred.

> **EARNINGS:** $18,000 national average for agents. $30,000 national average for brokers. But, for successful salespeople, income can go sky-high.
>
> **WORKSTYLE:** Office-based, but a big percentage of the workday will be spent in meetings and in showing properties. Set your own schedule in many jobs.
>
> **DIRECT INTERACTION OPPORTUNITIES:** Lunches and dinners for two, property showings, one-on-one meetings.
>
> **FOR MORE CAREER INFORMATION:** National Association of Realtors, 430 North Michigan Avenue, Chicago, IL 60611.

GENERAL SALES

52% are men   48% are women

+ Results count more than office politics in this career.

− There isn't much room for advancement. (And half the time when people do get promoted out of sales, it means a cut in income.)

Whether or not you meet men in a sales career depends very much on what you sell. When it comes to retail sales overall, seven out of ten workers are women. Eighty-three percent of all apparel sales employees are female. In a career in the intimate apparel department at Saks Fifth Avenue, you may make a lot of new friends, but there won't be much romantic opportunity to use your own merchandise.

When it comes to other specific products, however, men dominate the retail work force:

Auto and boat sales	91% male
Parts sales	90% male
Hardware/building supplies sales	77% male
TV/radio/hi-fi/appliance sales	74% male

Few beginners are assigned right away to high-ticket items like televisions and stereo equipment—you'll have to work your way up. If you take a department store job, for instance, your first department is likely to be an area that's mostly self-service, one in which very little informational or persuasive selling is required. Then all you'll have to learn right away is how to take payments, make out sales checks, hand out change and deal with an occasional merchandise return. Later, you'll move up to the departments with higher-priced merchandise, more real selling (and all the men).

Auto sales has its own special compensations. This is an image business, and many employers will present you with a "demo," a free car of your own, when you begin work.

Retail sales is good experience, but you may prefer to work in manufacturer's sales eventually. That could mean working for a cosmetics or pharmaceutical company, and "selling in" their products to drugstores, discount stores and other outlets in your geographical area. The estimated workforce breakdown in manufacturer's sales is 80 percent male to 20 percent female.

The dozens of possibilities include computer products and services, electronics, food products, building materials and housewares. No matter which industry you choose, you'll probably work on your own, driving from home to call on customers on a regular basis. If your geographical territory is very large, you might fly to see accounts instead. This career does give you some room for promotion, perhaps to district or regional sales manager, then to the headquarters sales administration office. If actually getting out there and selling is your strongest point, however, you may be much happier (and earn more money off your good commissions) by turning down promotions and staying in the field.

The best in the business say they got that way by doing their own research. "Companies in general don't know their own products or markets enough," says one successful rep. "So a little work on the salesman's part gives him an edge and makes him valuable."

What kind of man will you meet in this field? For one thing, he's likely to be from a relatively affluent family, according to one study. The average salesperson is male, 37 years old, has gone to college, has been on the job for seven years and earns just over $30,000.

JOB SECURITY: It depends on how good you are. In bad economic times, sales staffs definitely do get cut. The company's very best salespeople, however, are almost never let go. Because sales is a huge field (4 million or so workers) with high turnover, finding a new job shouldn't be difficult.

The Bureau of Labor Statistics foresees average occupational growth (27 percent), so there should be about 5.5 million retail and wholesale sales jobs by 1995.

MONEY: It goes from rags to riches. Most beginning retail sales clerks will start out earning the minimum wage. Retail sales workers earn a median of $9,880 per year in stores that don't specialize in high-ticket items, and a median of $15,600 in stores that do. The top ten percent of all retail salespeople earn at least $20,000. Of course, if clothes are your life, your discount as a store employee could help make up for a low salary. You'll probably be able to buy anything in the store, from Japanese fashions to Swedish crystal, for 10–25 percent off. Some retail workers are employed on a combination salary and commission basis.

At least 50 percent of all manufacturer's salespeople work on a combination salary and commission basis. The national average income is about $30,000; the national median income is $24,000. Trainee salaries can range from under $10,000 to over $25,000.

Experienced sales people in a number of industries can earn impressive salaries, even on the average: electronics, $26,000–$40,000; service industries, $29,000–$50,000; building materials, $24,000—$30,000. Computer salespeople average $23,000–$50,000, but almost every computer company has a few star sales reps who earned $100,000, $200,000 or more last year.

LIFESTYLE: The worst way sales work can affect your personal life is by cutting into your weekends with Saturday work. Otherwise you can enjoy all your discount purchases.

WHAT IT TAKES: Almost anybody who can pull it together to shower, comb her hair and smile five days a week can find a beginning retail sales job. To be good at sales, however, takes a knowledge of your product and a real ability to persuade. You've got what it takes if "you can bounce back from a rebuff with ways to help your customers," explains a suburban camera salesman. If it takes you two days to recover after a potential customer has refused to see you, please reconsider going into this career. Or at least stick to working in a self-service department, like greeting cards or food.

News flash: If you don't fit this description, even if you were the kid who used to knock on neighbors' doors and say, "You don't want to buy any Girl Scout cookies, do you?" there may be a sales career for you yet. Store owners and personnel consultants agree that computer sales calls for a completely different approach, and it might be one in which you could excel.

"The stereotypical buoyant, effervescent, outgoing salesperson who might succeed in short-term, quick-close situations such as life insurance or automobile sales, would not be adept at selling high-tech products," one personnel consultant told *The New York Times*. In a retail computer sale, a tendency to heavy persuasive tactics actually could work against you. What's called for instead is an image of stability, solidness and reliability. Most of the same rules are true of sales careers with hardware or software manufacturers too.

The difference is that computer sales are made slowly, usually after at least one prolonged customer-salesperson session. And sales follow-up may go on for months or years. You need to be a good listener, in order to really pinpoint the customer's needs, and you need to be willing to slowly build the sale step by step. Paperwork is important in this sales field, so excellent communication skills (written and oral) are even more important than in most other careers.

What do the people who hire say they're looking for? A warm, friendly personality, computer literacy and sales experience. If you haven't sold computers before, a background in high-ticket retailing (perhaps in the television/stereo department) is ideal.

EDUCATION: High school graduates are often trained for retail sales jobs. Manufacturer's sales reps more often have college degrees. Some college training is helpful in either area.

EARNINGS: $9880–$15,600 median in retail. $24,000 median in manufacturer's sales.

WORKSTYLE: A standard 40-hour work week for most retail employees, but with some evening or weekend work likely. Flexible schedules for manufacturer's sales reps, but with the likelihood of evening work and travel.

DIRECT INTERACTION OPPORTUNITIES: Regional sales meetings, district sales meetings, national sales meetings, daily department and customer contact.

FOR MORE CAREER INFORMATION: No professional associations do much in the way of career information for these jobs. Instead, write directly to manufacturers, department stores and other retail outlets in your area.

TECHNICAL WRITER

59% are men   41% are women

+ You're needed—and respected—by top management.

– You'll always be an outsider among the computer types.

> *"You are going to start learning Word Juggler IIE by using it to type a simple letter. In order to continue with this lesson you will need a blank diskette. Do not touch any of the exposed magnetic recording surfaces of the diskette. Fingertips can render the diskette useless."*
>
> —Word Juggler IIE User's Manual
> Quark Incorporated, 1983

One writer, when she is asked how she came to choose the Apple IIE computer on which she now composes all her articles and books, always answers, "It was good-looking enough that I knew I could stand to look at it all day. It was a name I knew. And the manual for the word processing program the store offered with it was written in English."

Not that the others were in Japanese, but they might as well have been. She had looked at other manuals and found that even the subheads contained technical terms she didn't know. (Of course, at the time, the most technical computer-age thought she had ever voiced was, "I'm just not programmed to do this.") In the Word Juggler manual, she found subheads like "Some More About Arrows," "Changing Things Around," "Numbering Your Pages" and "Moving Hordes of Text." She was in love.

The computer industry is just as enamored of the technical writers who spend their workdays making the highly technical language of the high-tech industry clear and easy to read for the average consumer. Chemical, aerospace, aviation, pharmaceutical and engineering firms feel much the same way.

Who will you meet if you decide to launch a career as a technical writer? The business world is of two minds about who to hire for this fast-growing specialty. Some take their engineers, chemists and other technicians and put them to work in marketing or communications departments. Others take people with journalism and other nontechnical backgrounds and introduce them to new technical concepts. The latter approach seems to be winning favor. "It is much easier to teach a writer how to be a technician," says one man in the computer industry, "than to teach a technician how to write."

You may meet a former philosophy major, an ex-music teacher or a writer who's made the switch because this is the only writing specialty in which the job market isn't glutted. "You really find a lot of nice, normal men and women in these departments," says a female technical writer. "They're very practical people, or they wouldn't have made such a pragmatic career choice. Most of them have learned to compromise. I don't know whether that's a sign of weakness or a sign of maturity. Maybe they're even a little bit disillusioned as a group—you know, about doing this instead of writing the great American novel or covering wars and famines—but isn't everybody by a certain age?"

Like writers in any corporate environment, technical writers face very real limitations. Little career advancement is available to them. And they tend to be outsiders, because they're among the least expert in whatever the company's technical area is. That near-ostracism is most apparent in the computer industry, where many employees speak computerese 24 hours a day.

These problems may be offset by one big plus: management knows the company needs the technical writers, and gives them front-office treatment more than writers in many other industries, generally including them on new product development almost from the beginning.

Your job might be writing brochures, documentation manuals, training books, reports or articles. Aside from working closely with the technical people, your work duties are much the same as in any corporate editorial job. You'll work with photographers, artists and printers. You may edit your own work and/or that of others. You may collect or contribute to charts, diagrams, illustrations and other artwork. You will have deadlines—and the printer will always swear the job is at the binder's.

JOB SECURITY: The Bureau of Labor Statistics doesn't make an official occupational growth forecast for technical writers per se. If the overall category of writers and editors is expected to grow by 35 percent (well above the average) between now and 1995, however, it safely can be assumed that this specialty will grow even more. It's estimated that 25,000 technical writers are now on the job.

MONEY: Starting salaries can range from $10,000 to $20,000, depending on your educational background and the kind of work you've done in the past. The average salary for experienced technical writers in the private sector is $25,000-$30,000. The 2,000 or so technical writers who work for the Federal government average $28,000.

Some of the people who are really cleaning up in this field are the authors of computer books. There were about 2,400 computer titles in print as of 1983. And although they don't tend to be blockbuster best-sellers (it's hard to imagine a mini-series based on uses for your Commodore 64), the tendency has been for them to sell steadily over the years. Rumor has it that a few particularly successful authors get $200,000 royalty checks every year—and will for some time to come.

LIFESTYLE: No problems here. You're probably not tied to your office as many of your technical co-workers are. You can live and work in almost any part of the country (although Texas, California and the Northeast offer the greatest opportunity) and you'll have enough free time to enjoy it.

WHAT IT TAKES: A good technical writer has all the same qualities any other kind of writer would need—only more so. You'll need to be able to make complex, detailed or very technical matters interesting and clear. Then you'll need great attention to detail and an ability to meet deadlines on a regular basis.

GETTING HIRED: The ideal educational background is one college degree in journalism or communications, and another in the specialty of your industry (computer science for computer companies, chemistry for pharmaceutical firms, and so on). The next best choice is a major in communications with a minor in the specialty field. If you left college behind you years ago, take some night courses in the technical specialty you want to write about. A portfolio of good technical writing samples (published or not) will give you a job-hunting edge.

Then you may meet a fellow writer in your new department, or you may find yourself drawn to the scientist, engineer or systems analyst down the hall.

EDUCATION: Bachelor's degree, but not necessarily in a technical subject. Writing ability and experience are more important.

EARNINGS: $25,000-$30,000 national average.

WORKSTYLE: Standard 40-hour work week, but with possible long hours when the deadline pressure is on.

DIRECT INTERACTION OPPORTUNITIES: Deadline work sessions with fellow writers, getting down to laymen's terms with the technical guys.

FOR MORE CAREER INFORMATION: Society for Technical Communication, 815 15th Street NW, Washington, DC 20005.

UNDERWRITER

52% are men   48% are women

+ Finding a man like this is like buying a piece of the rock.

− You had a pet rock once, and it never had much to say.

Let's say you're 18 years old with a long record of drug busts and you've totalled three cars since you got your license at age 16. Or let's say you're a new homeowner who's looking forward to your free time in the garage workshop where you'll be experimenting with small nuclear warheads. Or let's say you're a three-pack-a-day smoker with a cholesterol count of 320 and a new part-time job as an astronaut. Let's say you're applying for car, home or life insurance.

The underwriter is the guy who gets to turn you down—or charge you such a high premium that he might as well have.

"Do not think for a minute that this guy is a risk-taker," stresses an actuary (an insurance company's mathematical wiz who draws up the odds that the underwriters deal with). "People may think that insurance companies take risks and that a man who would become an underwriter has the fortitude of a gambler. Just the opposite. He's trained only to approve sure things."

Put more simply, the difference between an actuary and an underwriter is this: the actuary does the study to figure out the number of accidents 21-year-old Toyota owners are likely to have; the underwriter looks at the application of a particular 21-year-old Toyota owner, looks at the actuary's report on that subject, takes all other factors into account and decides whether the company should insure that person.

If stability, logic and common sense are the traits you look for most in a man, an underwriter may be the guy for you. Get him and get a piece of the rock. "Do not," the actuary adds, "ever expect him to jump into a fountain or a swimming pool with you with his clothes on." It's not that underwriters don't want to have fun. It's just that he knows that a reasonable chance exists that he might develop pneumonia as a result.

If and when you become an underwriter, analyzing information will be a big part of your work day. You may look at the insurance application, medical reports, actuarial studies and reports from loss control consultants before deciding whether to issue a policy or not. You may decide that the person isn't the very best risk, but that the company could afford to take him on if you charged him a $150 premium instead of the usual $50 one.

Underwriters specialize. You might go to work for a life insurance company, a health insurance company or a firm that handles both. If you go into property and liability insurance, you may specialize within that field—perhaps handling only fire insurance, auto insurance or workers' compensation.

You might become a commercial account underwriter, exclusively handling business insurance. This could mean insuring major capital expenditures, from an oil rig to new machinery for a large factory.

More and more insurance is sold through group policies. As a group underwriter, you'd analyze the entire group (5,000 employees of an oil company; 2,600 members of a professional association, whatever).

Coverage of computer crimes is a fast-growing insurance specialty. If you have computer background and knowledge, you might make the decisions on policies protecting companies against computer theft, stolen or lost data or loss of revenue from a crime-related computer breakdown. Two other growing specialties: kidnap and product liability insurance.

Here's one career where English and other liberal arts majors aren't looked at as throwbacks to another century. Some insurance company personnel departments may prefer to see a business administration degree, but overall the insurance industry is open to those with liberal arts education backgrounds. You even could get hired without a college degree at all. You'll need one, however, to have a chance at career advancement. Continuing education courses in your specialty will be important, too.

Insurance is big business and should continue to be, now and well into the 21st century. One reason is that the enormous Baby Boom generation has aged into the 25-44 age group, the largest market for insurance. There are at least 2,125 life insurance companies now operating in the U.S., and almost 3,000 property and liability firms.

The best-insured Americans, by the way, are in Washington, DC (carrying an average of $113,000 in life insurance per family), Delaware ($83,800), Connecticut ($70,000) and Hawaii ($69,300).

JOB SECURITY: The insurance industry is one of your best bets. Even when economic times are at their worst, most Americans try to hold on to their insurance policies. For that reason, the business is considered virtually recession-proof and underwriters are rarely laid off.

Job growth looks fine. Average occupational growth of 21 percent is forecast, bringing the total number of underwriters' jobs to 92,000 by 1995.

MONEY: According to the Bureau of Labor Statistics, underwriters in the property and liability side of insurance earn the following median salaries: $18,500, personal lines underwriters; $21,000, surety bonds underwriters; $23,400, senior personal lines underwriters; and $23,700, senior commercial lines underwriters. Underwriting supervisors are reported to earn between $26,500 and $28,000 per year.

LIFESTYLE: At least people won't run away from you at parties, as they sometimes do from insurance salespeople. Just introduce yourself and/or your husband as an "underwriter," and they probably won't even realize you're in insurance.

Otherwise, your thoroughly normal work week should leave you plenty of time for home and family, riotous living (if only you didn't know the risks) or some combination of the two.

If you go into life insurance, you're very likely to find yourself living in one of the industry's six big cities: Philadelphia, Dallas, Chicago, San Francisco, New York or Hartford, Connecticut.

WHAT IT TAKES: Good judgment is the first and most important criterion for an underwriter. You'll also need to be good at working with details, evaluating information and aggressively seeking out facts. Finally, if the thought of having to make a decision sends you into emotional paralysis, do not pass go. The underwriter's ability to make fast but logical decisions affects the entire company's success or failure.

Franz Kafka, Colonel Sanders (of fried chicken fame) and Spiro

Agnew all worked for insurance companies at some point in their lives. So who can guess what kind of man you may meet?

EDUCATION: College degree—with any major—preferred. High school graduates are sometimes hired as trainees.

EARNINGS: $18,500-$23,700 national median.

WORKSTYLE: Desk job with a standard 40-hour week. Some travel possible.

DIRECT INTERACTION OPPORTUNITIES: The usual inter-office work and play.

FOR MORE CAREER INFORMATION: American Council of Life Insurance, Health Insurance Institute, 1850 K Street NW, Washington, DC 20006 (for life and health insurance careers); Insurance Information Institute, 110 William Street, New York, NY 10038 (property and casualty insurance careers); National Association of Life Underwriters, 1922 F Street NW, Washington, DC 20006.

CAREERS WITH A LOT OF MEN—BUT YOU'D BETTER MEET THEM IN SCHOOL

My favorite, I might say, my only study, is man.
GEORGE BORROW
The Bible in Spain

CLERGY

94% are men   6% are women

+ You'll have stable community status in a rapidly changing world.

− Caesar's wife must be above suspicion, which can get on your nerves.

For a performance by an actor in a leading role as a man of God torn by temptation, the nominations are: Richard Chamberlain as Father Ralph de Bricassart, who loved Meggie Cleary but kept insisting that he loved God more, in *The Thorn Birds*. John Heard as the tortured Reverend Mister Dimmesdale, without whom Hester Prynne could never have worn her *Scarlet Letter,* in the television production of the same name. Richard Burton as Reverend Shannon, whose favorite aspects of his post-church career as a tour guide were under-age female tourists, in *The Night of the Iguana*. Burt Lancaster as the evangelist who brought God's love to female worshippers in very personal ways, in the title role of *Elmer Gantry.*

And the winner is—real life. From Pope Alexander VI, who had at least seven illegitimate children and took a 16-year-old mistress while in his sixties, to Congregational minister Henry Ward Beecher who was tried for seducing a married woman in his church office in 1874, men with the calling have heard the siren's song as well. Yet most of them have gone back to the pulpit, their followers as faithful as ever.

Verily, verily, we say unto thee. It is not blasphemy to suggest that a minister or rabbi is made of flesh and blood. And it shall come to pass that thou mayest meet such a man and lust after him. And ye must find him in a seminary; for once he's ordained, there'll be too much competition.

"The single minister is the object of much attention. The amount of matchmaking that goes on would make your head spin," reports an Episcopalian congregation member in Massachusetts. "Everyone wants to see the young minister fixed up." And his wife pregnant.

Even if you happen to luck into a congregation with an unmarried man at the pulpit, you'll have every other unattached female dropping handkerchiefs and home-cooked Sunday dinners at his feet. So get thee to a seminary, where you'll be surrounded by many intense, unattached young men.

The truth is, you may have a difficult time finding a pulpit of your own after graduation. With your theological training, however, you may find administrative work in the church that could be equally satisfying. And a two-clergyperson family would be very hard to job-place anyhow.

If you're Catholic, you might as well skip to another career section. There's that vow of celibacy to contend with, and the 11th century edict forbidding priests to marry. While it's true that almost 60 percent of all U.S. Catholics now say they favor a married priesthood and religious experts predict that it may come by the year 2000, by that time it will be too late for you.

Protestant seminaries report that many of their new students are mature men choosing the ministry after years in other careers. So if you're over 25 (decades over, even), you may find a man your age in your art-of-preaching class.

JOB SECURITY: Clergymen have to be aware of "office politics," just like every other kind of chief executive officer. And they do get fired. If your husband is a Protestant minister, finding a new job can be tough. Enrollment in Protestant seminaries increased 14.6 percent between 1979 and 1983; currently there are more graduates than there are churches in which to place them. The greatest number of new ministers are Southern Baptist. The clergy glut is greatest for Episcopalians and Presbyterians.

If you become a rabbi or marry one, the job picture depends on your branch. Orthodox rabbis face serious job competition; Conservative and Reform rabbis should have no problem, because their seminaries limit enrollments to keep supply and demand in balance.

Reconstructionist rabbis represent the fastest-growing branch of Judaism, and demand currently exceeds the supply.

MONEY: Protestant ministers earn a mean national salary of $20,790. Presbyterian ministers take first place financially with a mean of $24,420, followed by Episcopalian priests at $23,680. Lutherans come in third. The poorest ministers by far are the Seventh Day Baptists (as opposed to the Southern Baptists or the American Baptists) at $12,670 annually. Two out of three ministers have some source of income (including a working spouse, a second job or investments) in addition to their salaries, bringing the mean total income to $23,631. Salaries are highest in the South Atlantic, West South Central and Pacific states.

The Bureau of Labor Statistics reports limited information on the income of rabbis. Salaries appear to range from $20,000 to $50,000 per year. In addition to base salary, a rabbi may receive free housing or a housing allowance and other fringe benefits.

LIFESTYLE: The clergyman always has a special place in his (or, in rare occasions, her) community. The Sabbath (Sunday or Saturday, depending on your particular faith) is for formal religious services and possibly lunch with a congregation member's family.

Throughout the week, there are sick people to visit, funerals or weddings to conduct and counseling to offer church or temple members with problems. If you are the minister's or rabbi's wife, you're expected to be present and active at all those events. Minister's wives have been heard to complain of a scarcity of private time. They have also been known to suggest that not all those women really need their husbands' ear and consoling hand on their shoulder quite as often as they claim to. It comes with the territory; you'll have to learn to share him. Men of God will always have groupies.

WHAT IT TAKES: Every clergyman has to be a good speaker. You're your own boss (at least on earth), so the job calls for the initiative and self-discipline of the self-employed. If you didn't like studying, researching and writing papers in school, you probably won't like writing sermons. It also helps to be sensitive to other people's problems, a good listener and the very model of a moral and ethical person.

EDUCATION: In most religions and denominations, college plus three-to-six years of theological studies.

EARNINGS: $20,790 national mean, Protestant. $20,000-$50,000, Jewish.

WORKSTYLE: Long and irregular hours. "On call" for emergencies. Much sedentary work, including research and writing of your religious message.

DIRECT INTERACTION OPPORTUNITIES: After ordination, your best chance will be to work on a religious leader's staff in a large church or synagogue. So get him while he's still reading the scriptures.

FOR MORE CAREER INFORMATION: Write or call seminaries directly.

ATHLETE

82% are men   18% are women

+ He's bound to be in great physical shape.

− You won't be the only woman who knows it.

"Male athletes are just big studs," a female tennis pro told Studs Terkel in his book, *Working*. "They'd pick up girls and they'd rig it up so one guy would watch from the next room—and give points. They kept track. They made it a contest."

And these were "genteel" tennis players. One shudders to think what the football players are doing.

"Cynicism is a tool for survival," says one hockey player. "You know you're just a piece of property."

Baseball player: "You can be traded anytime they want to trade you."

Jockey: "I think we're all self-centered."

Hockey player: "We talk about our sagging egos. Are we really that famous? Are we really that good? We have terrible doubts."

Baseball player: "Most of us . . . who are over thirty are considered old men."

Baseball player: "A lot of ex-players go into insurance or become car salesmen."

If people who know professional athletes well—the athletes themselves—don't paint very pretty pictures, at least we can play psychologist and blame it on their insecurities.

The wives of professional athletes don't do much public complaining about the men they've married, but the lifestyle isn't always what it's cracked up to be. "There was hardly a glamorous moment," observed a baseball player's ex-wife, speaking on WABC-TV's *The Morning Show*. "In the eighteen years we lived together, we moved sixty times." Her husband, she added, always slept until noon because the games were at night.

He often comes home with injuries, a hockey player's wife reported. Athletes are away from home so much that the only way to have a real marriage is to "get a housekeeper so you can go on the road with him," another baseball player's wife suggested.

The wives know all about the groupies. In some cases, the idea of her husband's being unfaithful is not the most disturbing aspect of the phenomenon. "It was the demeaning way they treated those women," says one. If this was how he felt about women, what did he really think of her, she wondered.

If you marry him in his (and your) twenties, you may have ten years or so of travel, glamor, big money and public attention. Then age will force him into retirement. And according to one survey, about 50 percent of all athletes' marriages break up after he retires. "It's an adjustment for them, to go from being in the limelight," one ex-wife explains. Suddenly he's just an unemployed guy pushing 40. Suddenly no one is taking care of him or scheduling every moment of his day. If you're interested in a relationship with an ex-athlete, this may be the time to catch him single again.

Yet the athletes' wives know they are envied for having snared such desirable men. "People see it as winning the lottery," laughs one. Yes, and lottery winners also pay the taxes on their prizes.

Meeting a professional athlete isn't difficult. You just go to the games, ask around to find out which bars they frequent in your city and go there to hang out. "New York and Chicago are good cities," says one athlete's wife. "You get the American League *and* the National League." But that makes you a groupie, and that's not the most appealing option. A good job as a sportcaster or newspaper sports writer (see television, page 240) will get you into the locker room. An office job working for a major league team or the league itself is desirable work if you can get it. But your best bet is to find him in school, before his ego has been completely blown out of shape.

Go to college and major in physical education or perhaps exercise physiology. If men and women attend classes together, you're set. If not, at least you'll be hanging around the same classroom buildings and gyms.

What will you do with a degree in P.E.? If you're a superb athlete, you can turn pro yourself. Or you can teach, or open your own health club or spa. Fitness is big business—and all those gorgeous guys you hire as aerobics instructors will take your mind off your loneliness when your famous husband is on the road.

JOB SECURITY: Absolutely none. In professional sports, you produce or get out. And a man celebrating his 35th birthday probably will get his retirement gifts at the same party.

Every pro knows he'll have to have a second career after he's spent his youth on the playing field. The superstars end up doing television commercials, sportscasting or both. Some end up teaching phys. ed. and/or coaching at high schools or colleges. Some end up on construction jobs. The rest end up selling used cars or life insurance policies, if they're lucky.

MONEY: The average salary for National Football League players in 1982 was $95,000. The average quarterback earned $161,380. The average major league baseball player earned $241,497 that same year. The average National Basketball Association player earned $246,000; the average National Hockey League player, $120,000.

The point to remember is that making the major league in any sport is a major accomplishment in itself. As one athlete put it, "No one complains about how much the top 500 lawyers in the country earn." And that's what being a member of any of these teams amounts to.

Of course, the mega-superstars are in a class by themselves. Some of the top sports incomes in 1982 went to Chicago Bears running back Walter Payton, $700,000; the Yankees' Dave Winfield, $1,531,000; the Lakers' Kareem Abdul-Jabbar, $1 million; the Oilers' Wayne Gretsky, $500,000; tennis stars Ivan Lendl, $1,528,650, and Martina Navratilova, $1,194,055. Professional bowlers seemed to be the lowest-paid champions. Earl Anthony, the year's number one bowling moneymaker, earned only $134,760.

Athletes on minor league teams, however, often have to take menial off-season jobs just to pay the mortgage or the rent.

LIFESTYLE: Constant travel for out-of-town games, usually by plane, is the first fact of life the professional athlete has to face. In a way, the team becomes his family. Some wives and children do visit or move in during spring training, but even that can be difficult.

You can expect to run the house and the family's affairs yourself. If you decide this is the life for you, learn to love sexy long-distance talks late at night and romantic reunions whenever he turns up at your front door. You may also want to open a charge account with North American Van Lines or other mover; chances are you'll be packing up and moving several times during his career.

Of course, if *you* decide to become a professional athlete, you'll enjoy the attention but face the same stresses of competition and travel. And if your husband isn't a pro, he'll have to take charge of the home front. Of course, if the two of you are taking home big prize money, you can hire full-time housekeepers, nannies and traveling secretaries. Women may never make it onto the N.F.L.'s starting line-up, but there are other opportunities, particularly in tennis and golf.

WHAT IT TAKES: Extraordinary ability, youth and a good agent.

EDUCATION: Many professional athletes are drafted from college teams, which is the only real reason a college degree may be called for. Otherwise, no formal educational requirements.

EARNINGS: $100,000 and up average per year in the big leagues of all sports. Seasonal starvation wages otherwise.

WORKSTYLE: Television cameras, crowds, travel and constant pressure to win.

DIRECT INTERACTION OPPORTUNITIES: Until the big leagues allow women on the team, forget it.

FOR MORE CAREER INFORMATION: Write the professional association of the particular sport in which you're interested or check out the physical education department of your chosen college or university.

FORESTER

85% are men   15% are women

+ "Oh beautiful for spacious skies, for amber waves of grain. . . ."

− "What do you mean I can't get H.B.O. out here?"

When they show the film *Woodstock* on television, do you notice the beatific smiles more than the mud? Do you get misty every time you hear Crosby, Stills and Nash do "Suite Judy Blue Eyes" ("Don't let the past remind us of what we are not now," "Will you come see me Thursdays and Saturdays? What have you got to lose?") Would Amerika be a better place if Jerry Rubin had never put on a three-piece suit? Somewhere in the back of your closet, is there still a peace-symbol belt and/or the black armband you saved from the Moratorium? What ever happened to those intense young men in denim you used to know?

Some are in Amsterdam. Some have been lost to long-range planning. But we may have located some of them here.

Or let us put it this way: within the forestry service, Smokey the Bear is not the only thing in pants. But be careful.

"There are two basic types of forester," explains Elena Cromler, a former forestry worker in Oregon. "The ones that become professional foresters are idealistic types, with an ecological bent. They're well-educated, intelligent and find themselves in rural areas, left to their own devices."

And the others? "The ones that come from the rural areas and are usually forest technicians. Basically, they're redneck, conservative, back-to-the-earth types." Forestry makes strange bedfellows.

The job goal is simple: to plan and supervise the protection, growing and harvesting of trees. It may involve mapping forest areas, estimating the amount of standing timber or protecting trees from fires, insects and disease. The forester has to be an expert on the interrelationship of trees, plants, forest soil, air, water, wildlife and animals.

And who do foresters interact with every day, besides technicians or loggers or the occasional tourist or hunter? "Each other," says Cromler. "They don't come into contact with women much. There are a few in the office, but the best thing for a male forester to do is bring his own." She is more than half-serious.

As a woman forester, you may meet the man of your dreams across an uncrowded glen. Or you may end up in an observation tower for one, looking out at nothing but whispering pines. Your best bet is to find him at one of the 50 U.S. colleges and universities that now offer degrees in forestry. Brush up on your study habits; with all those male students, you can always find someone who needs help with his forest biology homework.

In Saturday morning cartoons and in the National Park Service, there always seem to be plenty of park rangers. But in the U.S. Department of Agriculture Forestry Service, the term "ranger" has a different meaning. Making it to the level of district ranger is a real career accomplishment and a big job—being in charge, perhaps, of 100,000 acres or more.

One more possibility is a career as a forestry technician. You might help fight forest fires, supervise surveyors or road-building crews, measure logs, inspect trees for disease or do any number of projects under the supervision of a forester. At last count, about 80 colleges and technical schools offered forestry technician training. A one- or two-year course is all you'll need.

JOB SECURITY: About half of all foresters and conservationists work for the Federal government, about one-fourth work for State governments, and most of the rest have private industry jobs (perhaps with logging, lumber, paper companies). Although the government is certainly a stable employer, they have budget limitations in this area. The greatest job opportunities are expected to be in private industry. Overall, the Bureau of Labor Statistics sees below-average occupational growth for the field, with only an expected increase of nine percent in new jobs between now and 1995.

MONEY: Starting salaries in Federal government jobs are about $13,000-$16,500. The national average for experienced foresters is $27,900. To earn more, you'll have to advance to regional forest supervisor or move up into management with a private company.

LIFESTYLE: There really are forestry jobs in or near urban areas, but most will put you in the great outdoors, far from the madding crowd. If you love it, no career could be better. If you don't, a little welcome solitude can turn into catatonia faster than you might expect. Lots of people try a summer job in forestry before plunging headlong into a lifetime of communion with nature.

WHAT IT TAKES: Naturally, you have to like the outdoors. It's also important to be in good shape physically (there aren't many aerobics classes out there) and to be willing to move. The Department of Agriculture—like any corporation—can hand you a transfer.

Good communication skills are important here. Even if you spend a good deal of the time on your own, you may work with loggers, landowners, tourists and your own employees, the forestry technicians.

Happy note: the man supply in this career may be even better than the figures at the opening of this chapter indicate. The Bureau of Labor Statistics' most recent figures list forestry and logging occupations together, and the combined figure is 97 percent male. Maybe logging is something to think about, too.

EDUCATION: Bachelor's degree in forestry minimum. Many employers now prefer advanced degrees.

EARNINGS: $27,900 national average for Federal foresters.

WORKSTYLE: Outdoor work in all kinds of weather, sometimes in remote areas. There is people contact, however.

DIRECT INTERACTION OPPORTUNITIES: Getting to and fro in the helicopter or the jeep. Long, slow days in the tower. And what could bring two people closer than tagging trees side by side?

FOR MORE CAREER INFORMATION: Society of American Foresters, 5400 Grosvenor Lane, Bethesda, MD 20814.

Chapter **3**

Careers Where You Can *Meet* a High Percentage of Men

"I want to meet a tall, dark and handsome airline pilot,
not be one."
"I could make a beautiful life with a cop, but if I never
hold a gun in my hand, it will be too soon."
"No man is worth three years of law school."

Okay. There are other ways. In fact, your fellow professionals aren't the only people you'll come in contact with on company time. Some men you'll meet may be clients, cutomers or co-workers who have very different jobs from your own. Flight attendants meet just as many pilots as female pilots do (and *they* get to check out the passengers as well). Medical journalists meet doctors. And you don't have to become an attorney to work just a law book away from scads of junior partners.

Consider these careers, most of which require minimal educational retraining—or none at all.

228

THE AIRLINE INDUSTRY

"Poor Muffin," all her friends said when they heard. What was to happen to her, pushing 30 and suddenly divorced? She'd even lost custody of her child.

Muffin was not cut out to be a 1980s woman. She'd been a real beauty in college, the sort of blonde destined to be a fraternity sweetheart and to coax C's out of smitten professors. If she missed sorority events, it was because she was away in Hawaii as the state winner in a swimsuit company's beauty contest, or in New York losing to Cybill Shepherd in the Model of the Year pageant. She was the sort of girl who, when asked what career she wanted after college, replied "What do you mean?" She married two weeks after graduation.

So it was with great sympathy and a few snickers that her women friends greeted her news. Now that she was a single woman again, she'd signed on with a major airline—as a flight attendant. No. Muffin actually called herself a "stewardess," unaware of the semantic advances of the decade just past.

We clucked among ourselves. Should someone tell Muffin that she'd chosen a dead-end career, that no one considers the flight attendant's life glamorous anymore, that smart women have gone on to far better things? Well, no, we decided, it was probably the best she could do. She'd never been an intellectual giant, remember. At least the poor thing had kept her looks.

The next time we heard from Muffin, it was in a letter on stationery from the Palace Hotel in Gstaad. She and her fiancé were on a Christmas skiing trip and would be stopping briefly in Hong Kong before returning to their new home in Beverly Hills. The fiancé, of course, was a businessman, successful beyond the bounds of good taste, who'd been a First Class passenger on one of her flights.

Moral of the story: (1) That old line, "Coffee, tea or me?" still works; (2) You don't have to become a pilot to make good in the airline industry.

Flight Attendant

One of the reasons the new job title has caught on so well is that at least 15 percent of today's airline flight attendants are men. If it's the only traditionally female career that men have jumped at the chance to enter (98 percent of all secretarial jobs are still filled by women), maybe it's because the career really has a lot to offer.

Veteran stewardesses will tell you, in no uncertain terms, that things aren't what they used to be. With all the passengers the jumbo jets can carry, food service has become a challenge of space and time. It's not as easy to chat and flirt with passengers as it used to be. And the layovers in glamorous cities are shorter than in the past. Still, you're seeing the world free, all by flying an average of 75-85 hours per month (averaging a 20-hour work week).

Most airlines require only that you be a high school graduate and at least 19 years old. To get hired in today's very competitive atmosphere, however, being a college graduate gives you a big edge. So does work experience in dealing with the public. If you're interested in an airline with overseas routes, fluency in a foreign language is the ticket. Study French for the most glamorous routes.

After being hired, you'll be shipped off for four to six weeks of training. As you get started on the job, seniority will be hard to come by. That's because the flight attendants are no longer required to retire as early and some are now showing passengers snapshots of their grandchildren. Hang in there.

Despite all those changes and all the industry's well-publicized financial problems, job growth looks steady. The Bureau of Labor Statistics forecasts an increase of 29 percent (about average) in the number of new jobs between now and 1995.

National average income: $21,000 plus travel privileges for yourself and your family.

Airline Reservation and Ticket Agent

When you call an airline to make a flight reservation, you talk to a reservation agent working in a large central office. When you arrive at the airport and have to check your luggage or pick up your ticket, you see a ticket agent at the airline's front desk. Then, when you go to the gate for takeoff, you find a gate agent or two. They may check passengers in, give seat assignments and assist passengers in boarding. This is probably your best career spot for meeting handsome frequent flyers and crew members.

About 60 percent of all these agents are women, but you're not taking the job to meet your co-workers. The workforce figure that's more important—and most discouraging—is this: forecasted job growth of only two percent between now and 1995, according to the Bureau of Labor Statistics. That's about as far below average as you can get, without actually losing jobs. The reason for this bleak job picture is automation. Computers are making it possible for fewer people to accomplish more.

Getting a job with an airline is a competitive proposition, primarily because of the appealing air travel benefits, but there are ways to give yourself an edge. If you're a college graduate, you're already ahead of the game. Although this is technically a clerical occupation, a high percentage of people in the job have degrees. Good typing, word processing and computer skills are important. Business experience, either in dealing with the public or working in the transportation industry, is a big plus. If you can't get an airline job right away, start as a reservation agent for a railroad, bus company, auto club, steamship line or hotel instead, then try to switch horizontally into the airline industries. When you're hired, you'll be trained, formally or informally, in all the specifics of the industry.

Finally, polish your public image. Looking good, dressing well and having a pleasant speaking voice can make a difference. Of course, if you're hoping to meet great men, you weren't going to show up without blusher and lip gloss anyway.

National average income: $23,140 for reservation agents; $25,584 for gate agents.

For More Career Information:

Get in touch with airlines directly. For a list of airline addresses, write Air Transport Association of America, 1709 New York Avenue NW, Washington, DC 20006.

THE RESTAURANT BUSINESS

In an average week, he works 58.5 hours. Although he probably doesn't have a college degree, he earns $35,100 a year and owns and operates a $1 million restaurant. He's 43 years old, less likely to be married than corporate restaurant chain types and his greatest dream is to be a millionaire.

Here are some inside tips on impressing him:

"*Customers are so fickle*. They'll switch to a new restaurant for no reason at all." This is the average restaurant owner's greatest disappointment in his chosen field.

"I'm not saying I'll never go out with other men. I am saying, though, that *I'll never lie to you* about it." The thing that makes him angriest is dishonesty.

"*I really admire a man who's taken a risk* and opened his own business, and who has enough fight and ambition to make a go of it." The average restaurant owner thinks of himself as competitive, ambitious, outgoing and daring.

"*I collect rare coins.*" More than 47 percent of all owners invest in art, antiques, coins or stamps.

"*You're working too hard,* you know. Lie down. Let me give you a massage." His biggest career worries are that he's living with too much stress and that his hours are too long.

"*Gosh, I love to eat out* at a nice restaurant almost as much as I love working in one. It's my idea of a perfect date. Otherwise, I'd rather just sit at home with a good book, or watch television with the man I love." His favorite forms of after-hours recreation are dining out, reading and television.

If you are a teetotaler and/or believe that alcohol is the devil's tool, a man in the restaurant business may not be for you. His favorite vices are work and liquor.

Of course, meeting the man who owns or runs the restaurant isn't the only reason to go into the food service business. There are the waiters and bartenders—out-of-work actors or students struggling to pay the rent now, but perhaps the million-dollar-a-picture stars or corporate tycoons of tomorrow.

There are the chefs, almost always male. What better marriage can be imagined than one in which your husband is a fabulous cook and won't allow you near the kitchen?

And there are the customers.

One of the best choices for meeting great men is a big-city restaurant right in the middle of the business district—one that's popular with executives on expense accounts. You tend to get to know your customers, because they often choose one or two favorite restaurants at which to entertain clients. When you greet him by name, ("And how are you today, Mr. Bonzo? Your regular table? The usual from the bar?") he's made an impression on his guest and will be grateful to you.

Working the lunch shift may be the best choice. You're more likely to find men alone or with male business associates at that time of day. On the dinner shift, you may spend your time trying to move hot plates back and forth between hand-holding couples with visions of sexual conquest dancing in their brains. (And with each other, not you.)

At any time of day, you're at least as likely to meet bachelors as married men. Singles spend almost half their food budget on eating out. And the 35- to 44-year-old age group spends 36 percent more than the average consumer on restaurant meals.

If you're patient enough to wait for the right job, you can even choose your target market. Do a little investigating to find out where the doctors, lawyers, stockbrokers, celebrities or advertising executives hang out at lunchtime or cocktail hour in your city (asking other waiters and waitresses about their clientele usually turns up the required information). Then apply for a job there.

There is one major hitch. The more expensive and/or elegant a restaurant likes to consider itself, the more likely its management is to hire only male waiters. It may go against every notion of equal employment opportunity, but they get away with it. But don't despair; these three- and four-star dining places often hire women as hosts, maître d's or in restaurant management.

The restaurant business is growing fast. Demographers say one reason is the growing number of women in the work force. Couples would rather eat out than cook at home, when both have put in a full work day already. And two paychecks make eating out more affordable. So does the trend in today's generation toward marrying later and having fewer children. By 1990, almost six out of ten households will consist of only one or two people.

By 1995, the Bureau of Labor Statistics says there will be more than 2.2 million waiters and waitresses on the job, an increase of 34 percent from today. The number of cooks and chefs will have risen 33 percent to more than 1.6 million. The number of bartenders will have gone up by 32 percent to just over 500,000.

Even the number of restaurant managers and proprietors is growing faster than the average rate. An increase of 38.3 percent is expected by 1990.

The overall growth picture for all restaurant industry jobs is an increase of 32.6 percent by 1990. That's compared to an average increase of only 18.9 percent for all U.S. industries. This means almost 6.4 million people will be making their living in the food service industry by the beginning of the next decade. Or if you count the food service employees in hotels and other institutions, as the National Restaurant Association does, the figure comes to almost 8 million.

Restaurant managers earn a median of $19,000-$44,000, depending primarily on the size of the operation, according to the Roth Young Wage and Salary Review. Assistant managers earn $16,000-$29,000. Chefs earn $23,000-$50,000 and cooks, $11,000-$21,000. According to a *Restaurant & Institutions* survey, executive chefs average $23,667 nationwide while managers average $20,926.

Waiters and waitresses earn median salaries of only $8,200 per year, with the top ten percent earning at least $14,800. Tips, however, increase their incomes considerably. Waiters in busy big-city restaurants can earn $400-$500 per week in tips. Bartenders earn a median salary of $10,200—plus tips. Most people who work for restaurants also get free meals on the job.

You could get your training on the job, too. Many beginning waiters and waitresses do. And you might work your way up to a job as captain, maître d' or host. Bartenders generally need some formal education, perhaps from a vocational or technical school. If you have your eye on restaurant management—or even on owning and managing a place of your own—a bachelor's degree in hotel and restaurant management could be your best bet.

The fast food industry is the fastest-growing segment of the restaurant business, and we'll admit that many teenage romances may have blossomed over a Big Mac assembly line. If you are over 21, however, this is probably not the place for you.

Women are beginning to outnumber men in the food service industry as a whole. Sixty-two percent of the restaurant labor force was male in 1970, according to one survey; that figure has plummeted to 36 percent today. Men do outnumber women in one entry-level job, however. Seven out of ten newly-hired dishwashers are male.

For More Career Information:

National Restaurant Association, 311 First Street NW, Washington, DC 20001.

THE LAW BUSINESS

Your parents would be so proud if you married a lawyer. You'd have money, status, security and someone to write nasty letters for you whenever you're wronged by the dry cleaners or the business client who won't pay up.

But you don't want to be an attorney. You've heard too many stories of people coming close to nervous breakdowns in law school. You hate getting up to talk in public. You look terrible in gray flannel. Besides, when you were in group therapy, half the patients there were lawyers, and one of them always got seriously depressed whenever she lost a case. And all another one ever talked about was his dream of giving it all up to open a restaurant in the Village.

Thankfully, there's a way to work with lawyers all day without becoming one.

Law Office Administrator

Back in the old days, when law firms were smaller and the world was a simpler place, attorneys took care of business themselves.

They either assigned one staff attorney to handle things or they took turns making sure the bills were paid, the new office space was contracted for, and the hiring and firing was carried out. Many things have changed since then. Computerization has evolved, for one thing. Now legal firms are churning out an incredible number of records, reports and forms. Telecommunications advances have been made too: now legal firms can tap into huge data bases of court cases. Growth has occurred, along with a major trend toward mergers, so law offices are larger than ever and have been spawning branch offices across the country. Finally, advertising and marketing have happened in a big way. Maybe it was considered less than professional to openly seek new clients a few years ago, but even the stodgiest firms are beginning to warm up to the usefulness of the media.

That's why, according to executive search consultants, more and more law firms are asking them to find business experts to act as office managers or administrators, and some of these jobs qualify for the big time. Salaries, say the headhunters, can range from $25,000 and up and up. One firm of 13 attorneys recently hired an administrator in the $50,000-$60,000 range. And one of the nation's largest law firms (with more than 300 attorneys) pays their administrator more than $300,000

Is it for you? Yes, if you're good at people management and don't mind a frenetic work pace. At the moment, law firms are taking managers from a variety of backgrounds—everything from data processing, finance and accounting to the military. An M.B.A. is a plus, but not at all necessary. A background in marketing or advertising would be an asset, too.

Corporate legal departments are also hiring administrators. In a corporate environment, your title might be manager of legal services. Your duties would be essentially the same, but you'd have the entire corporation's support to call upon.

This is a field so new that the Bureau of Labor Statistics doesn't report on it. Still, there's strong evidence that it's growing fast. The Association of Legal Administrators was founded in 1971 with 25 members. Today's membership is over 4,000.

Legal Assistant

Look for it in the classified ads under this title or under "paralegal." Expect to find salaries as high as $38,000 in big cities. The national median income is $21,200, but ten percent earn $30,000 or more. Federal government paralegals average $26,300 and start at $13,000 or $16,100, depending on training and experience.

But that isn't even the best news. Legal assistants are part of the second-fastest-growing career in the country (topped by computer service technician). By 1995, the number of paralegal jobs will have increased a stunning 94 percent— to a total of 88,000 jobs—according to the Bureau of Labor Statistics. Warning: Competition is growing commensurately.

Your job will be to do everything a lawyer does, with four notable exceptions. You can't set legal fees, accept a client on your own, give legal advice or present a case in court. What you can do is all the background work. You might investigate the facts in a case, analyze the information and write a report. The attorney you work for will use that report in deciding how to handle the case. You may obtain affadavits, prepare legal arguments, help draft contracts and mortgages, plan estates and assist the attorney or attorneys during a trial.

A few law firms continue to train paralegals on the job, but most now look for candidates with a formal education in the field. Most legal assistant courses take two years. They can be found in all kinds of institutions: four-year colleges, junior and community colleges, law schools and business schools. You can become a C.L.A. (Certified Legal Assistant) after a certain amount of training and experience by passing a two-day exam. Certification is voluntary, but some employers may ask for it.

If you're thinking about this career, do be prepared to specialize. Even your formal education may concentrate on a certain area of law, and you'll have to declare a major. Possibilities include litigation, corporate, real estate, trademark, and trusts and estates.

The ideal legal assistant knows her field, knows her legal terminology backward and forward, and has excellent research and communication skills. Opportunities for advancement are limited. The

best you can hope for is supervising other paralegals, perhaps delegating attorneys' work to and among them. Your opportunities for
working elbow-to-elbow with lawyers, however, are wide open.
Choose a large legal firm for a larger field to play. The big ones pay
best, anyway.

For More Career Information:

American Bar Association, Standing Committee on Legal Assistants,
1155 East 60th Street, Chicago, IL 60637; Association of Legal Administrators, 1800 Pickwick Avenue, Glenview, IL 60025; National
Association of Legal Assistants, 1420 South Utica, Tulsa, OK 74104.

THE JOY OF "TEMPING"

TEMPORARY M/F

Register today—work tomorrow.
Free IBM PC and Wang training
& typing brush-up programs.
Daily pay. Medical benefits. Free training.
Work a day or two, a week at a time,
a month or more.
Flexible hours. Vacation pay.
$100 bonus after 70 hours.
Receive $75 bonus after only 25 hours work.
$50 bonus after 8 hours completed.

The temporary employee business is booming, to the tune of about
600,000 temporary job assignments with a 30 percent annual growth
in the number of jobs projected. In 1984, temps took home a payroll
of more than $5 billion. And luckily for you, there's an enormous
shortage of qualified employees—as the classified ad excerpts above
indicate. A good temp can just about name her game.

Why should you even consider making a living this way? Aside
from the freedom and flexibility she gets, the temp can avoid office
politics altogether. And there couldn't be a better arrangement for
meeting men at the office.

"On most assignments, you're there for one or two weeks, a month at the most," explains a veteran temporary secretary. "That's just long enough to meet the people in the department and have a chance for a couple of personal chats—just long enough for you to see if anyone really interests you, and to see if they're interested too.

"If you do meet somebody, that's great because you're leaving and there aren't any complications about having an office romance. And if you happen to get assigned to a company where there are no interesting men, at least you're not stuck there for a couple of years. Just relax. There'll be a whole new office full of men next Monday."

There's only one problem, you say. You're not a secretary. In fact, you've made it a point of sexual politics never to learn to type.

Not every temp is a secretary. About forty percent of all temporary jobs today are for nonclerical assignments. There are companies specializing in giving and getting work assignments for accountants, engineers, architects, computer specialists and medical personnel. One data base specialist estimates that he's earned as much as $90,000 per year in temp jobs. Plus he can take off a month or two whenever the mood strikes him. (This may sound like delusions of grandeur, but the head of a temp firm admits that they've paid up to $50 per hour for systems analysts.)

You can take home pretty impressive paychecks as a typist or secretary, too. A temp with word processing training but very little work experience could make $4.50-$9.00 or more per hour, according to one industry source. According to a representative of the National Association of Temporary Services, the pay scale is even higher: $7.50-$15 per hour. For a 37-1/2-hour week, that could mean as much as $562.50 per week. You could earn almost $25,000 in ten months—and take July and August off.

But you don't know the difference between a word processor and a microwave oven, you say. Not to worry. Many temporary agencies offer free training and are delighted to teach you the ropes. One claims that they can have you trained, productive and ready to go out on your first word processing assignment in eight hours.

Well, fine, but you'd have no medical insurance or other employee benefits, you say. That's changing too. Some of the temporary services now give medical coverage, paid vacations and other perks to their "employees."

Mobility is another great benefit. With a favorable recommendation from your local office of Manpower, Kelly Girls or other national temporary services firm, you can turn up at their branch in Houston or Los Angeles or Boston and be welcomed with open arms. Spend next winter in a sunny climate, or drive cross-country, working as you go to pay the bills.

What kind of man will you meet on temp jobs? Every kind, if you do secretarial work. If you're good at what you do and if the current supply-and-demand situation remains the same (lots of demand, very little supply), you probably can tell the agency just what kinds of companies appeal to you. For sheer numbers of men, of course, you should ask to be assigned to engineering firms, architectural firms, hotel chains, medical offices, law offices and financial services companies.

The only clear reasons not to become a temp are if you already have a career you love or if you want a career with a clearly-marked corporate ladder to climb. Good point. But then you could always temp at night or on weekends. Almost 5 million Americans today hold two jobs.

For More Career Information:

National Association of Temporary Services, 119 South Saint Asaph Street, Alexandria, VA 22314.

TELEVISION JOURNALISM

"If you end up with a man in television, you'll never be bored. He'll take you to wonderful openings where you'll rub elbows with the rich and famous," says Martina Gold, a former CBS employee. "He'll be spontaneous. He'll think fast and move fast. And when he gets home, he probably will not want to sit in front of the TV and watch the ballgame."

Being part of the TV industry, or being married to someone who is, confers instant status, Gold admits. "You'll be the envy of all your friends. Whenever I used to flash my CBS I.D. card, I always got the best tables at restaurants or clubs. For all they knew, I might have cleaned the toilets there." But they would have been network toilets!

Whether you're working in a major market like New York or Los Angeles or at a local station in a smaller city, you're likely to meet three distinct types.

• *The On-Air Anchorperson*. There he is—Mr. Glamor. He's the talk show host, the newscaster, the name and face that everybody recognizes. For every Johnny Carson or David Letterman, there are a hundred local celebrities—all dreaming of that network shot someday. Insiders describe the type as "very self-centered, self-absorbed, preoccupied with his looks. He's afraid of getting older, so he'll be frightened if you look older." For that reason, you will often see the on-air man with younger women.

The woman he's most likely to marry is someone social who can help him make contacts and will reflect well on him. "She'll be someone who's distant, not genuine and friendly," suggests a female talk show producer. "The on-air people are performers, and part of the charisma is mystery. A revealing wife would reveal them, too."

• *The Producer*. Actually he might be a producer, director, production assistant or hold any number of other titles. He's part of the staff that puts the show together, and he lives or dies by his ratings.

You'd recognize him by his casual dress, says Martina Gold. He'll wear jeans and a sports jacket, as opposed to a suit. "The production type's self-image is creativity," she explains. "The on-air person's self-image is power."

Sometimes the producer or director you date may seem to be living at 78 rpm while you're still on 33. "People in TV think real fast," Gold explains. "They don't finish sentences because they're always visualizing as they think."

The women they marry often are those with impressive academic credentials. "It's because *they* don't have master's degrees or M.B.A.'s," says Gold. "It elevates their status. It doesn't matter whether you have a law degree or a doctorate in art history. You've proved yourself academically."

Corporate work backgrounds seem to impress them, too. "It shows you're a real person. You're an adult. A lot of them think TV is a sham, not real grown-up work," observes Gold. Being from a 'good family' impresses as well.

• *The Management Type*. The men and women in television station management offices are said to be the most stable of the bunch.

They are more like people in business than people in entertainment. They change jobs less often, bump into fewer celebrities and are less affected by the glare of the spotlight. "They look at the creative people as a little childish," says one female producer. The man in management offers stability, tremendous power and a great expense account.

Getting a job in this competitive industry can seem about as easy as penetrating the K.G.B. And you'll probably have to start at the bottom, even if you've been running a department in some other industry for years. "If they say 'OK, you can work here as a security guard,' take it," advises Martina Gold. Once the first door opens to you, you can become an insider.

"They promote from within," she explains. "TV people have an intense loyalty to their own. You get an instant family, and it's incestuous. It fosters co-workers dating each other."

People may feel drawn together by the pace of the television industry. Everything, it often seems, is an emergency. Part of the bond also may be the high pressure. Thanks to the rating system, you're constantly getting instant feedback; if the ratings were high the day they used your idea you'll feel great, but if they weren't, it can feel like the end of the world. Or perhaps television people come to feel close to each other because of the subject matter they deal with every day. "It's either death or sex," points out one observer. When you've just come from a program conference in which you discussed what kinds of questions to ask the author of *The Ultimate Orgasm* on tomorrow's show, a certain professional distance has to disappear.

There is one big advantage to a career in television: Women appear to be treated more like human beings here than in most other fields. "They're not very role-defined. TV is much more androgynous. They're accustomed to working with women in power."

The only problem is that he'll cheat on you like there's no tomorrow. He can't help it; the opportunities are endless. The minute he announces what he does for a living, every would-be actress, newscaster and co-host will do anything she can to encourage him to help her career. Of course, when you're in TV, all those men you meet at parties will feel the same way about you.

The Interview As Blind Date

If you had your own talk show, you wouldn't meet most of your guests until the moment they walked out onto the set. At best, you'd have dropped by the Green Room just before air time to shake hands and introduce yourself. And if you're interviewing your city's handsome bachelor mayor that day, the two of you will do the eight-minute segment, you'll shake hands and thank him—and he'll be out of the studio before the commercials are over. If you were hoping to get something started, the only possible way is to schedule him as the last guest of the day. Then pray that he isn't rushing to his next appointment (probably scheduled 15 minutes after yours).

Of course, in some cases someone will pre-interview the mayor for the show. In that case, you'd be better off with a job as assistant producer or whoever handles that duty. Unfortunately, you might do it over the phone—which just doesn't give you the same opportunities. Or you might have a chance to sit down with hizzoner for a half hour or so to go over possible topics and questions that could be part of the on-air interview. Just the two of you, alone, talking about his favorite subject: him. Now that's the kind of setup that encourages follow-up questions—over dinner.

Being a print journalist can offer better opportunities. If you're writing a magazine or newspaper article, you're more likely to set up an in-person interview date. You can meet the subject at his hotel room, office, publicist's apartment or perhaps over lunch at a great restaurant. It may be just the two of you. At the most, he'll have a publicist or manager along—perhaps to help him out of tough questions, perhaps to protect him in case you make unwanted advances, or even to convey the message later that he's interested. We're told Howard Hughes never asked out a woman directly; he sent an employee to tender the invitation.

Unlike broadcast journalists, magazine and newspaper writers tend to spend a reasonably long time with their interview subjects. You might have an hour, two hours or an afternoon with him. Once in a while, however, you might be forced to suffer through an entire interview in the stretch limo as he races to the airport. It's true that many interviews are done by phone, but that's often up to you.

Broadcast journalists have one important advantage. They may meet and interview 10-20 celebrities a week for a daily talk show. Magazine and newspaper writers may work on only one or two "people" assignments per month.

Politicians and movie stars aren't the only people who get interviewed and written about, of course. You might interview authors, doctors, scientists or business executives. Being fascinated by a man and by his work is a real head start on romance. It worked for Hart Bochner playing a *Rolling Stone* writer assigned to do a feature on a successful author (Jacqueline Bisset) in *Rich and Famous*.

For More Career Information:

Broadcast Education Association/National Association of Broadcasters, 1771 N Street NW, Washington, DC 20036; Women in Communications, P.O. Box 9561, Austin, TX 78766.

THE TRAVEL BUSINESS

"It's a terrific job for escaping reality, escaping responsibility," says an East Coast travel agent, male. "We call ourselves in the office 'the Jewish under-achievers.' We should have been doctors or lawyers, but we're not willing to make the commitment to that kind of career."

So if you're looking for a man who turns blue with fear at the thought of commitment or responsibility, here's the place to find him.

"There are a lot of gay travel agents," observes a female agent from Minneapolis. "They're working in an industry where there are many more women than men. But male or female, they all live their jobs. You have to have enthusiasm for sales and for travel. You have to pay attention to details. And you have to be a workaholic because travel agents work long hours."

There are the kids right out of school sitting at their computers and checking the fares. They don't make much money. They've gone into the business for the glamor of free travel.

And there are the doctor's wives. "In Florida, you find every chiropractor's wife is a travel agent," says a New York agency owner.

Obviously, they don't need the money. They've gone into the business for the glamor of free travel.

And if you decide to become a travel agent, you'll go into the business for the glamor of free travel, too. And to meet male clients.

You may go into the *retail* side of the business, helping individual clients plan their vacations. If you do, you could end up spending your work days talking to happy couples planning their honeymoons or other romantic getaways. Don't. The solution: specialize in singles' resorts, singles' cruises and other destinations that appeal to the unattached. Make it a point to get to know everything about Club Med's villages around the world, for instance. Then all those single and newly-divorced men will find their way to your desk.

Or you may go into the *commercial* side of travel agenting, working with corporations and business owners. This way, most of your work will involve handling business trips. Business clients tend to work with a single travel agent again and again, so you'll have a chance to get to know the men for whom you're making arrangements. Ask him the kind of hotel he's looking for, what's important to him in a hotel room (you?) and what time of day he prefers to travel. Get personal, it's your job.

Many corporations award all their travel business to a single agency. In fact, 62.9 percent of the companies responding to the American Express Survey of Business Travel reported that they use only one agency. According to the survey, the average company spends $10,200 per year on each frequent traveler.

A single Philadelphia agency handles more that 400 corporations, including DuPont which spends an estimated $80 million annually on business trips. The agent's job is to save the corporation money, primarily by obtaining bulk airfares and corporate hotel rates. One agent, who now heads corporate sales, advocates making the travel arrangements first, then scheduling the necessary meetings around them. If the first flight of the day leaves at 9:50 a.m. and arrives at 11:03, it's foolish to set up a meeting for that morning at 10. It would just mean flying there the evening before and spending money on an extra hotel night. Instead, book the flight that arrives at 11:03 a.m. and schedule the first meeting for 11:30 or noon. The most lucrative specialty is group and incentive travel. "You make more money and more contacts, you get to travel more and you need more experience to handle group and incentive," says an agent from the Midwest.

Group travel is self-explanatory. You might arrange vacation trips for alumni associations, corporate travel clubs or almost any kind of group. Or you might arrange conferences or conventions, working with corporate meeting planners.

Incentive travel means company-paid trips given as rewards or incentives to certain employees, clients or suppliers. The Glamor-puss Beauty Company, for instance, might sponsor a European trip for the owners of the 25 salons that bought the greatest amounts of their products last year. Or the Load-and-Store Computer Company might reward its 50 top salespeople by treating them to a Caribbean cruise. Incentive travel is big business, and getting bigger all the time.

• *Travel Agent*. Chances are you won't get rich as an agent. Average salaries are between $10,000 and $20,000. But it's the perfect entry to the travel industry, and a relatively easy job to get. That's because it's one of the country's fastest-growing occupations, expected to grow 43 percent to a total of 88,000 jobs by 1995.

Even if you have higher ambitions, getting sales experience as an agent is a great place to start. You may answer phones, type letters, file destination brochures, build window displays (a Paris theme for April, Hawaii in January?) or all of the above. You'll definitely need to learn one of the computer reservations systems; American's SABRE system is the most frequently used.

• *Corporate Travel Manager*. As head of a corporate travel department, you may supervise other managers and dozens of assistants, or you may run a one-woman show. Either way, your job is to keep track of travel costs and keep them as low as possible while arranging all the business trips employees need to take. You may work with one or more travel agencies, or you may function as an in-house agency. In addition to keeping track of airline routes, discount fares and the like, you may arrange for employees' passports and visas. Many travel managers arrange conferences too, so you'll either work with meeting planners (see page 185) or act as one yourself. Travel managers' salaries range from $15,000 to $35,000 and up, depending on department size and the company's travel budget.

• *Travel Company Management*. Then there are the big travel companies—American Express, Thomas Cook and the like. A background as a travel agent gives you a big edge in getting hired here, whether you want to work in planning, promotion, public relations or sales.

• *Tour Operator*. If three relatives are coming to visit your city for the first time and staying a week, what would you show them? Maybe you'd start by driving them around the city for an overall impression, then take them to your favorite Italian restaurant (the one with the view of the water) for dinner, then arrange to spend the next morning at the art museum. That's exactly what you'd do as a tour operator. You'd put together packages and itineraries, run the tour buses and employ the guides. Then you'd promote your tours to travel agents, who'd in turn sell them to the public.

• *Travel Writer/Editor*. Your job is like that of any other editor, reporter (see page 169) or freelance writer. It's just that you specialize in travel stories, and you have to see the places to write about them.

Whether you work as a writer, agent, manager or have some other job in the travel industry, the people who want to impress you are those with destinations to sell. They're the people who'll invite you on free or very inexpensive "fam" (familiarization) trips, a practice that the majority of publications condone. One travel industry specialist lists these trips among those she's taken in the line of duty recently:

• A week in Sweden to attend the Nordic Travel Mart in Stockholm and to see the glories of the glass country around Kalmar. Sponsored by the Scandinavian Tourist Board.
• A month in the Bahamas to research a guidebook. Arranged by the advertising/public relations agency that handles the Bahamas account.
• A long weekend at the Tryall Golf and Beach Club in Jamaica, to prove that tourism in Jamaica is alive and well again. Co-sponsored by Tryall's P.R. firm and the Jamaican Tourist Board.
• A long weekend in London to see the newly-refurbished Mayfair Hotel. The group also got tickets to *Starlight Express*, the hottest show in town. And they caught a glimpse of Diana, Princess of Wales, shopping at Harrod's. Co-sponsored by Inter-Continental Hotels and British Airways.

Whatever travel career you choose, your best education is a bachelor's degree in travel and tourism, with a minor in marketing, communications or business.

For More Career Information:

American Society of Travel Agents, 4400 MacArthur Boulevard, Washington, DC 20007.

DIVORCE MEDIATOR

+ You'll never have to furtively sneak a peek at a ring finger again. If he's in your office, he's about to be available.

− A man never marries the *first* woman he meets after the divorce.

It's the American dream wedding, statistically average in every way. She's 22; he'll be 24 in about six weeks. They'll take an eight-day honeymoon in California, Florida or Pennsylvania, spending $1700 in the process. They'll make the retailing industry very happy, as they and their relatives run up bills for china, silver, crystal, furniture, linens, luggage and kitchen appliances with European names. Their marriage will last exactly seven years.

Strangely enough, medians and averages and statistics being what they are, she will be 29 when they split up and he will be 31.5. An average of .97 of a child will be involved in the divorce.

Then there's the good news. At age 32, she will remarry. At age 35, he'll do the same. If you want him, you'll have to catch him quickly—within that crucial three-and-a-half-year period. Otherwise, you'll have to wait for a second divorce to bring him on the market again.

Would you like to be first in line when these poor, bedraggled ex-husbands are ready to start dating again? If so, become a divorce mediator, a new occupation that didn't exist 15 years ago and the use of which is now law in at least 20 states. As a mediator, you might be the most important woman he'll see during the divorce proceedings. (If his attorney is female too, just pray that she's 30 years older than he, and wears orthopedic shoes.)

No, a divorce mediator isn't a lawyer. A number of attorneys have become mediators too, and have added it to the services they offer. But just as many psychologists and social workers have gone into the field.

John Haynes, the man who essentially created the new career, was originally a labor-management negotiator. When he made a career switch to teaching, he became a professor of social welfare at Stony Brook University, specializing in family policy. "One of the things I thought about as I was teaching was how little we do for families," Haynes recalls, "and how many of the things that we do are destructive, like divorce. Then I asked myself why we couldn't take all the techniques that we know about labor-management negotiations and apply them to divorce negotiations? I began to put the two together, I developed the idea, tested it with a family agency and wrote a book about it."

Why should people come to you, a divorce mediator, rather than handle everything with a lawyer? Haynes sees four major advantages.

• *It doesn't take as long.* Even a relatively normal divorce takes nine months or so, he approximates, when both husband and wife have their own attorneys. A typical mediation takes 12-15 hours to complete over a six- to eight-week period. Most sessions are two hours long.

• *The couple gets to take control of the situation.* "That plays itself out in a number of interesting ways," Haynes remarks, describing one possible scenario. The two may have been in litigation for a year or two. The husband angrily asks "What about that petition that you filed? You accused me of being homosexual!" The wife, equally furious, replies "What about that petition that you filed that said I was abusive to the children?" Each then says, "Well, my attorney told me to file that." When people work through attorneys, they can do things without taking responsibility for their actions. When two people sit facing each other in the same room, they're in control of their divorce and they're responsible for what happens.

• *It's cheaper.* According to Haynes, the standard retainer for a New York City matrimonial lawyer is $2500 for each party. That's an initial cost of $5000—and the couple goes from there. A New York mediator would charge perhaps $100 per hour, a 15-hour mediation adding up to $1500. With each of the two involved attorneys charging $350-

$500 to draw up the necessary legal documents, the maximum cost for this mediated divorce is $2500. (Note: Legal retainers are lower in smaller cities, and so are mediation fees.)

• *It makes for "more successful" divorces.* There may be American ex-husbands running around owing billions in unpaid child support, but studies so far show that about 90 percent of all mediated support agreements are honored. "In mediation, there's always more intensive parenting on both sides," Haynes believes. "The more active the parenting, the more likely he is to pay."

There are no legal or licensing requirements for the divorce mediator's career yet, although there is a membership association. If you want to, you can have cards printed and call yourself a mediator tomorrow. Doing it this way, however, you'll probably meet only very foolish men who would put important matters in a so-called expert's hands without checking her out.

If you already have a master's degree in one of the "helping professions" (psychology, social work and so on), good. The Academy of Family Mediators will accept you as a member only if you do, or if you have a law degree. You also must have undergone a certain amount of specialized education in mediation.

Clients will find you in one of several ways. They may be referred to you by their attorney, their therapist, or the Academy of Family Mediators. The mediation may even be court-ordered. "Around the U.S., there's a big move on to mandate mediation," says Haynes. "In California, you cannot go to court on any issue involving children. In Maine, you have to mediate both the financial and the child issue."

You could meet almost any kind of man in your work as a mediator. One day, your clients might be a couple who earn $20,000 together and have very few assets to split. The next day, you might be working with an affluent couple who have to split up a business, two homes, investments and a great deal of other property.

Choose the attorneys and therapists you work with very carefully. The kinds of clients they attract will be the kinds you'll spend your days with—and the group from which you may be choosing your next great love.

You can practice in just about any state, because the divorce rate is high from coast to coast. It's true that Nevada has by far the highest rate of all—13.9 marital split-ups per 1,000 population—but many of these people establish residency in Reno strictly for divorce purposes.

The highest true divorce rates are in Wyoming, Oklahoma, Arizona and New Mexico (from 7 to 7.8 per 1,000 population). The highest total number of divorces per year are in California and Texas, followed (not so closely) by New York, Ohio and Illinois. All we learn from these statistics, however, is that states with big populations have a big divorced population too.

Divorce mediation is too new a career to have official Bureau of Labor Statistics figures on its work force. Based on the people who have signed up for his Learning Annex adult education course on the career, Haynes estimates that the occupation is now about sixty percent female and forty percent male. Most students are former attorneys or mental health professionals in their 30s and 40s.

Of course, you won't be spending your work days with other mediators. You'll be behind closed doors with unhappy couples— most often in a meeting for three. Occasionally, however, you may do "shuttle diplomacy" between the two. And every one of those men is about to become single again.

Don't worry if you hear that the really handsome guy you're attracted to has asked for the divorce because he's in love with the upstairs maid. As the women's magazines tell us, some newly-divorced men are in too much psychic pain to make another commitment so quickly. Lots of those earth-shaking, home-wrecking romances never make it to the altar. Wait six months for that relationship to fizzle out, then send him an invitation to a dinner party. Serve champagne.

For More Career Information:

Academy of Family Mediators, 111 Fourth Avenue, New York, NY 10003.

ENTREPRENEUR

The truth is, you're not cut out to be an employee. Your career dream and your realistic plan is to become your own boss.

That's great. As head of your own company, you can always hire a whole staff of fascinating men. (Note: Try *not* to think of your male employees as a harem. Reverse sexism is *so* unbecoming.)

Unfortunately, however, most entrepreneurs don't get their start by spending all the receipts on payroll. If you plan to be a one-woman show, for a while at least, male clients will have to be the answer to your prayers.

Consider these entrepreneurial possibilities. Or use your own imagination to found a business that will bring you both financial and social satisfaction.

Skin Care Salon for Men

So you're a beauty expert or know you could learn to be one. Then why waste those magic hands and all those facial and shoulder massages on female clients? We already have Georgette Klinger, Janet Sartin and Elizabeth Arden. Get your training, open a salon with masculine decor and start teaching the businessmen in your city just what professional skin care can do. They'll look younger and healthier as a result. And they'll look forward to the regularly-scheduled pampering you give them. It's a real hands-on career opportunity to meet men.

Barber

Some men don't like getting their hair cut at unisex salons where the atmosphere is all punk rock music and designer robes. Some would really rather go to an old-fashioned barber shop, as long as the cut is excellent and the feel of the place (barber shop-ese for "ambiance") is right. In this essentially all-male world, there's no reason the barber can't be a woman—you.

Career and Outplacement Counseling

The average executive let go by his company is a 47-year-old man who has worked for the same corporation for more than 15 years, according to a client survey by an outplacement consulting firm, Bushnell, Cruise & Associates. They point out that this man may be going through mid-career crisis, he may have lost at corporate politics on the highest levels or he may be re-evaluating his personal life. As an outplacement counselor, you can help him define his goals and assist him in effectively merchandising his skills and experience on the job market. When he's happily ensconced in a new $75,000-a-year job, he'll remember how you helped him and will want to thank you. Allow him to take you to dinner.

Retail Shop

A men's clothing store is the ideal choice. You can even control the kind of men you'll attract by the kind of merchandise you carry. Put mannequins in classic, conservative suits in the window, and you're most likely to attract a devoted following of bankers, stockbrokers and other traditional types. If your ideal man is a trendier sort— maybe someone in advertising, public relations or the media—do just the opposite. Stock the store with more avant-garde fashions and the lines of unconventional young designers.

Personal Shopper Service

This is big business in big cities, but all the services seem to be for executive women. You can change all that. It works like this. The poor man is too busy (running his Greek shipping empire or an international bank, we hope) to go all over town shopping for his own clothes. Or maybe he just feels better having a woman handle things for him. You go to his home, go through his closets, throw out all the things that don't work and talk to him about himself, his lifestyle and his tastes. You go shopping for him and pick out clothing that will work for him, including things to go with items he already owns. Then he meets you at the store to try it all on. You get a flat fee, with almost no overhead, and perhaps a new friend.

Restaurant

It's the next best thing to giving a dinner party at home every night— with someone else doing the cooking and clean-up. Choose a business neighborhood where you're sure to draw executive lunchers or diners. Take all credit cards. Encourage corporate accounts. Then establish your image as the glamorous hostess. The chef may be a prima donna, and you may work 60 hours per week, but you'll be very visible as you greet interesting men every day.

Bar

You could open a place near the business district in order to meet tired businessmen stopping for drinks on their way home. Or you could open a glitzy sort of pub in a residential neighborhood heavily populated by singles. Just think, you'll be the only woman in this singles bar who can't be accused of being there because she's desperate. Yet there you are in the middle of all those men, every one of them hoping to meet a great woman. Smile, be sympathetic and take your pick.

For More Career Information:

Associated Master Barbers and Beauticians of America, 219 Greenwich Road, Charlotte, NC 28211 (skin care salon, barber);

National Mass Retailing Institute, 570 Seventh Avenue, New York, NY 10018 (retail shop);

American Association for Counseling and Development, 5999 Stevenson Avenue, Alexandria, VA 22304 (outplacement and career counseling);

National Restaurant Association, 311 First Street NW, Washington, DC 20001 (restaurant, bar);

National Association of Women Business Owners, 500 North Michigan Avenue, Chicago, IL 60611 (general).

Chapter **4**

Geography Lessons:
Where the Men Are

Accept this one hard, cold fact: women outnumber men across the board. In the United States, there are only 94.5 males for every 100 females. Statistics show that we have the edge in very few metropolitan areas. *Fringe Benefits* offers, however, these ten cities where you might start a new life with an almost equal chance.

Rankings are based on combined statistics in four areas: the highest ratios of men to women overall, the highest percentages of single men among all males in the population, the highest percentages of divorced men among all unmarried males in the population and the lowest percentages of married men among all males in the population.

The Top 10 Business Cities

1. LAS VEGAS, NEVADA
   100.6 men to every 100 women
   Population: 164,674

   Take a gamble on Vegas with a career at one of the hotels or casinos on the Strip. A greater proportion of dancers and musicians live here than in any other major city in the U.S. The man you meet here also might be in mining, tourism (Hoover Dam, Lake Mead, Death Valley) or the Air Force. And nice weather is a bonus. Las Vegas is the least rainy major city in the U.S.

2. LONG BEACH/ANAHEIM, CALIFORNIA
96.1 men to every 100 women
Population: 361,334/221,847

Welcome to a whole cluster of southern California cities with real potential. If he's not a high-tech type, the man you meet here may be in oil refining, food processing, aircraft and shipbuilding, or marine research. Or he may be a soldier. Or he may work at Disneyland.

3. ANCHORAGE, ALASKA
107.7 men to every 100 women
Population: 173,017

Look, it's not *that* cold. And the whole state is full of men (112.8-100 overall), making money from defense projects, oil and other natural resources. Alaska has a lot to offer: the fastest job growth in the country (up 94 percent between 1973 and 1983), the highest per capita income in the U.S. (of course the cost of living is also one of the highest in the country) and the highest percentage of residents in the 25-44 age range.

4. SAN DIEGO, CALIFORNIA
104.1 men to every 100 women
Population: 275,741

He could be in aerospace, electronics, shipbuilding or oceanography. He could have something to do with the military and naval bases. San Diego Bay is beautiful almost any time of year. And you can go to the San Diego Zoo on your first date.

5. DENVER/AURORA/COLORADO SPRINGS, COLORADO
100 men to every 100 women (Colorado Springs)
Population: 491,396/158,588/215,150

Here, in the shadow of Pike's Peak, find yourself a man who earned his money in the stock market (livestock, that is). There are ski instructors, military types and your basic businessmen. Aurora is one of the country's youngest cities, with a median age of 26.1 years.

6. PHOENIX, ARIZONA
96.1 men to every 100 women
Population: 789,703

Get yourself a fellow in agriculture, mining, timbering, tourism, the military or one of the various manufacturing industries here. Financial analysts predict employment in Phoenix will grow faster than in any other U.S. metropolitan area this year. And it's the sunniest major city in the country.

7. HONOLULU, HAWAII
97.5 men to every 100 women
Population: 364,048

In the 1820s, you might have met a handsome whaling captain or sandalwood trader in Honolulu. Today you might find an ad man or a banker here in the middle of the Pacific. The biggest industries include manufacturing—sugar, pineapple, clothing, steel, aluminum, oil, cement—plus tourism, transportation and the military.

8. WICHITA, KANSAS
96.1 men to every 100 women
Population: 279,272

Forget the Wichita lineman. Your new love might be connected to the oil refineries, aircraft construction, the nearby Air Force Base or any of the diversified industry here.

9. TULSA, OKLAHOMA
96.1 men to every 100 women
Population: 360,919

Here's your golden opportunity to land an oil man. More than 800 major oil companies (at last count) have plants and offices here. In addition, you can meet men in the aviation-aerospace industry, or at Oral Roberts University.

10. SACRAMENTO, CALIFORNIA
96.1 men to every 100 women
Population: 275,741

It's too late to meet the boys who stopped here at the end of their Pony Express route. But you'll be able to find yourself a gentleman farmer (they're big on agricultural production here) or a nice man in food processing, printing, the military, aerospace or state government (this *is* California's capital city).

Dishonorable Mentions

Special honors go to New York City, where the ratio of women to men is highest (53.37 percent female, or approximately 112.7 women to every 100 men). The runners-up were Yonkers, New York; Jackson, Mississippi; Birmingham, Alabama and Boston. In San Francisco, there are 99.1 men for every 100 women. Unfortunately for the single women of the Golden Gate City, 24 percent of the adult males there identify themselves as homosexual or bisexual. Gay men may be some of our best friends, but they don't make the very best husbands.

Mr. Congeniality Awards:
5 Small Cities with Lots of Men.

1. AMES, IOWA
   111.3 men to every 100 women

   A great place to meet sensitive young veterinarians and husky young farmers.

2. CHEYENNE, WYOMING
   97.2 men to every 100 women

   Find yourself a wealthy cattle baron or someone in oil, chemicals or plastics. Cheyenne's nickname used to be "Hell on Wheels."

3. FARGO, NORTH DAKOTA
   95.7 men to every 100 women

   Big business here: farm implements, fertilizer, meat-packing plants and stockyards.

4. MISSOULA, MONTANA
   96.8 men to every 100 women

This is where you'll find that nature-loving forester (see page 224). Look also for men in lumber, paper milling, beet sugar and the dairy business.

5. RAPID CITY, SOUTH DAKOTA
98.7 men to every 100 women

He'll be a rugged outdoor type, probably in mining, agriculture or lumber. If you don't get lucky, at least you'll get to see Mount Rushmore.

Thank God He's A Country Boy

These are hard times for farmers, with land values shrinking, but many still are doing right well, thank you, ma'am. Looking for the states where people worth half a million or more make up the greatest percentage of the population? North Dakota takes first-place honors, with 24 citizens per 1,000 worth at least that much. The runner-up states are Nebraska, Iowa, Wyoming and Montana.

If that doesn't start you thinking about a new lifestyle in wide open spaces, maybe this will. According to the Census Bureau, there are 134 single men in America's Farmbelt for every 100 single women.

All the farm girls, it seems, want to leave home and move to the city. The men *are* a little unavailable during planting and harvesting seasons. But you know that just gives you more free time to pursue your own interests—and appreciate each other more "off season."

There aren't many cultural differences nowadays. Half of today's farm wives come from nonfarming backgrounds. Take a teaching job somewhere in the heartland. "A good-looking teacher, she doesn't last too long," reports one Montana rancher. "One came last year, and six ranch boys were calling her up. One drove 60 miles to take her out."

Warning: When he tells you how many acres he owns, don't let him see your eyes light up. Wear sunglasses.

International Affairs

Just how far will you go to find a home city where you can be the belle of the ball?

Think twice before applying for a work visa to start a new life overseas. The nations with the best ratios of men to women are as follows:

United Arab Emirates	68.96% male
Qatar	63.62% male
Kuwait	59.62% male
Bahrain	58.38% male

To the best of our knowledge, a single woman would have a hard time getting a visa to enter most of these countries. Anyway how great do you look in veils? The only other country with good stats that we can honestly recommend for American women is

Greenland	54.28% male

True, it's a little chilly in Greenland, but they have a literacy rate of virtually 100 percent, a divorce rate of 2.6 per 1000 (ours is 4.9) and a rate of 35.9% of women participating in the work force. They speak Danish, and 97.8 percent of the citizens are Protestant (primarily Lutheran). Read up on the Vikings before you buy your ticket.

And Now for Something Completely Different

- The "typical" American male is 29.1 years old and earns $31,459 as a professional, administrator or salesman. One out of three American men live in the South.
- There are now 4.9 million divorced men in the U.S., a group that has grown more than 700 percent in the past 45 years.
- Four out of five fathers are present in the delivery room, compared with only one in four a decade ago.
- There is a bachelor boom in America. In 1960, only 23 percent of men ages 25–29 were single. Today, a full 38 percent are still unattached.
- And, no small thanks to *Dynasty*, lots of them have older-woman fantasies.

WHERE THE MEN AREN'T

If a ratio of 95 or 98 men to every 100 women doesn't sound so great to you, then you may not be aware of how bad the ratio can be. Herewith, a sampling of other U.S. cities.

Baltimore, Md.	87.6 men to 100 women
Baton Rouge, La.	91.3 men to 100 women
Billings, Mont.	92.6 men to 100 women
Birmingham, Ala.	84.4 men to 100 women
Boise, Id.	93.3 men to 100 women
Boston, Mass.	89.3 men to 100 women
Burlington, Vt.	83.4 men to 100 women
Cambridge, Mass.	94.6 men to 100 women
Charleston, S.C.	87.5 men to 100 women
Charleston, W.V.	83.3 men to 100 women
Charlotte, N.C.	89.5 men to 100 women
Charlottesville, Va.	88.1 men to 100 women
Cincinnatti, Oh.	85.5 men to 100 women
Chicago, Ill.	90.5 men to 100 women
Cleveland, Oh.	88.4 men to 100 women
Dallas, Tex.	92.8 men to 100 women
Detroit, Mich.	89.8 men to 100 women
Duluth, Minn.	89.7 men to 100 women
Indianapolis, Ind.	90.7 men to 100 women
Jackson, Miss.	86.7 men to 100 women
Kansas City, Kan.	90.1 men to 100 women
Kansas City, Mo.	89.5 men to 100 women
Knoxville, Tenn.	87.9 men to 100 women
Louisville, Ky.	85.7 men to 100 women
Manchester, N.H.	87.8 men to 100 women
Memphis, Tenn.	88.1 men to 100 women
Miami, Fla.	88.0 men to 100 women
Milwaukee, Wisc.	89.9 men to 100 women
Minneapolis, Minn.	88.8 men to 100 women
Nashville, Tenn.	89.5 men to 100 women
Newark, N.J.	86.5 men to 100 women
New York, N.Y.	
Manhattan	88.3 men to 100 women

The Bronx	83.1 men to 100 women
Staten Island	93.1 men to 100 women
Newport, R.I.	91.4 men to 100 women
Omaha, Neb.	90.0 men to 100 women
Philadelphia, Pa.	86.4 men to 100 women
Portland, Ore.	91.7 men to 100 women
Portland, Me.	83.1 men to 100 women
Providence, R.I.	86.2 men to 100 women
Richmond, Va.	83.0 men to 100 women
Salt Lake City, Ut.	93.2 men to 100 women
Santa Fe, N.M.	90.8 men to 100 women
Seattle, Wash.	94.7 men to 100 women
St. Louis, Mo.	81.7 men to 100 women
Terre Haute, Ind.	88.5 men to 100 women
Washington, D.C.	86.1 men to 100 women

Chapter 5

Marrying Down

Just take a moment now to think quietly about Bruce Springsteen. Think about him sliding out from under the car, all greasy and sweaty from the day's work, in his video, *I'm On Fire*. Think about that cute little crooked smile. Then think about him getting all cleaned up at the end of the day and driving to your house to return your newly-repaired car.

Now does the idea of your being attracted to an auto mechanic sound far-fetched?*

Not every terrific man can be found in the executive suite. Many of the mostly male occupations, in fact, are strictly blue collar.

In construction occupations, there are practically no women at all. Men constitute 99.7 percent of all brickmasons, 98.8 percent of all electricians, 98.7 percent of all carpenters and 98.9 percent of all plumbers, pipefitters and steamfitters. They're running all the heavy machinery too—as 98.8 percent of all operating engineers, 98.4 percent of all bulldozer/grader/scraper operators, and 97.6 percent of all crane and tower operators.

A full 97.3 percent of all mechanics and repairers are men, for

---

*OK, we'll admit that the real Bruce Springsteen could buy and sell a town full of real auto mechanics. But love is about fantasies and images too. And Springsteen has done more for the dignity and public perception of the American working man than anyone we can remember.

example. That includes auto and aircraft engine mechanics, auto body repairers and the people who fix everything from small engines to industrial machinery. Then there are the electrical and electronic equipment repairers, an occupational group that's 94.2 percent male. That includes the man who fixes the computers and the copying machines at the office, the telephone installers, line installers and the guy downtown who knows what to do when the Cuisinart refuses to slice mushrooms anymore. Once he's fixed it, show him what a Cuisinart can do. After all, in the land of the blue collar, the way to a man's heart still starts where it always has.

"Men are only good for two things," says a spirited New England newspaper reporter that we know. "Sex and home repairs." And although we don't take her completely seriously (after all, she's one of the few women we know who owns her own quarter-inch drill, and her last big romance was with an art critic), the philosophy has a certain appeal.

Men have been marrying down for centuries, maybe longer. Millionaire executive Cary Grant whisks unemployed Doris Day away for a romantic tryst in Bermuda, buying her mink coats and a new Paris wardrobe along the way. This being one of Doris' virgin movies, you'll recall, she holds out for marriage in the last scene. Dudley Moore as *Arthur* finds the happiness that all his money couldn't bring him by falling in love with waitress/acting student Liza Minnelli. *Love Story's* Oliver Barrett IV elevates Rhode Island baker's daughter Jenny Cavilleri a few giant steps up the social ladder by making her his bride. Of course she doesn't live long enough to enjoy it, and we have to say we're sorry.

In real life, some may raise their eyebrows slightly when successful businessmen choose to spend their evenings with waitresses, manicurists, sales clerks or secretaries, rather than with the women considered their social and intellectual equals. But we recognize a stellar tradition when we see one. When the chorus girl marries the producer, we cheer her on, especially if she really loves him. She's accomplished just what her mother hoped for her.

So let's look at your life realistically. If you have a successful career, if you're paying the rent, buying nice clothes, taking yourself out to dinners and the theater and jetting away for island vacations once or twice a year, do you really need a man for his money? If he's secure enough to handle it, you can always take him out to dinner and buy him overpriced clothes with Italian labels. And when you're both in swimsuits in Barbados, no one will be able to tell whether he's a loading machine operator or an investment banker. Anyway, who cares?

You need intellectual stimulation, you say? "I always thought it was funny when my girlfriends asked how I could talk to Dave on the same level," recalls a New York woman who dated a construction worker for more than a year. "I always wanted to ask them, 'When was the last time you and your husband sat down and discussed Sartre?' I'd just as soon hear about the troubles on the building site as I would the corporate politics in the trust department. In fact, I'd rather."

A blue collar lover or husband won't leave you alone by taking long business trips, won't drag you to corporate parties where you have to play office wife and won't bring his office pressures home. To find him, try these options.

1. Go into construction work yourself. Most specialties don't require brute strength. For information, get in touch with local contractors or with the local office of the U.S. Department of Labor's Bureau of Apprenticeship and Training.

2. Go into repair work yourself. Get in touch with the local office of your state employment service, or write one of these organizations: Automotive Service Industry Association, 444 North Michigan Avenue, Chicago, IL 60611 (auto mechanics, auto body repairers); Computer and Business Equipment Manufacturers' Association, Human Resources, 311 1st Street NW, Washington, DC 20001 (computer and business machine repair); International Union of Electronic, Electrical, Technical, Salaried and Machine Workers, 1126 16th Street NW, Washington, DC 20036 (for industrial machinery repair, among other things).

3. Find an administrative or secretarial job with a construction company, a factory, a utility or another kind of company that employs lots of blue-collar men.

4. The next time your car breaks down, take it around for at least ten estimates.

And if you do decide to "marry down," don't worry so much about money. Electricians earn an average of $16 per hour; plumbers, $15.50; and bricklayers, $14.80. The guys who repair computers have a median income of $430 per week ($22,360 per year), and the top ten percent in the field earn $665 a week or more. That, my dear, is just over $34,000—which is more than many programmers and systems analysts are making these days.

Chapter 6

Do Men Still Marry Their Secretaries?

Why, Miss Jones, you're beautiful.

Derwood Dashing, Executive Vice President for Important Matters at Glamour Conglomerates, was engaged to marry the beautiful but cold Dorrian Debutante when his new secretary, Miss Jones, came to work for him. She was a shy, unassuming young thing, quiet as a mouse and just about as noticeable. She wore thick, horn-rimmed glasses—all the better to take impeccable shorthand and type perfect letters. And she pulled her hair back in a tight, neat chignon—all the better to look professional. Then, one night Mr. Dashing asked her to work late.

Well, you know the rest. She takes off her glasses, lets her thick chestnut hair tumble lovingly over her shoulders and they live happily ever after.

But does that sort of thing still happen, now that *Secret Hearts* comics have disappeared from the stands and women's role in business has changed so dramatically? Yes. And no.

Secretaries have never been so well-paid, so badly needed and so looked down upon.

When Rona Jaffe wrote *The Best of Everything*, no one was surprised that the main character, a recent Radcliffe graduate, would

267

be thrilled with her secretarial job in publishing. That's what nice young women did in the 1950s. But then nice young women also wore little hats and white gloves to the office.

Today Radcliffe graduates go into management trainee programs along with Harvard men, and Princeton women, and Vassar men. There *are* women with master's degrees still sitting at typewriters and reception desks. But for the most part, those jobs are left to women who never considered a formal education beyond high school. And thus a new class-consciousness is born.

"As a rule, the secretarial work will be a waste of time," advises a New York City bank officer, when asked about meeting male bankers on the job. "You're dealing with people who are socially upwardly-mobile. They're going to be interested in marrying 'their own kind'—women recently out of college. She can't be in a clerical position, or she'll be untouchable."

"I've seen it change completely since I was twenty-one and started out as a secretary," reports one woman in her late 30s. "We all did it then. But today you look at the secretaries in our department, and the married ones' husbands are cops and telephone linemen, blue-collar types. And the men in the office would never think of going out with the single ones."

This attitude doesn't exist in every part of the country. A publicity specialist living in Atlanta had been married for eight years to an insurance salesman who was home every evening without fail at 5:15 p.m. Until he announced that he was in love with his 28-year-old secretary. Nothing had happened, he explained, but they were going away that weekend "to see if they were sexually compatible." It is assumed that they were; as soon as his divorce was final, they got married.

They didn't have to "do anything" to fall in love. A man and his secretary, or a woman and hers, have the closest thing to a marriage that exists in the corporate culture. No wonder so many romances begun with "Take a letter, please," were nourished by business trips *à deux* and ended up at the altar.

Only time will tell whether secretaries are able to upgrade their collective image. Organizations like 9 to 5, with its 14,000 members, are working hard to make this happen. Unfortunately, sometimes it seems that it is more realistic to try getting promoted out of secretarial work altogether.

If that's what you're looking for, studies show that small companies, especially manufacturing firms, are most likely to give you a chance. This means real promotions, too, not just a title change to office manager or administrative assistant. Others point out that the real problem with secretarial jobs is their too-close link with the status of the boss, rather than the experience of the secretary or the complexity of her particular duties.

Meanwhile, the job market is wide open and salaries are still rising. According to one estimate, 20 percent of all secretarial jobs go unfilled. The average secretarial salary ranges from $15,548 in the South to $17,784 in the West. Secretaries working for middle management people in large companies average more than $18,200 nationwide. And big-city papers like *The New York Times* often run classified ads for executive secretarial jobs paying $25,000–$28,000 and more.

Occupational growth is continuing, although it's leveled off at about 2.5 million jobs, after tremendous growth over the past decade. The Bureau of Labor Statistics now forecasts average growth (an increase of 29 percent) between now and 1995 in the number of secretarial jobs.

A high school diploma may be all it takes to get started, although formal secretarial training and/or some college background will help. And word processing training not only helps you get hired; it practically guarantees you a higher salary offer.

Secretaries Wanted:

GET THEE TO AN OIL RIG

"I love the pay and the lifestyle," said the woman at the heliport. "I earn more than twice what I did teaching. Also, where else can you find a job where you work seven days and have seven days off?"

A former assistant professor at the University of Oregon, this woman took a secretarial job—but not just any secretarial job. Her office is an oil rig in the Gulf of Mexico off Morgan City,

Louisiana. Her co-workers, approximately 35 of them, include only three other women—and that is considered liberated.

On the first day of every work week, she gets on the helicopter that takes her out to the rig, making stops at several rigs before returning to the heliport. Not long ago, she met a man on the helicopter. He worked on another rig but was on her schedule. They kept running into each other, and now they're going to get married.

You might meet a blue-collar man working on an oil rig. There are roustabouts (entry-level laborers), roughnecks (who operate the machinery), mechanics, electricians, welders and cement mixers. There are computer operators and office clerks. And of course there are caterers; otherwise, the crew would have to bring a suitcase full of ham sandwiches to last through each shift. Engineers don't live on board, but they visit regularly to test the oil and the systems.

It's impossible not to get to know the people you work with here. This is shipboard living without the luxuries or the shuf-fleboard tournament. Alcoholic beverages are absolutely forbidden, since the crew has to be alert at all times in case of storms or other emergencies. Luckily, there's an activity room where you and the boys can play cards and watch tapes of movies on a television monitor.

Of course, secretarial work isn't the only career possibility in this setting. Women reportedly began coming into the off-shore labor force in the mid-1970s, and today are represented in every kind of job, from cementer to engineer. Although major oil companies lease the rigs, most crew members are technically employees of smaller supplier companies instead.

You'll look gorgeous in a hard hat.

For More Career Information:

Professional Secretaries International, 2440 Pershing Road, Suite G10, Kansas City, Missouri 64108; 9 to 5, 1224 Huron Road, Cleveland, OH 44115.

Chapter 7

New Directions Without Changing Careers: Options and Opportunities

What if you're perfectly happy in your career? Then you're either one of the minuscule number of Americans who have always known exactly what they wanted to do. Or you were lucky enough to find your career niche early on.

Nobody is suggesting that you give up a satisfying professional life just to meet prospective husbands and lovers. If you aren't meeting men in your current job, though, there could be a way to change that without turning your life and career upside down.

Just find another subspecialty.

Let's say you're a *public relations account executive* at a medium-sized P.R. firm. Because you handle beauty and fashion industry accounts, you spend a lot of your work day with female executives (who happen to dominate cosmetic and fashion P.R. departments). When you do a media tour or set up a special event, the experts you work with are hairdressers, makeup artists and fashion designers. And whether this makes you guilty of stereotyping or not, you're sure a number of these men are gay. Great friends. No romance.

Then it's time to break out of your own stereotype. If you're a

271

good P.R. woman, you can handle publicity expertly for any kind of client. Make a switch, within this agency or by changing jobs, to handling clients in industries with a larger percentage of available men. Possibilities include an oil company, computer or other high-tech company, financial services or a medical or pharmaceutical account.

You may have some initial trouble making the switch, because of the way the job market works today. It's not that these aren't sought-after specialties. In fact, in a recent *New York Times* classified employment section, 12 of the 20 advertised P.R. jobs that specified a certain background called for financial, medical/scientific and high tech expertise. But your current boss, prospective employers and even the executive search people themselves are bound to argue: "But you've spent the last eight years getting to know everybody in and everything about the cosmetics business. Why do you want to throw that away?" It may be difficult to explain that yes, you *have* met everybody in the industry—and their husbands, and their 2.2 children. That's just the problem.

To make the switch easier, learn everything you can about the new industry in which you want to work. Attend seminars or workshops on the subject, clip newspaper articles about industry trends and even interview some executives in the field. You just might make a job search contact while you're gathering research. And in a month or two, you could find yourself planning a multi-media presentation for a predominantly all-male group of metallurgical engineers or recombinant DNA biochemists.

It can work this way in almost any career. One personnel manager, who had come to the big city in her early 20s, had jobs at a major women's clothing store, the children's book division of a major publisher and a nonprofit art association. She enjoyed the work, got regular promotions and even had a decent social life—thanks to men she met at parties and through her roommates. But it was only when she accepted a similar personnel job at a large teaching hospital that she met the man she married. A soon-to-be heart surgeon, no less.

If you're a *travel agent* and you're sure that, if one more engaged couple comes in to plan their honeymoon you're going to throw a wall rack of Hawaii brochures at them, it's time to make a switch.

Do some investigating and find a way to specialize in singles cruises or Club Med vacations or incentive travel packages (where many of your clients will be male executives.)

If you're an administrative assistant or an accountant or a staff attorney and your current job is on a sewing and crafts magazine, with a business and professional women's foundation, or at an unwed mothers' home, you may want to start composing your letter of resignation. You could be doing the same kind of work in an insurance, engineering or investment banking office instead.

You'll use the same skills, be able to show off the same expertise and enjoy the same workstyle. But the change in your nine-to-five environment can open up all sorts of new possibilities. "When the ratio of men to women changes, everything is different—whether it's at a party or at the office," says a woman who made just such a career switch. "You can feel it in the air."

Chapter 8

Volunteer Jobs (If You Don't Really Have to Work—Or if You Don't Want to Change Careers)

Of course, some women don't have to work at all. Maybe your trust fund keeps you very nicely in white wine, taxi fares and this year's fashions. Rent? Why, the townhouse has been in the family for goodness-knows-how-long.

Maybe the only thought you give to money is when the bank calls every year or so to update your net worth. Maybe you made a million in software development when you were 22, invested the royalties wisely and will soon be listed in *Forbes'* list of the 400 richest Americans.

You poor thing. Where are *you* going to meet a nice man?

The debutante season is over, and everyone else works these days. Even Jacqueline Onassis has a job. On weekdays, you, your grandmother the golfer and the corporate wives are the only people at the country club. (Well, there *is* that darling little tennis pro—but what would the neighbors say?)

Or maybe, like most of us, you do work for a living. And you love what you do. No, you don't want to change careers. And no, you don't want even to change the specialty in which you've built up your reputation and knowledge. But you're tongue-tied at parties, a failure at co-ed health clubs (you just don't feel you're attractive when you're bathed in perspiration) and singles bars make you break out.

All is not lost. There is a way for you to meet men in the dignity and calm of a work setting. Part-time volunteer jobs can be the answer.

No matter where you choose to work, volunteers tend to do the same sorts of things. They answer phones, make calls, answer questions, stuff and lick envelopes, type, file, make coffee, hand out pamphlets and open the mail.

True, these things you'll do for free are all the same things that women have been underpaid to do for decades. But this is different. Most organizations have male volunteers pulling the same duty. And you're old enough now to have a strong sense of identity. Even as you're collating the campaign-promise letters, you realize that tomorrow morning you'll be back managing a $10 million shampoo brand or running a diversified department.

There is a special advantage. Unpaid volunteers can job-hop to their hearts' content, without its looking bad on their employment records. If you don't like the men you're meeting in one place, just move on to the next.

Some possibilities follow.

• *Alumni Associations*. All the members will be college graduates. And all will be hometown boys, in a way.

• *Architectural Preservation Groups*. Someone has to help save Grand Central Station—and the more elegant old buildings in your city. You'll meet architects, urban planners and people rich, bored or interested enough to make time for this sort of thing.

• *Community Action Groups*. Meet the press. Also politicos and lawyers.

• *Hospitals*. Great for meeting doctors and patients. And you're never too old to wear candy stripes.

• *Libraries*. At least you'll know he's literate.

• *Museums*. Reputed to be great pick-up spots. Manning the information desk makes you very visible.

• *Parents Without Partners*. Or a similar group. For meeting divorced daddies. Requirement: at least one child.
• *Parks and Zoos*. Any man who loves animals, nature or both can't be all bad.
• *Political Campaigns*. Meet politicians, lawyers, future politicians and intense people from all walks of life.
• *Professional Associations*. Pick your career. If you want to meet stockbrokers, answer phones at a securities industry association's local office. If you're attracted to bankers, do the same for the local banking association. And so on.
• *Tenants' Groups*. Lawyers, landlords and neighbors. Maybe real estate developers too, if they're threatening to tear your building down.

Tips for making the most of your volunteer career:

- Look your professional best when showing up for work. If you're a bank vice president who's volunteering to type letters and run the Xerox machine on Tuesday and Thursday nights, dress like a bank vice president.
- Stay on the job long enough to really get to know people. Some nice guy that you didn't like at first may grow on you, or vice versa. Remember, if you wanted snap judgments, you'd be looking for men at a bar or disco.
- After a while, vary your schedule. If you're working Sunday afternoons and the perfect man for you only comes in on Saturdays, you may never meet him.
- Don't go out with the first man who asks you. You might be immediately "paired off" in everyone's minds. Go out for a drink or a cup of coffee with groups of co-workers for a while, until you've had a chance to look over the field.
- If you want to ask out a man you've met here, make up a professional excuse. Say you want to interview him for a publication or a research paper you're doing. Or you'd like to meet with him to discuss—allegedly—(a) a panel you'd like him to speak on, (b) an organization you'd like to join, (c) your own career ambitions in his field. Try to make it a nighttime meeting, outside your volunteer-job office. And wear perfume.

Chapter **9**

But Is He Your Type?

What? You've met a wonderful single neurosurgeon, but he can't discuss Proust in as much detail as you'd hoped? Well, who said that doctors had time to read?

You're probably not going to meet a literary genius with a medical degree—or a fabulously wealthy man working on a college campus (unless he inherited the money)—or a famous actor working in the back office of a trucking company—or a trucker working in a hairdressing salon, for that matter.

If the man of your dreams has a specific type of personality, background or paycheck, go looking for him where he's most likely to be found.

THE BEST JOBS FOR MEETING MEN WITH AT LEAST A MASTER'S DEGREE.

College Teaching. He can't even stand in front of a freshman class as a lowly instructor until he has a master's in his subject. And unless he plans to teach only at a junior college level, he'll be at work on his Ph.D. faster than you can say "publish or perish."

Economist. It's just that kind of specialty. To get all but the most basic jobs, even in corporations, he'll need a master's in economics or an M.B.A. Ph.D.'s are common in this field, too.

277

Educational Administrator. A master's is a must for every job, from elementary school principal to district superintendent. And any man with ambition will at least start work on his Ph.D. Meet him by becoming a teacher or by going into administration yourself.

Foreign Service Officer. Only half of all recent appointees held master's degrees, but almost one out of four had graduated from an Ivy League School. Of the same group, more than one in ten had a law degree. Six percent had Ph.D.'s.

Scientist. Employers won't let most of these fellows touch a test tube until they have Ph.D.'s. You could find him on a college campus, at a research institute, or in the research and development department of a large corporation.

NOTE: Doctors do not make this particular list. Emerging from med school able to describe simple conditions polysyllabically in a dead language does not necessarily make for a Renaissance man. As for attorneys, you said you were looking for an educated man—not a pedant.

THE BEST JOBS FOR MEETING ATHLETES

Firefighter. How about an amateur athlete for starters? These all-American heroes have to stay in shape to keep their jobs. And they tend to do it by becoming weekend warriors of one sort or another. If you don't look good in a helmet and hip boots, see page 46 for alternate ways of meeting those men in blue.

Fitness Specialist. If you're after a professional athlete, take a job at a sports training facility in a city that has one or more professional teams. Then your job will be to keep your eye on all those muscles. You could fall in love with your work—literally.

Sportscaster/Sports Writer. The way to an athlete's heart may be through his ego. Your job will be to ask questions and put his name in print or his face on the air. And what better way to get into the locker room?

NOTE: We knew one young woman who took a job as a stadium usher to meet star athletes. She ended up marrying the local sportscaster instead.

THE BEST JOBS FOR MEETING CELEBRITIES

Media escort. Just imagine picking up that handsome actor at the airport, showing him to a waiting car, then driving him to all his interviews while he's visiting your town. If he's on a publicity tour to plug a movie or book, he'll need a local contact. To get yourself started in the business, work with a local media escort/publicity liaison company or establish your own. Then let movie studios, public relations firms and book publishers know that you're available.

Model. We don't know why they're getting all the stars, and we don't like it. We simply point to the evidence: Mick Jagger and Jerry Hall, Keith Richards and Patty Hansen, Billy Joel and Christie Brinkley, Bruce Springsteen and Julianne Phillips. To break into this career, try to be 5'9", 110 pounds, have blue eyes, straight blonde hair and perfect teeth. (At the very least, you might meet a nice dentist while you're having all that cosmetic work done.)

Publicist. Work for a television network, movie studio or outside public relations firm that specializes in entertainment clients. Then you'll be the go-between for the stars, who are your clients, and all those journalists who want interviews and news. P.R. people like to say a lot of their work is "hand-holding." But if Jeremy Irons is your client, who's complaining?

THE BEST JOBS FOR MEETING SEXIST (OR MACHO) MEN

Airline Pilot. These fellows probably can't help being sexist. They've gotten used to the men sitting up front and flying the plane while the "girls" serve drinks and smile prettily. Let's face it, any man who has your life in his hands at 30,000 feet should be given a chance to mend his ways. Admire him, move in with him, then get your commercial pilot's license and raise his consciousness to new altitudes.

Construction Work. Those guys in the hardhats aren't whistling and calling you "baby" so you'll stop for a while to discuss Kierkegaard. Get yourself an apprentice's job in any construction specialty (bricklayer, carpenter, drywall installer, glazier), then play dumb. Try holding your hammer by the wrong end. Whimper when you break a nail. You'll lose your job, but you might get lucky and lose it *after* you've met Mr. Macho.

FBI Agent. Every one of the Bureau's special agents has had firearms training. And all are college graduates, many with law degrees. But then you may want to think twice about marrying a lawyer with a gun.

Firefighter. Many of the dashing young men don't want you on their big red firetruck. They'd rather think of you as a damsel in distress. Humor them. A good man who can think clearly while suffering smoke inhalation is hard to find.

Photographer. Maybe their unfortunate attitudes toward women come from telling beautiful models when and which way to turn their heads—and being obeyed. After you marry him, launch a new project of your own: photographing nude male models for a calendar. There's more than one way to cock a shutter.

THE BEST JOBS FOR MEETING RICH MEN.

Financial planner. The average planner earns $76,200 per year, and at least 15 percent of those in the field earn over $100,000. He may be a self-made man without a college degree, but so was Henry Ford. Bonus: If you're a planner, your average client will be a 43-year-old man who earns at least $80,000.

Health Care. Doctors, who average a net income of $100,000 per year, are tied (with investment bankers) for the title of best-paid workers in the country. Lots of other health care professionals are high on the list, too, including dentists, optometrists, podiatrists, veterinarians and even chiropractors.

Wall Street. Investment bankers reap the highest financial rewards in America's securities industry, but the others are no slouches. If you're looking for a stockbroker, pick one who handles institutional accounts; they earn about twice as much, on the average, as those who work with individual investors. Or consider a romance with a securities trader. If he doesn't burn out before making his first few million, he may retire rich at age 35 and whisk you away to an island paradise. You could learn to handle servants, couldn't you?

FINAL NOTE: Also consider jobs in the oil and gas industry, real estate development, finance and media. According to *Forbes'* annual list of the 400 richest Americans, these are the fields that have produced the greatest number of multi-multi-millionaires. And on the most recent list, 331 of the 400 are men.

Of course, if you've been alone this long, it might be too great a shock to take on a constant companion who's always underfoot. In that case don't even consider going out with a novelist. He'll only leave the house twice a year, if you're lucky, to deposit his royalty checks. But open your mind to the joys of life with an airline pilot, an obstetrician or a traveling sales director, all of whom have highly irregular schedules.

WHERE TO MEET MEN WHO ALWAYS WORK LATE

Educational Administrator. He'll always be at meetings—with the P.T.A., community groups, the board of ed. So you can watch *Dynasty* without his sarcastic comments.

Insurance Salesman. He has to meet with clients over drinks and dinner, when their sales resistance is lowest. When he does, you

282

can just pick up something for dinner—say, a two-pound box of chocolates—on the way home.

Investment Banker. (See travel section below.)

Lawyer. The average attorney works more than 50 hours per week, and goes into the office at least one Saturday per month. That's all the time you need for a meaningful "happy hour."

Musician. (See weekend section below.)

Product Manager. If he ever hopes to run the company (and all product managers do), he'll rarely leave the office before seven p.m. And during marketing plans weeks, Johnny Carson may come into your living room before he does.

WHERE TO MEET A MAN WHO WORKS WEEKENDS

Editor/Reporter. Whether he's helping to put the Sunday morning paper to bed or getting out a weekly newsmagazine, he got used to working weekends long ago. (The only trouble is, with seniority will eventually come a better schedule.)

Firefighter. Accidents and arsonists don't take weekends off, so neither can the local fire department. This gives you the chance to watch as many consecutive movies as you want.

Musician. When do you think they hold all the weddings and Bar Mitzvahs he plays at? Or the greatest number of concerts, rock or classical? Many musicians work at night as well as weekends and holidays, so you could be married for years without learning what time he likes to eat dinner.

Police Officer. Same as for firefighters. He may draw weekend duty, night duty or both. Crime never takes a holiday.

WHERE TO MEET A MAN WHO TRAVELS A LOT

Airline Pilot. He'll probably only log 18 hours a week or so of actual flying time, but he has to rest between flights, jetting home. It may be painful to imagine him spending layovers (an unfortunate term) with a bevy of flight attendants in Paris or L.A. If it is any compensation, his travel privileges will be treating you to near-free vacations for the rest of your married life.

Buyer. That "made in U.S.A." label has gotten pretty rare, so buyers for all kinds of goods tend to spend a lot of time in the Far East. At the very least, he'll be leaving town for trade shows all the time.

Investment Banker. One executive in this field reported the following during a two-month period: five round-trips from the East to West Coast, 16 business-related meals and 21 all-night work sessions at the office.

Meeting Planner. Better double-check before making an emotional commitment. Many planners are constantly on the road, but he might have a job in which he only plans one or two big meetings a year. In that case, he'll be living in your house the rest of the time, making all sorts of unpredictable demands.

Photographer. If he's a sports photographer, be glad that football, basketball, hockey and baseball seasons all blend together nowadays. If he's a fashion photographer, be glad that some of the top models today are only 14 years old and chaperoned by their mothers. His brain may sometimes seem to be in his zoom lens, but his darkroom will keep him home but out of the way.

Sales Rep. Make sure he has a wide sales territory. Otherwise, he might drive back home most nights.

WHERE TO MEET A MAN WHO'S NEVER HOME

Doctor. From his residency days onward, he'll sleep at the hospital at times. And you can rest assured that he's much too tired to be unfaithful. Obstetrician-gynecologists and all kinds of surgeons are good bets. Do not make the mistake of marrying a dermatologist. He will be home so often it may give you hives.

If all else fails, try a *commuter marriage.* You live in Washington, D.C., he lives in Dallas and you visit each other on major holidays. Or *you* can take a job that demands enormous amounts of travel. After enforced intimacy and the rigorous demands of today's relationships, nothing will restore you to mental health faster than a spacious hotel room with just you, a terrycloth robe, a club sandwich from room service and a Cary Grant movie on TV.

Chapter 11

Meeting Him Away From the Office: Optional Approaches

She was an accountant for a television station in Manhattan. He was an English professor at a college in New Jersey. They probably never would have met, were it not for the commuter train system.

They met the way couples always did in 1930s movies. It had something to do with passengers nearby playing Trivial Pursuit, a long line in the bar car, a misunderstanding with the conductor over tickets and probably a great deal of luck. It just proves that meeting a man through work, directly or indirectly, doesn't have to mean finding him at the office.

Commuting:

How to Meet a Man on a Train

Meryl Streep and Robert DeNiro met on a commuter train in the 1984 movie, *Falling in Love*. Even the film's final scene took place on the train.

In a way, commuter trains are like extensions of the office. Everyone is dressed for business and has to be there. And everyone arrives

286

at about the same time every day, so you see the same faces on the 8:14 week after week, month after month, often year after year.

If you've recently moved to a suburb or started a new job, you might want to try different train schedules every few days for a while, until you've spotted a man or men who interest you. Then start taking the same train every day, until you've seen each other often enough to feel free to say hello.

"It's easier to meet men on the afternoon trains going home," says one female commuter. "Then the work day is over, everybody wants to loosen up, some even have a drink." The bar car *is* one of the friendliest parts of the suburban railroad system.

Drawback: A vast majority of men on commuter trains will be married. Still, some separated or divorced men do take apartments in the suburbs, perhaps to be closer to the kids on weekends or just because the setting is familiar.

What if you live right in the city, five blocks from your office? Try visiting your married sister and her family on weekends. That will give you the Friday night and Monday morning trains to scout out new possibilities.

Car pools also can be good places to get to know men on the way to and from work. Try changing car pools every six months or so. Then just let friendships develop naturally.

Subways do not work. As long as they arrive every three minutes or so, you can never be sure of being on the "same" train every day. And it's difficult to make friends with a man while standing with his elbow in your eye and his briefcase hardware pulling runs in your pantyhose.

After Hours:

Meeting Him at His Favorite Watering Hole

Have you got your heart set on meeting a successful lawyer? In Chicago, look for him at Ambria, Le Perroquet or Nick's Fishmarket. In Boston, check out Anthony's Pier 4 or Legal Seafoods. In New York, try Lutéce, The Four Seasons, Tavern on the Green or Windows on the World. That's where they take clients to lunch or dinner, according to a survey of 8,000 attorneys by the *ABA Journal* (published by the American Bar Association).

If you're in Philadelphia, check out Bookbinder's or Le Bec Fin. Or if an advertising or P.R. man is more your style, head for Bogart's. To meet bankers or other "East Coast WASPs," wrote Ben Harte in *Frequent Flyer*, have a drink at the Barclay Hotel on Rittenhouse Square. If you were looking for the same sort of bankers in Honolulu, you'd be most likely to find them at Arthur's. And according to one Manhattan-based lending officer, nearly all New York bankers go to the Oak Room at the Plaza.

Hangouts for various professions and occupations can change rapidly. Restaurants and bars open and close before our eyes. But if you'd feel comfortable meeting the man of your choice when he's having a business lunch or stopping for a drink after work, it won't be hard to determine where he and his crowd go.

Proximity is almost always the key. If you think it would be fun to date a reporter, for instance, just locate the local newspaper office. Then take a walk to the bars within a two-block radius. It won't take long to find at which one (or two) the journalistic set congregates. Then you can make it your own special place.

Rules: Don't go alone, unless you're exceptionally good at this sort of thing. Do ask a friend, male or female, to meet you there— but always arrange to get there ten or fifteen minutes ahead of time. Wear business clothes to establish acceptability. Carry a book, preferably a hardcover, to get their attention. Who knows? That good-looking reporter across the way might have written it.

Business Trips:

How to Meet a Man on a Plane or in a Hotel

Have we got a group of guys for you!

Almost all of them are business managers or professionals. They have an average household income of $109,300. More than one out of ten is a millionaire. And more than one out of three is top management—a company president, chairman or owner. One out of four sits on at least one board of directors. A full 93 percent are college-educated. And the majority of them take 20 or more airline roundtrips per year, almost exclusively on business. They're the nation's *Frequent Flyers* according to a poll by the magazine of the same name.

The number of women business travelers has increased in recent years, but the friendly skies are still a man's world. In 1981, TWA estimated that 11-12 percent of its business travelers were female, but only three percent of its *frequent* business travelers were women. And a full 92 percent of the airline's Ambassadors Club members were men.

And that's as good a place as any to start. If you're flying on business, join at least one airline club. It gives you various privileges, the most important of which is use of the private club lounges in airports around the country or around the world. You can get away from the crowds, have a drink (often free), do some reading, make telephone calls and—most important—find yourself surrounded by male business travelers.

Try to fly First Class or at least Business Class whenever possible. That's where you'll find most of the male executives you'd like to meet. If your employer won't pick up the tab for more than the economy fare, it might be worth it to pay the difference yourself. Joining the airlines' frequent flyer programs can sometimes help. On Delta, for instance, members can upgrade an economy ticket to First Class for just $10-$30 each way.

Dress like a businesswoman—to prove you're one of the boys. Get some work done on the plane; 80 percent of frequent flyers say that they do. In fact, nine out of ten travel with pocket calculators and almost half take along dictation machines when they fly. One way to get a man's attention, in fact, is to pull some new electronic gadget out of your briefcase. He can ask you about it as his opening line, and let the conversation go from there. Best bets: personal computers, and attaché cases with unusual gadgetry built in.

Meeting men at hotels can get a little sticky. Prostitutes do work most business hotels, and it's easy to be mistaken for one if you're too friendly—particularly in hotel bars. If you're attending a formal conference or convention, do wear that awful nametag everywhere. It's literally your badge of respectability. So is drinking and dining with a group of co-workers, preferably co-ed, and asking another man or group of men to join you.

Stick to meeting on planes. In fact, to meet the cream of the executive crop, try taking the Eastern shuttle which runs hourly between New York's LaGuardia Airport and Washington, DC. According to journalist Peter Davis, writing in *Esquire*, the 8:00 a.m. flight is the Power Shuttle. "Assistants and managers take the 7:00; C.E.O.'s and senators take the 9:00 or 10:00. . . . The action is on the first section of the 8:00."

Davis talked to an investment banker, a telephone industry lawyer, a developmental psychologist, a P.R. man, a computer executive, two Treasury agents and a television producer, among others, on one flight. One of the flight attendants had married a Secret Service agent she'd met on this route.

When Davis tried counting and categorizing the passengers, he got as far as 77 white males, six white females, four black males, one black female and four Japanese males. "You are surrounded," shrugged a middle management woman in a gray suit. The official count was 169 passengers, of which 163 were males.

Let's hear it for the wings of man.

Chapter 12

Sizing up a Company's Man Supply

A lot of terrific men work in a lot of different corporations, and you may want to check out the supply—and its general quality—before formally accepting a job. Or you can do the same sort of research in those first few crucial weeks of work.

Initial Spying: Before the Interview

You have a job interview scheduled. The executive search firm or the company itself has given you the address, date and time. But don't wait until the day of the interview to go there.

At lunchtime or at the end of the work day, when plenty of people are sure to be streaming in and out of the building, go to that address and do some serious man-watching. If you live in a walking city, just stroll there, stop in the lobby or right outside the main door and pretend you're waiting for someone. Otherwise, drive to the building and do the same. Try to be discreet if possible; make your observations from the driver's seat. In any event, look your best (in business clothes, just in case you're spotted) and glance down impatiently at your watch now and then to maintain the ruse.

What you're looking for is quantity, primarily. How many appear to work there? How old are they? Who are their lunch dates—

women, other men, large groups? How do they seem to relate to their co-workers? You probably can't tell if the men are married or single without getting a lot closer to their ring fingers, but you can tell something about how they relate to the women they work with. Just try to read their body language.

This is a good time to size up the competition too. Do there seem to be a lot of executive women, or do the majority appear to be clerical workers? How old are they, how do they relate to the men around them and how do they dress? In fact, if you're feeling a little uncomfortable about this reconnaissance mission, keep in mind that this is dress-for-success research, too. You're just checking out the corporate culture and the company dress code so that you'll be sure to wear the right thing at the interview.

At the Job Interview

Job search experts will warn you: never arrive more than five minutes early for an interview. However, being late for the interview is a crime often punishable by unemployment, so do leave your home or office far earlier than normal. Then, if you don't run into traffic gridlock or a blizzard, you'll have some time to kill in and around your destination.

Take a walk or a drive around the block. Stroll into the nearest newstand, drug store or coffee shop. Whatever you do, don't stop into the nearest bar. Even worse than your turning up at the interview with white wine on your breath is the possibility of being spotted by the head of personnel or your future boss who has snuck down there to fortify him/herself for the ordeal of meeting and judging you.

While you wait (briefly, we hope) in the reception area, keep your eyes open for male employees and male business visitors coming in and out. Look busy, of course, scribbling in your appointment book or going through some papers. But look up now and then to check things out. After all, each time you look up, you expect it to be the person with whom you have the appointment.

During the First Week at Work

Once you've taken the job, you have some time to relax and look more carefully at the environment you've gotten yourself into. And there are numerous opportunities for man-watching (most of which can fall under the guise of do-it-yourself employee orientation): the personnel department, where you'll have to fill out all those benefits forms; the company cafeteria and/or executive dining room; even the elevators.

If a coffee wagon makes the rounds every day, making several stops per floor, be mobile at those times of day. That way, you can find yourself standing in line with a different crowd each time. (If you're working for one of those misguided companies in which all the male executives have their female secretaries stand in line for coffee and doughnuts, take another approach. This is the one time the office doors are unguarded. Poke your head in, pretending to be looking for somebody else.)

Finally, do not hesitate to have your photo taken for the employee newspaper or bulletin board. We honestly know of a man who was reading the company paper, saw a photo of a new female employee whose looks appealed to him and picked up the phone. "My friend and I have a bet," he began, "that, with your rosy cheeks, you come from Ohio." Well no, she was from New Jersey, and this was the corniest line she'd heard since college. But what the heck, she married him anyway.

Honorable Mention:

Companies that Throw Their Employees Together

According to *The 100 Best Companies to Work For in America*, the best employee parties in the country are given by Advanced Micro Devices, Leo Burnett Advertising, Hewlett-Packard, Odetics, Tandem Computer and Time Inc. Some other corporations, however, offer just the right ambiance and opportunities for you to turn a handsome co-worker into something more.

• *DuPont* (that's E.I. Du Pont de Nemours of Wilmington, Delaware, and points west) has a U.S. work force of 100,000. Nearly

7,000 of those employees are married to each other. Maybe that's happened because Du Pont people tend to socialize with each other—at their country clubs, in particular, where they can play golf, tennis or dive into one of several pools. So you can see right away how all those engineers and chemists look in swimsuits.

• *IBM* employees spend a lot of off-hours time in each other's company too. And if they move you to a new city often enough, you're sure to find someone you like.

• *Procter & Gamble* is known more for its marketing expertise than for great company picnics. Yet a significant number of P&G employees end up side by side at the altar. Some say it's the intensity of the work experience that does it.

If you're young enough (or theatrical enough), consider a full-time or summer job at one of the *Walt Disney* theme parks. If the kind of guy you're looking for talks and dresses like one of the Johnny Mann Singers, this is the place to be. There are 8,000 young or youngish "cast members," dressed up like Mickey and Minnie Mouse, Goofy, Donald and all the rest. And according to inside reports, many of the cast members end up marrying each other in real life. Your location choices: Disneyland (Anaheim, California) or Disney World (Orlando, Florida).

There are good social opportunities, even if you take a more standard kind of corporate job at the Disney Studios in Burbank. The Mickey Mouse Activity Center there arranges employee trips, sports teams and tournaments.

Some companies just don't go in for old-fashioned company picnics, team sports, special events or much of anything besides a half-hearted office party at Christmas. And in some corporations, only the clerical and production level employees participate. If you find yourself working for that kind of employer, beat the system by instituting events on your own.

One of the safest methods is to suggest something with a real purpose—a farewell party for a departing department member, or an anniversary dinner for the man who's worked there for 20 years. If you have a secretary or assistant, make him or her the organizer. If not, you'll have to do it yourself. Then make it the biggest success possible, so others will follow your lead.

Chapter 13

How to Handle Dating at Work

When one corporation discovered that two employees were having a romance, they called them to a secret meeting in a public park. Someone must have seen too many spy movies.

When a Texas police department suspected that two officers (one male and one female) had become romantically involved, they rented an apartment across the street from the man's apartment in order to spy on them, assigning four detectives to the "case."

When a female marketing manager at IBM fell in love with a co-worker and he left to join a competing firm, the company demanded that she end the relationship or be fired. Their reasoning: she might reveal company secrets to him. Oddly, the company allowed him to continue playing on the IBM softball team.

Meeting a fabulous man at work is only the beginning of your love story. No woman should consider dating a co-worker, however, until she's taken a realistic look at the situation's possible pitfalls and given some thought to just how she plans to deal with them.

Office romances aren't new, but they have changed and multiplied in recent years as more women have entered the work force, particularly at the managerial level. There are strong opinions on both sides of the issue. And the rules, from informal corporate policies to legal decisions, are being made and changed as we go along. The courts appear to be on the side of lovers and the rights to privacy.

• *Legal decision:* "Dating an employee of a rival company is not a ground for firing."

The former female IBM marketing manager won $300,000 in damages for emotional distress. IBM had alleged a conflict of interests. A California state appeals court considered its action a breach of contract, because it violated IBM's stated policy of noninterference in employee's personal lives.

• *Legal decision:* "A company cannot be sued for negligence if it fails to stop an illicit affair."

A woman whose husband had divorced her to marry a co-worker sued his employer, U.S. Steel, for allowing it to happen. The court ruled that a company has no obligation to monitor its employees' private lives.

On the other hand, the two police officers who were spied on by their own department were forced to give up their careers. At first, both were temporarily suspended, and the man was demoted from sergeant to patrolman—after 13 years with the force. Finally, conditions at work became so unpleasant that the couple turned in their resignations.

• *Legal decision:* The Supreme Court refused to hear the case, upholding a lower court ruling that said the police department had not violated the couple's right to privacy.

"So the Supreme Court hasn't yet decided on your right to romance," summarized ABC-TV correspondent Sylvia Chase in reporting on the case, "but this area of law is changing daily, as more employees challenge companies' rights."

Other cases involving office liaisons are still in litigation.

Company Policy

Many corporations have reversed their positions on employee dating and marriages, if only because they're afraid they might lose good employees otherwise. Other companies have always felt employees personal lives are their own business, even when it involves dating a co-worker. "It's none of our business," says the editor of a metropolitan newspaper. "That is all kid's stuff. We feel that our staffers are adults."

"All but the most conservative companies choose not to interfere, as long as the affair isn't hurting performance," summarizes the president of the American Society for Personnel Administration (A.S.P.A.).

Of 547 corporations that responded to an A.S.P.A. survey in late 1984, more than half (58 percent) said they were relaxing rules about hiring and placing spouses and other close relatives. As for couples working for the same company who choose to live together, 265 companies reported that they ignore such arrangements, rather than risk being charged with violations of the employees' rights to privacy. (Of course that leaves 282 corporations that might step in and take action.)

Corporate paternalism is alive and well. A New York banker reports that when two employees there decide to make it legal, one has to resign. If an exception is made, it will only come after one employee has, in essence, asked the company for the other's hand in marriage. "It's so very feudalistic," he laughs. "It's like getting the approval of your 'lord' before you can get married."

Companies that oppose inter-office dating have a point, of course. Office love affairs do complicate things, spark jealousies and sometimes lower productivity. "A love relationship constitutes a threat to business," says Eliza Collins, a senior editor of the *Harvard Business Review* whose 1983 article on the subject is considered the Bible for those opposed to office affairs. And one study showed that, in ten percent of all such situations, one partner in the romance was fired—usually the woman.

But the reverse of the situation is that, in nine out of ten cases, no one was fired. And in many cases, employee productivity actually goes up. "There's a good argument to be made for an increase in the couple's competence," offers psychologist Arthur A. Witkin. "In responsible employees, an office romance can cause increased excitement about work."

Or as Helen Gurley Brown put it back in 1970, "Managements who think romances lower the work output are right out of their skulls. A girl in love with her boss will knock herself out seven days a week and wish there were more days. . . . A girl with a crush on any co-worker jumps for joy at having to work overtime with him." (Historical note: The word "girl" often was used to describe females of all ages in an earlier era.)

All in the Family

To many people, the work organization is like a family. It has its own culture, structure, values and codes of behavior. Self-help articles point out that you may see the boss as your mother or father—and may recreate your family role (as the smart older child or the bratty kid sister) at work. And if the office equals family, then office romance equals incest.

"Yes, a lot of people do see it that way," agrees New York psychologist R.D. Banner. "That's why a lot of employees feel betrayed and genuinely shocked when they find out you're sleeping with the boss. You're sleeping with *Daddy*. But, for heaven's sake, that's their psychological fantasy, not reality." And if magazine articles can teach us how not to act like the bratty kid sister, surely they can remind us all that corporations and families are very different structures. If fellow employees find it less upsetting when you date a man from another department or another company location, rather than a close co-worker, maybe that's because he's more like a distant cousin. And that's just aristocratic intermarrying, a lesser crime than incest.

Certainly your life would be simpler if you could meet your future mate at a church social or be introduced by mutual family friends at Thanksgiving dinner. But some of us fare better with the opposite sex when we have time to get to know a person before one or both of us has to decide on the other's desirability.

A good job may be hard to find, but good men are even scarcer. And you probably didn't plan to work for one company for 20–30 years anyhow. Ideally, your marriage will last at least that long.

Office romances are serious business, however. To give both your relationship and your career the best possible chances for survival and growth, consider these guidelines.

THE FRINGE BENEFITS RULES
FOR OFFICE ROMANCE

1. *Be very, very discreet.*

   As much as possible, spend your evenings together at home—yours or his. When you do go out, try to choose restaurants or theatres outside the office neighborhood and/or outside the usual tastes of your co-workers. Bring props with you. If your table is strewn with papers, reports and computer print-outs, the co-workers who catch you are more likely to believe that you're meeting for business purposes. This method probably will not be totally convincing, however, at a disco or a champagne picnic in the park.

   Taking a vacation together can be a dead giveaway. If you both ask for the first two weeks in July and announce separately that you're finally going to see Venice, you're just asking to be caught.

   Two consumer products company employees almost got away with it, because they worked in separate departments (art and information services) and no one had noticed. Then each was approached individually by their department reporters for the company newspaper and asked about any recent personal news. When the next month's issue came out, announcing several paragraphs apart that each had "recently spent the first two weeks of July in romantic Venice, Italy," friends quickly put two and two together. They might as well have been in the *National Enquirer*. The romance fizzled shortly afterward, she left the company, and nobody is talking.

   Solution: She should have taken off the first two weeks in July and had him take off the second and third week of that month. She could have flown to Paris, spent a week there, then taken the Orient Express to Venice. Meanwhile, he'd have flown to Rome or Milan, then taken a train or rented car to meet her in their room overlooking the Grand Canal. The resulting employee newspaper items about her July vacation in Paris and his in Milan would have looked much less suspicious, and they might be together today.

2. *Be very, very choosy.*

Do not go out with every man in your company. If you say no because you're not sure you're interested, you can always change your mind next week or next month. You have time to get to know him better, through office contact and drinks or lunch with a whole group from the office. The worst thing for your career and your office reputation is to "date around."

Breaking this rule didn't seem to keep the young woman mentioned in our section on lawyers (page 77) from her goal. Although a co-worker reports that she slept with several attorneys in her office, and virtually everyone in the office knew about it, she ended up marrying one of them.

Another young woman tried bed-hopping with co-workers and now regrets it. "It was my first job, I was 22, living in the city and feeling I'd just been let out of prison into the grown-up world," the woman recalls. "During the year and a half I was there, I had brief affairs with three men. Luckily, they were all in different departments, so I don't think they ever knew about each other. But my boss became aware of it, and I think it had a lot to do with his opinion of me as very young and flighty and out for a good time, not serious about my work."

She was fired from that job under unusual circumstances. "For some reason that I couldn't understand, I was always being excluded from the design meetings that were held in Los Angeles. My boss would go and my boss's boss. If the meeting was in New York, Chicago or Washington, then I'd be invited too." If it was in L.A., however, she was always given a reason requiring her to stay behind. Finally, she was given a chance to attend a West Coast meeting, but was told up front that she couldn't take a room at the Bel Air, where both her supervisors always stayed. "It's full," her boss informed her curtly. "Ask the travel department to put you in the Beverly Hills instead."

She went, but just before the next Los Angeles trip, her boss gently asked her to resign. In a closed-door meeting, he told her that his boss, a married man, was having an affair with a woman that he always met at the Bel Air. And he admitted that that was exactly the reason they hadn't wanted her along on the L.A. trips.

"I was furious," she recalls. "For years, I saw it as discrimination against me because I was young and female. They didn't think I should be 'allowed' to know. As time passed, though, I realized that it was my behavior that led them to treat me that way. Anyone who ran her own personal life as casually and openly as I did couldn't possibly be trusted with somebody else's secrets." Today this woman says she'll go out with a co-worker only if she thinks he has the potential to be the love of her life.

Even when the right man comes along, and you know it, take your time. Find reasons to be together for business purposes, yes, but be sure you're both sincerely interested before turning that important corner.

3. *Act like a virgin.*

You have never had a better excuse to say no to a man (even if you very badly want to say yes). Just explain that, while he's becoming very important to you, your career also is important and you're afraid that having casual sex with a friend from the office wouldn't be a good idea. If and when you both agree that there's nothing casual about it, do what you will.

Despite the double standard, even men can get a "bad reputation" for too many in-house conquests. One male personnel director had flings with several secretaries, including one in his own department. Unfortunately for him, she fell in love with him. And when she realized that these deep feelings weren't reciprocated, she became so emotionally distraught—and so visibly enamoured—that she was politely but firmly encouraged to seek employment elsewhere, and he lost a good deal of esteem.

The secretary wasn't the only person hurt in this incident, however. For years, the personnel director had been groomed for the V.P.'s spot. When the position became open, about six months after the aforementioned affair, top management passed him over and hired from outside instead. He left the company within the year.

Oddly enough, the business world doesn't seem to object to one-night stands nearly as vehemently as they do to true love. Boys will be boys, the old men in the executive washroom say with a smile. One-nighters are not the best idea, however, in cases where you think it's an out-of-town fling and he thinks it's the first act of *Romeo and Juliet*. Rule of thumb: When you drink, don't flirt. When you flirt, don't drink.

4. *Consider the organization chart.*

The biggest difference between 1950s and 1980s office affairs is that most of today's couples are peers, not male boss and female secretary. Two Level 6 managers dating each other probably have a relationship based on equality and common interests.

The ideal situation is a romance between two people in departments or divisions that have little or no contact. Such a relationship can break a lot of the other rules and still be tolerated by the company. A female publicity manager and a male R&D executive met at a company sports event and fell in love. Both were married to other people. The publicity manager divorced her husband. The R&D man left his wife and children. The couple moved in together, made no secret of their affair and continued to work for the same company for several more years.

"Sure, people gossiped about it a little, but that's all," a former co-worker recalls. "They were just accepted as a couple. But it helped a lot that none of us in publicity ever had much direct dealing with R&D. The two of them even worked in separate office buildings, almost an hour's drive apart." And they lived happily ever after. Twelve years later, they are still together and have advanced in their careers.

Falling in love with someone you work closely with every day can be a different matter. If you find yourself attracted to your supervisor—or to a man even higher up—understand that power may be part of his appeal. If he serves as your career mentor, that's wonderful. You may learn a great deal about the business through him.

But no matter what your personal relationship may be, he's still the boss at the office. To ignore that or try to change it could endanger the relationship and, perhaps worse, arouse the suspicions of co-workers.

If you're the boss and are interested in dating your male assistant, secretary or other subordinate, he has to be willing to respect your title and responsibilities at work. If other employees even suspect the relationship, you could stand accused of an abuse of power or even of sexual harassment.

Let's say you're attracted to a male subordinate and *you* make the moves to turn your professional relationship into something sexual. He seems perfectly happy about the idea and the two of you become a hot item. But what if he honestly feels he can't turn you down without jeopardizing his job? "Men have done things for years because they feel women have pressured them into it," one businessman points out. "There's nothing new about that. What's new is that more women have power at the *office* than before, and they can be just as guilty of power plays and sexual politics as men."

A man charging a female boss with sexual harassment may sound like a cartoon situation to you, but keep this in mind: the courts say you can be guilty, even if he seems to be ready and willing.

• *Legal decision:* "Employees who give in to the sexual advances of supervisors do not forfeit their right to compensation under the Civil Rights Act of 1964.... Even though a victim voluntarily submits to the advances of a supervisor, the real issue is where her (or his) toleration of his (or her) conduct was a condition of employment." (A U.S. district court ruling, upheld by an entire U.S. appeals court.)

5. *Break Up with Him First.*

If you see that the relationship is going nowhere or has insurmountable problems, summon up the courage and end things in as civilized a manner as possible. Psychologists say women often avoid taking this step, letting men do the dirty work when it comes to saying goodbye.

"I knew he didn't want me anymore," one woman recalls of an affair with a department head. "I could tell from the last few times we'd been together. But I felt desperate, so I'd find reasons to go into his office for closed-door meetings or to hang around the secretaries' desks in his department, just so he'd see me. I called him constantly, which I know made his secretary suspicious. I ended up just making a fool of myself, and it hurt worse because I was sure everybody knew I'd been dumped."

The advantage in your making the break is that, with your pride intact, you may find it easier to stay on civil terms with him at the office. Keep your emotional distance from him, but don't stop speaking. You'll find it uncomfortable seeing him every day, but it won't kill you—and you will get over it. Both of you will.

Whether your title is executive secretary or executive vice president, whether you're just beginning an office romance or getting over one, one of the worst mistakes you can make is to let your work suffer. Part of your responsibility as a participant in a workplace-based affair is to give your company its fair share of your time, effort and mental energy. You're being paid to do a job, and you're on the line to prove to others that you're doing it efficiently, objectively and well.

But what if you'd love to have the kind of trouble this chapter has described? You've spotted an interesting man at the workplace, but he doesn't seem to have spotted you. "Don't just ask him out," one psychologist warns. "Most men still don't react well to direct social invitations from women. He may go, but he also very well may never reciprocate. Most men still like to believe they discovered you, instead of the other way around."

What you can do is ask him to a meeting—and insist on scheduling it at opportune times. "When we got assigned to work on the project together, he couldn't understand why I had to set up every meeting for five o'clock or five thirty," interior design specialist Jean Barrett laughs. "I just kept telling him that I was very tightly scheduled and anything else was impossible. But it finally worked. We'd start to end the meetings with a drink, then with dinner and so on." They moved in together six months after the first meeting and were married two years later.

If he has any Yuppie tendencies at all, try to impress him with your credentials, career future and earning power—not just your perfume. Leave your Stanford diploma lying around. Excuse yourself from meetings by announcing that you have to call your broker.

If he tends to work late, do the same. There's nothing like sunset over a row of empty offices to inspire a friendly chat. This is the time of day when executives often do their own Xeroxing; the copy room is a fine and private place to talk. Offer to pick up coffee or a sandwich for him while you're downstairs getting yours. Spend your overtime dinner allowances together.

If he has drinks after work at a certain nearby bar, start showing up there too (always in a group). Even if he's with five other co-workers, you can go up and say hello to one of them. Stay just long enough to be noticed, then rejoin your table. Next time, you can sit down for a while. Just remember that all of this has to stop once the relationship has been established. Then it's time to be discreet and keep all the other rules for office romances in mind.

Even if everything goes wrong, of course, you still could have a happy ending. When Mary Cunningham was fired from her executive job at Bendix because of an alleged affair with the company's chairman, things must have looked bleak. But she got more job offers than she could count, wrote a book to tell her story and still married the guy. (She does insist, however, that the relationship began only after she left Bendix.)

The worst thing that has happened to Mary Cunningham, it seems, is that she's doomed to be mentioned in every book, article or dissertation ever written on the subject of office romance. That probably won't happen to you.

Chapter 14

Is There an Office Romance in Your Future?

Just how much opportunity for meeting men does your present job offer? It all depends—not only on your occupation, but on the opportunities in and around your workplace. To find out, answer the ten questions below as accurately and honestly as possible.

1. The percentage of men in the work force of your company is about:

   (a) 0-30%
   (b) 31-79%
   (c) 80-99.9%

2. At the business-lunch restaurant nearest your office, the percentage of tables usually occupied by an all-male group is:

   (a) 0-20% (one out of five tables at most)
   (b) 25-50% (one of every two or three tables)
   (c) 51% + (there are always more men than women eating there)

NOTE: Deduct two points if the best restaurant near your office is Burger King.

306

3. The last time you got into an elevator at work, most of the passengers with you were:

   (a) other women
   (b) men wearing T-shirts, jeans and messengers' caps
   (c) men in business suits

NOTE: Deduct two points if your building has no elevator.

4. How many possible ways could you get to work, if you felt the need for variety?

   (a) car only
   (b) one kind of public transportation (train or bus only, for instance)
   (c) at least two methods of public transportation

BONUS: Give yourself two extra points if it's possible to reach your workplace by train, bus, ferry and car pool. Add five points if your commute is 45 minutes or longer.

5. Write down the names of ten co-workers, male or female, at random. How many of them appear to be happily married?

   (a) 0-2
   (b) 3-5
   (c) 6-10

NOTE: Deduct five points if there aren't enough employees in your company to come up with the names of ten co-workers.

6. In your present career, how many professional associations exist for both women and men in your occupation? And if you can't accurately answer this question, do your homework. You're probably overlooking an untapped source of men.

   (a) None
   (b) 1
   (c) 2 or more

BONUS: Give yourself two extra points if your company is willing to pay the dues.

7. If you decided to take a seminar or evening course related to your work, your company would:

    (a) wish you well, but not shell out a penny
    (b) pay partial tuition
    (c) foot the entire bill

8. When it comes to fitness for its executives, your employer:

    (a) isn't interested—or, at the most, has an all-male softball team
    (b) at least contributes to the cost of a nearby health club
    (c) runs a company gym

9. Write down the names of the last five people outside your company (clients, suppliers, professional colleagues, etc.) with whom you've had meetings. How many were men?

    (a) None
    (b) 1-3
    (c) 4 or 5

BONUS: Give yourself two extra points if any of the meetings with men were held at the end of the work day.

10. The last time you set off on a business trip, you went:

    (a) by car
    (c) by plane on an average commercial flight
    (c) on the Eastern shuttle between New York and Washington, DC.

NOTE: Deduct two points if you went by air, but the plane was at least half-filled with happy families and/or noisy vacationers. Give yourself five extra points if your employer sends you First Class. If you have never been on a business trip, deduct two points.

SCORING

Give yourself 5 points for every "A" answer, 10 points for every "B" and 15 points for every "C". Be sure to add in your bonus points and deduct points where necessary.

40-75 points: *Executive Wallflower*
If you haven't missed your local television station's *Saturday Night at the Movies* in five years, it's no wonder. You aren't meeting anybody. Take a career aptitude test and hope you come out in the 98th percentile for engineering. Of if you're completely happy in your present work, at least take a volunteer job at the hospital.

76-135 points: *Bridesmaid Revisited*
Well, you've probably met an interesting man at work once or twice— but you're not getting nearly enough workday exposure to the opposite sex. If a career change isn't feasible, at least consider changing companies or start working with some new clients—all male.

136-166 points: *Belle of the Office Ball*
Someone must have given you this book as a joke; you're virtually surrounded by men at and near work. If you haven't met a great man yet, it's only a matter of time.

Bibliography

AASA Job Bulletin, January 21, 1985. American Association of School Administrators.

Admissions to Schools and Colleges of Optometry, Fall, 1986. American Optometric Association, St. Louis. Association of Schools and Colleges of Optometry. Washington, D.C., 1985.

AIA Membership Survey: The Status of Women in the Profession. The American Institute of Architects, Washington, D.C., 1983.

AOA News, "Optometric Income Fails to Keep Pace With Inflation", August 1981.

Ayres, B. Drummond, Jr. "A New Breed of Diplomat," *The New York Times Magazine,* September 11, 1983.

Ayres, Mary Ellen. "Moonlighting," *Occupational Outlook Quarterly,* Spring 1983.

Barlow, Ellen. "Opportunities in Health Care," *Business Week's Guide to Careers,* Spring/Summer 1984.

Barmash, Isadore. *The New York Times.*
"Despite Recession, Salesmen Can Still Smile," October 17, 1982.
"High-Tech Salesmen: A Different Breed," March 25, 1984.

Basta, Nicholas. *Business Week's Guide to Careers.*
"Job Market: Human Resources Managers," Fall/Winter 1983.
"Job Market: Insurance," February/March 1984.
"Job Market: Law Office Manager," October/November 1984.
"Job Market: Purchasing Agent," February/March 1984.
"Job Market: Securities Industry," February/March 1984.
"The Wide World of Marketing," February/March 1984.

Bennett, Robert A. "Cashing In on the New Business of Banking," *The New York Times,* October 16, 1983.

Best Report (The), Editors of *The Book of Bests*, Andrews, McMeel & Parker, 1983.

Birnbach, Lisa; Roberts, Jonathan; Wallace, Carol McD.; Wiley, Mason. *The Official Preppy Handbook*, Workman, New York, N.Y., 1980.

Bly, Robert W. and Blake, Gary. *Dream Jobs*, John Wiley & Sons, N.Y., 1983.

Boone, Louis E. and Kurtz, David L., *Contemporary Marketing*, Dryden Press, Hinsdale, IL., 1974.

Brinkley, Joel. "Physicians Have an Image Problem—It's Too Good," *The New York Times*, February 10, 1985.

Brooks, Andree. *The New York Times*.
"At Work: Problems of Couples," June 17, 1985.
"The Secretary: Still a Nowhere Woman," October 11, 1981.

Brown, Helen Gurley. *Sex and the New Single Girl*, Bernard Geis Associates, N.Y., 1970.

Brown, Peter and Gaines, Steven. *The Love You Make: An Insider's Story of the Beatles*. McGraw-Hill, 1983.

Brown, Sue. "Why The Gender Gap in Earnings Remains Huge," *Medical Economics*, February 18, 1985.

Carroll, Mary Bridget. "It's Okay to Be a Secretary," *New Woman*, March 1985.

Chambers, Marcia. "Law's New Venues: Computers and Space," *The New York Times*, March 25, 1984.

Chemical & Engineering News.
"1985 Employment Outlook," October 22, 1984.
"1984 Salary Surveys," July 2, 1984.

Chi, Judy. "Onward and Upward! How Women Might Change the Face of Pharmacy," *Drug Topics*, March 7, 1983.

County and City Data Book, U.S. Department of Commerce, Bureau of the Census, 1983.

Davis, Peter. "The High and the Mighty Crowd," *Esquire*, June 1985.

Davis, Dr. Sandra. "Danger! Love at Work," *Business Week's Guide to Careers*, Spring/Summer 1984.

Dettinger, Judith A., editor. *The American Express 1984/85 Survey of Business Travel*, 1984.

Dowst, Somerby. "Purchasing's Salary Survey '84," *Purchasing*, December 13, 1984.

Dranov, Paula. "Women in the Foreign Service," *Cosmopolitan*, June 1982.

Drucker, Peter F. *Management: Tasks, Responsibilities, Practices.* Harper & Row, New York, N.Y., 1974.

Drug Topics Employee Pharmacist Compensation Survey, Medical Economics, Oradell, N.J., 1984.

Durniak, Anthony. "Job Market: Computer Programmer," *Business Week's Guide to Careers*, Spring/Summer 1984.

Employment and Earnings, Department of Labor, Bureau of Labor Statistics, January 1985.

Encyclopaedia Britannica, Encyclopaedia Britannica Inc.
  Macropaedia, Knowledge in Depth, 1979.
  Micropaedia, Ready Reference and Index, 1979.
  1982 Britannica Book of the Year
  1985 Britannica Book of the Year

English, Carey W. "Behind Hiring of More Temporary Employees," *U.S. News & World Report*, February 25, 1985.

Esquire
  "Soul Search: Home on the Range," June 1985.
  "Soul Search: The Work Ethic," June 1985.

Fadner, Kenneth. "The 1984 Salary Survey," *Adweek Annual Salary Report*, June 1984.

Ferguson, Scott. "The Planner Defined," *Financial Planning*, June 1984.

Forbes, "The Forbes Four Hundred," Special Issue: The Forbes Four Hundred 1984 Edition, October 1, 1984.

Foreign Service Careers, Department of State Publication 9202, Department and Foreign Service Series 249, June 1984.

Fowler, Elizabeth M., *The New York Times*
  "Accounting Moves Into New Fields," March 11, 1981.
  "Business Realty's Challenge," October 19, 1983.
  "Computer job Scene Changing," September 19, 1984.
  "Computer Law: New Specialty," April 20, 1983.
  "Computer Science Prospects," November 2, 1983.
  "Economics as a Field to Enter," March 6, 1985.
  "Engineers and Quest for MBA," January 9, 1985.
  "Finding a Niche in Music," May 28, 1985.
  "Giving Investors An Edge," December 14, 1983.
  "Lawyers in Pursuit of Jobs," May 18, 1983.
  "Managing Brokerage Houses," April 12, 1983.
  "Prospects Better for Architects," March 20, 1985.
  "Science Jobs for Women," September 5, 1984.
  "Toxicology Is Found 'Neglected'," December 12, 1984.

"Training Hospital Managers," February 13, 1985.

"Wanted: Law Firm Managers," March 21, 1984.

"Where Engineers Are Needed," March 27, 1985.

Freed, John C. "Glut of Doctors Creating a Patient's Market," *The New York Times*, April 8, 1985.

Freedman, Alix M. "Programmers: Writing Their Own Ticket," *The New York Times*, National Recruitment Survey, October 11, 1981.

Frequent Flyer, "1983 Frequent Flyer Poll Report," September 1983.

Giambanco, Jacqueline. "Taking Off in a Fast-Paced Industry," *Working Woman*, April 1985.

Goldman, Ari L. "'Sorry, No Experience' Line Begins to Include Computer Jobs," *The New York Times*, Careers '83 supplement, October 17, 1982.

Goodman, Ellen. "Getting Women on the Front Page," *The Boston Globe*, April 23, 1985.

Grant, Priscilla. "The Real Truth About Office Romances," *Glamour*, July 1985.

Gray, Paul. "New Information Careers," *Business Week's Guide to Careers*, Spring/Summer 1984.

Green, David S. and Strohm, Paul (staff and faculty editors). "The Annual Report on the Economic Status of the Profession, 1984–85," *Academe: Bulletin of the American Association of University Professors*, March-April 1985.

Gross, Jane. "Against The Odds: A Woman's Ascent on Wall Street," *The New York Times Magazine*, January 6, 1985.

Grossman, Ellie. "Soaring High: Careers in Aviation," *Working Woman*, May 1980.

Hall, Peter. "What It's Like to Work for IBM," *Business Week's Guide to Careers*, Fall/Winter 1983.

Hannibal, Edward, *Chocolate Days, Popsicle Weeks*. Houghton Mifflin, Boston, MA., 1970.

Harrop, David with Geeslin, Ned. "Who Makes What $," *People*, March 25, 1985.

Harte, Ben. *Frequent Flyer*.

"Who's Drinking Where in Honolulu," April 1983.

"Who's Drinking Where in Philly," November 1982.

Hayes, Cynthia A., "The Adweek Poll," *Adweek Special Report. Women 1984: Trade-offs and Payoffs*, May 1984.

Hazard, John W. "Before Picking Your Financial Planner," *U.S. News & World Report*, November 12, 1984.

Hazerjian, Margie. "1984 Salary Hikes Hit 6.1%; Average Pay Tops $30,000," *Meeting News*, November 1984.

Hollie, Pamela G. "Market Is Wide Open for Marketing Experts," The Occupational Outlook, *The New York Times*, October 16, 1983.

International Musician, "Help Wanted," April 1985.

Jackson, Patrick, editor. "Twentieth Annual Survey of the Profession, Part II: Salaries," *PR Reporter*, October 15, 1984.

Jacquet, Constant H. Jr. *Clergy Salaries and Income in 1982 in Eleven U.S. Denominations*, National Council of Churches, circa 1983.

Jessen, Gene Nora. "Sue Ranney: Corporate Pilot," *99 News*, April 1983.

Johnson, Sharon. "Paging Physicians' Assistants," *The New York Times*, March 25, 1984.

Josephson, Nancy. "Job Market: Hotel-Motel Management," *Business Week's Guide to Careers*, October/November 1984.

Jurney, Dorothy. "Women Editors Advance to 11.1 Percent," *ASNE Bulletin*, November/December, 1984.

Kirk, Kenneth W. and Shepherd, Marvin D., "Women in Pharmacy—Where Are We Now?" *American Pharmacy*, February 1983.

Kleiman, Carol, "'Associating' Could Be a Working Idea," *The Chicago Tribune*, August 5, 1984.

Kleiman, Dena. "Young Doctors' Problem: Too Many Doctors," *The New YorkTimes*, August 16, 1983.

Kleinfield, N.R., *The New York Times*.

"Companies in Search of Bionic Man," November 20, 1983.

"How a Company Does Its Shopping," January 17, 1982.

Kondracke, Morton. "The Foreign Service Is Looking For a Few Good Diplomats," *TWA Ambassador*, August 1981.

Kushner, Dan and Feierman, Rueben. "Class of 1984: More than 60%, Record High, Will Work for Chains, Hospitals or Manufacturers," *American Druggist*, June 1984.

Langley, Monica. "Executive Sweets: Office Marriages Win More Firms' Blessings, But Problems Crop Up," *The Wall Street Journal*, October 16, 1984.

Lee, Tony. "Salaries Up, Jobs Fewer for Corporate Attorneys," *National Business Employment Weekly*, April 7, 1985.

Levering, Robert; Moskowitz, Milton; and Katz, Michael. *The 100 Best Companies to Work for in America*, Addison-Wesley, Reading Massachusetts. 1984.

Levine, Judith. "Can A Girl Get a Date in Silicon Valley? (Where The Boys Are)," *Mademoiselle*, March 1985.

Machlowitz, Marilyn. "Management/Business Advice: Velvet

Ghetto?" *Working Woman*, November 1981.

Maloney, Lawrence D. with Phillips, Kathleen. "What's Behind a Growing Shortage of Priests," *U.S. News & World Report*, June 18, 1984.

Margolick, David. "Less Pay for New Lawyers Urged," *The New York Times*, February 3, 1982.

Marlin, John Tepper. *The Book of American City Rankings*, The Council on Municipal Performance, 1983.

Martin, Gail. *Occupational Outlook Quarterly.*
"Careers in Associations," Spring 1983.
"You're a What? Travel Manager," Winter 1982.

McInnes, Mary and MacNeill, James H. *The Supply of Accounting Graduates and the Demand for Public Accounting Recruits 1985*, American Institute of Certified Public Accountants, 1985.

"Medicine: More Than Just Pill Counters," *Time*, October 12, 1981.

Miller, Bryan. "Diner's Journal," *The New York Times*, May 10, 1985.

Miller, Larry. "Sex in the Office: Taboo or Not Taboo?" *Cosmopolitan*, August 1984.

Minorities & Women in the Health Fields, U.S. Department of Health & Human Services, Washington D.C., September 1984.

Molloy, John T., *The Woman's Dress for Success Book*, Warner Books, New York, N.Y., 1978.

Nash, Nathaniel. "Computer Route to the Executive Suite," *The New York Times*, March 27, 1983.

New York Times, The.
"Assessing the Afflicted, and What They Want," June 2, 1985.
"Women in Clerical Jobs Band Together to Learn 9-to-5 Rights," February 20, 1985.

Niepold, Cecelia, *NRA News.*
"Expanding Job Opportunities in Eating and Drinking Places," October 1983.
"Getting Ready for Customers in the Year 2000," October 1984.

99 News, "Women Pilots in the United States," April 1983.

Occupational Outlook Handbook, U.S. Department of Labor, Bureau of Labor Statistics, Washington D.C.
Bulletin 2205, April 1984.
Bulletin 2200, April 1982.

Owens, Arthur. "Are You Still Losing Out to Inflation?" *Medical Economics*, September 17, 1984.

Pearce, Carol Ann. "New Career: Meeting Planning," *Working Woman*, July 1980.

pHilter, The. "I Know You're a Chemist, But What Do You Do?," Fall 1982.

Piontek, Stephen. "Why IAFP Keeps Growing, Growing," *National Underwriter*, September 10, 1983.

Prevailing Financial and Data Processing Starting Salaries 1985, Robert Half International Inc., 1985.

Priestland, Sue C. "Women Move Into Executive Slots But Salaries Lag Behind," *Association Management.* August 1983.

Proctor, Jo. "The Path to the Top," *Public Relations Journal*, June 1983.

Rand, Ayn. *The Fountainhead.* Bobbs-Merrill, New York, N.Y., 1943.

Reck, Dr. Ross R. "Some Comparisons of Men and Women Purchasers," *St. Louis Purchaser*, October 1981.

Reckson, Alyse. "Nonprofit Organizations Offer Profitable Work," The Special Groups, *The New York Times*, October 16, 1983.

Reinhold, Robert. "The New Engineering: Computers Print Out A Brand New Industry," *The New York Times*, March 25, 1984.

Restaurants & Institutions.
  "R&I Labor-Cost Index," March 20, 1985.
  "Salaries at the Top," March 14, 1984.

Ross, Nancy L. "Financial Planning Industry Has Taken Off," *Washington Post*, November 4, 1984.

Rothman, David H. "Making a Temporary Job Pay," *Business Week's Guide to Careers*, April 1985.

Roth Young Wage and Salary Review, Hospitality Industry, 1985.

Salmans, Sandra. "New Trials in Test Marketing," *The New York Times*, April 11, 1982.

Sanger, David E. "Technical Writers Can Write Their Own Ticket," *The New York Times*, March 27, 1983.

Scherschel, Patricia M. "Here They Come—The 'Nonbank Banks'," *U.S. News & World Report*, December 24, 1984.

Schultz-Brooks, Terri. "Getting There: Women in the Newsroom," *Columbia Journalism Review*, March-April 1984.

Seixas, Suzanne. "The Payoff for Working Under Fire," *Money*, April 1985.

Serrin, William. "Engineering: Outlook Is Rewarding In Most Specialities," *The New York Times*, High Technology Employment Outlook, March 24, 1985.

Shern, Stephanie. "The Lively Life of an Accountant," *Business Week's Guide to Careers*, Fall/Winter 1983.

Simmons, Nicole. "Biotechnology Industry Offers Specialists a Flurry of Jobs," *The New York Times*, March 25, 1984.

Skrzycki, Cindy. "Troubled Days for Commuter Airlines," *U.S. News & World Report*, December 24, 1984.

Sloane, Leonard. "Financial Planners on a Rise," Occupational Outlook supplement, *The New York Times*, October 11, 1981.

Spillman, Susan. "Latest Insurance: Computer Crimes Covered," *USA Today*, October 4, 1984.

Statistical Abstract of the United States 1985, U.S. Department of Commerce, Washington D.C., 105th edition, December 1984.

Steele, William. "Career Options: Women Who Buy the Big Stuff," *Working Mother*, February 1985.

Steger, Pat. "Four Hotel Managers Who Work At Home," *San Francisco Chronicle*, November 23, 1983.

Stodden, John, Ph.D. *Business Week's Guide to Careers.*
"Business Economists," Fall/Winter 1983.
"The Changing World of Banking," October/November 1984.

Stucker, Jan Collins. "A Financial Planner: Worth the Investment?" *Ms.*, December 1983.

Swindell, David. "The Drillers: Life Aboard Sabine II," *Compass*, Fall/Winter 1981.

Terkel, Studs. *Working*, Pantheon Books, 1972.

Time, "A Remarkable Job Machine," June 25, 1984.

Toffler, Alvin. *Future Shock*, Random House, 1970.

20/20, "Love At Work," ABC News, transcript of program aired November 1, 1984.

U.S. News & World Report.
"Hunting for a Job? Here's Where to Look," August 13, 1984.
"Looking For Work? Lots of New Jobs," June 18, 1984.
"Millionaires: They're Almost Commonplace Now," October 3, 1983.
"News-Lines," December 31, 1984/January 7, 1985.
"News-Lines," June 10, 1985.
"The American Male," June 3, 1985.
U.S. Business: Trends That Shape The Future, "Demand for Pilots Takes Off," March 11, 1985.
U.S. Business: Trends That Shape The Future, "Where Jobs Will Grow Fastest," March 4, 1985.
"Where Jobs Will Multiply," March 18, 1985.
World Business: A Fresh Perspective from Overseas, "Airline Earnings Take Off," February 4, 1985.

Wallace, Irving; Wallechinsky, David; Wallace, Amy; Wallace, Sylvia. *The Book of Lists 2*, William Morrow and Company, 1980.

Wayne, Leslie. "The Year of the Accountant," *The New York Times,* January 3, 1982.

Wedemeyer, Dee. "Women as Developers: Four Who Made It," *The New York Times*, March 10, 1985.

Weinstein, Bob. "What I Do on the Job," *Business Week's Guide to Careers*, October/November 1984. Page 18.

Wellborn, Stanley N. "Race to Create a 'Living Computer'," *U.S. News & World Report*, December 31, 1984/January 7, 1985.

Wiener, Leonard with Morse, Robert J. "The Swelling Ranks of U.S. Millionaires," *U.S. News & World Report*, March 18, 1985.

Williams, Winston. "Glory Days End for Pharmaceuticals," *The New York Times*, February 24, 1985.

Working Woman, Editors of. *The Working Woman Report*, Simon & Schuster, 1984.

Wright, John W. *The American Almanac of Jobs and Salaries*. Avon Books. New York, N.Y., 1984.

Yarrow, Andrew L. "Emerging Careers: Helping Our World to Come Clean," *The New York Times*, March 25, 1984.

Young, Stephanie. "Women Right Now: Can Your Company Tell You Who to Date?" *Glamour*, June 1985.

Zanker, Alfred. "Why World May Be Near Another Economic Boom," *U.S. News & World Report*, August 20, 1984.

Zaslow, Jeffrey. "A Growing Question: How Can you Keep Women on Farms?" *Cosmopolitan*, January 1985.